D1271039

eBoys

The First
Inside Account of
Venture Capitalists
at Work

Randall E. Stross

CROWN
BUSINESS

Copyright © 2000 by Randall E. Stross

All rights reserved. No part of this book may be reproduced or transmitted in
any form or by any means, electronic or mechanical, including photocopying,
recording, or by any information storage and retrieval system,
without permission in writing from the publisher.

Published by Crown Publishers, New York, New York.
Member of the Crown Publishing Group.

Random House, Inc.
New York, Toronto, London, Sydney, Auckland
www.randomhouse.com

CROWN BUSINESS is a trademark and the Crown colophon is a registered
trademark of Random House, Inc.

Printed in the United States of America on acid-free paper

Book design by Helene Berinsky

Library of Congress Cataloging-in-Publication Data is available upon request.

ISBN 0-8129-3095-9

2 4 6 8 9 7 5 3 1

First Edition

For Rebecca and Martin

Contents

The Cast

The Benchmark Partners

Dave Beirne   previously, founder of Ramsey Beirne Associates, an executive search firm in Ossining, New York

Bruce Dunlevie   previously, general partner at Merrill Pickard, a venture capital firm in Menlo Park, California

Bill Gurley   previously, general partner at Hummer Winblad, a venture capital firm in San Francisco, California; joined Benchmark in 1999

Kevin Harvey   previously, founder of Approach Software, in Redwood City, California

Bob Kagle   previously, general partner at Technology Venture Investors (TVI), a venture capital firm in Menlo Park, California

Andy Rachleff   previously, general partner at Merrill Pickard, a venture capital firm in Menlo Park, California

Selected Individuals Mentioned

Bill Atalla   son of TriStrata founder John Atalla

John Atalla   founder, TriStrata

Louis Borders   founder and CEO, Webvan

Eric Greenberg   founder, Scient

Bob Howe   CEO, Scient

Jerry Kaplan   CEO, Onsale

Bill Lederer   CEO, artuframe/Art.com

Burt McMurtry   general partner, Technology Venture Investors

Pete Mountanos   CEO, Charitableway

Pierre Omidyar   founder and chairman, eBay

Tom Perkins   retired general partner, Kleiner Perkins Caufield & Byers

Danny Shader   Benchmark entrepreneur in residence; founder and CEO, Accept.com

Rob Shaw   founder, Newwatch/Ashford.com

Jeff Skoll   cofounder and vice president, eBay

Paul Wahl   CEO, TriStrata

Jay Walker   chairman, Priceline

Steve Westly   vice president, marketing, eBay

James Whitcomb   president, Newwatch/Ashford.com

Meg Whitman   president and CEO, eBay

Selected Companies Mentioned

(Partner representing Benchmark)

Accept.com (Bruce Dunlevie)   payment systems for electronic commerce

Ariba (Bob Kagle)   online ordering of materials and supplies for businesses

Art.com [originally named artuframe] (Bob Kagle)   posters and frames sold via the Web

Ashford.com [originally named Newwatch] (Kevin Harvey) watches, pens, leather bags, and other luxury goods sold via the Web

Charitableway (Andy Rachleff)   online for-profit solicitor for non-profit organizations

Critical Path (Kevin Harvey)   hosts e-mail services for large organizations

eBay (Bob Kagle)   online person-to-person auctions via the Web

ePhysician (Dave Beirne)   prescription ordering for doctors via a PalmPilot

Juniper Networks (Andy Rachleff)   manufacturer of high-speed routers for the Internet

Newwatch [renamed Ashford.com; see above]

Priceline (Dave Beirne)   online bidding for airline tickets and hotel rooms

Red Hat (Kevin Harvey)   distributor of Linux, an alternative operating system to Windows

Scient (Dave Beirne)   technical consulting services to e-tailers

Toysrus.com (Bruce Dunlevie)   aborted joint venture to sell toys via the Web; to have been cofounded by, but organizationally separate from, Toys "R" Us

TriStrata (Dave Beirne)   security software for data networks within large corporations

Webvan (Dave Beirne)   groceries sold via the Web and delivered to the home

Introduction

When eBay, a small Internet auction company based in San Jose, California, sought venture capital, it had to pass an informal test administered by the venture guys before they would consider making an investment: Was there a reasonably good likelihood that the investors could make ten times their money within three years? In eBay's favor, the company displayed some mo—momentum measured in revenues and profitability. It did not have much visibility in the public at large, however, and the growth potential of its business—what seemed to be nothing more than a flea market online—was unproven. There was risk that the best that could ever be said about it would be that it was a good little business, with the emphasis on *little*.

The venture capital firm that in the end backed eBay was Benchmark Capital, itself a start-up, then only two years old. When Benchmark invested $6.7 million in eBay in 1997, the auction company's valuation was put at $20 million. EBay grew, prospered, went public. In September 1998, after the first day of public trading, eBay's market capitalization was $2 billion, and Benchmark's original $6.7 million stake was now worth $400 million. Little more than three months later, the stock had gained more than 1,300 percent. By the next spring, the company was valued at more than $21 billion; the value of Benchmark's stake had grown 100,000 percent in less than two years' time, making it the Valley's best-performing venture investment ever.

■

The eBay story happened to unfold right in front of my eyes—and my tape recorder; I must confess I was as surprised as anyone.

A year before eBay knocked on Benchmark Capital's door, I had knocked there, interested in writing a book about a corner of the financial world whose inner workings remained shrouded, even to those in other precincts of professional money management. Yet venture capitalists, who were concentrated in Silicon Valley, were entrusted with ever increasing amounts of capital by institutions, such as university endowments and charitable foundations, to invest in newly formed companies. In 1996 venture funds attracted $10 billion in capital; in 1997 the total jumped to $20 billion; and in 1998 it passed $26 billion.

It was a form of investing that brought higher risk than investing in shares of publicly traded companies found in the stock market, but it offered the prospect of higher returns, too. As for the venture capitalists, they received a significant cut—at least 20 percent—of any resulting gains in the portfolio's investments, so in flush times their personal wealth, on paper at least, grew as fast as the valuations of the new companies they funded.

Anyone who had followed the rise of Netscape, Amazon, and Yahoo—all were venture-backed—had already figured out that the venture guys were seated at the center of the New Economy. Endowment-fund managers who had not previously developed connections to the top venture capital firms pounded their fists on closed doors, begging for entry, but even with recent increases in size, the funds were already oversubscribed.

Business-school graduates headed to Silicon Valley in numbers never seen before, spurning six-figure salaries with management consulting firms to seek their fortunes with venture-backed start-ups. It appeared that entrepreneurial fever was spreading well beyond business schools, too. One in twelve American adults surveyed in the spring of 1999 said that they were at that moment trying to found a new business, and some unknowable multiple of that number surely daydreamed of such. Entrepreneurship was increasingly touted as a panacea, the best means of fighting poverty, according to advocates in nonprofit initiatives that sprang up to teach entrepreneurship in neighborhood classes, schools—even in kindergartens.

And all of these entrepreneurs and would-be entrepreneurs and institutional investors and individual investors—the entire money culture—trained their attention on the venture capitalists, who were the gatekeepers to the world of high-tech start-ups, the place where new firms grew the fastest and investors reaped the greatest returns. The venture guys made decisions that appeared to have oracular power. By the approach of the year 2000, the venture guys comprised the symbolically preeminent profession that served to define the zeitgeist in the nineties in the same way that investment bankers had in the eighties, investigative journalists had in the seventies, and hippies—as the antiprofession—had in the sixties.

■

Buyout firms, the sector of finance that had its own moment in the sun in the 1980s, also wanted to get into venture capital investing. Buyout funds had the same patrons, the same partnership structures, and a similar cut in profits. But where the buyout guys made a business out of what appeared to others to be detritus—decrepit auto-parts plants and ailing retailers—the venture guys worked in a nicer neighborhood, funding the brand-new and the not-yet-invented. The buyout guys rummaged around the stuff that comprised our yesterday (and slashed jobs with chilling efficiency); the venture guys were the financiers of our tomorrow (and got to create jobs in heartwarming numbers, as John Doerr, the best-known venture capitalist, never tired of reminding any reporter who would listen).

It was easy for the finance world to fall in love with venture capital in the late 1990s: The average return in 1998 for venture funds that concentrated on start-ups at the earliest stages was more than 25 percent, and leading funds were returning well in excess of 100 percent annually. This was a world in which the investment criteria used by the venture capitalists themselves were calibrated not in percentages but in multiples, as in "ten times our money."

Everyone who knew of their existence wanted a piece of their capital, their attention, and their blessing. Even nonentrepreneurs paid increasing attention because of a spreading understanding that the venture guys are the ones who stand closest to the spot that will remain of interest tomorrow. It is the venture guys who fund and guide the companies whose technology is most likely to diffuse and endure in a historically significant way. Fifty years from now it is unlikely that the leveraged buyout of RJR Nabisco will be remembered by anyone. But the early stage in the diffusion of any powerful new communications technology will always be of interest to future historians, regardless of the rise and fall of individual company fortunes or collective stock prices in the interim.

So at least it seemed to me, a historian who was struck by how that moment appeared to mark the apotheosis of the entrepreneur, the first time since the arrival of Big Business in the post–Civil War years that small business, in the form of high-tech start-ups, had regained the preeminent position of status in the business world. This was new and piqued my curiosity.

The offices of venture capitalists are concentrated in my hometown of Menlo Park, California, and I sought an inside vantage point so that I could observe at close range the financial alchemy at the heart of venture capital and determine which parts should be credited to human agency and which to impersonal forces at work in the larger financial environment—that is, sort out skill from luck. I resolved to arrange for access over an extended period while retaining unencumbered editorial control; I also wanted to work with the youngest renegades I could find, and those happened to be at Benchmark Capital. It took me a year of entreaties before I was able to gain entry. Ultimately, our agreement was sealed with a handshake—no written NDA (nondisclosure agreement), no attorneys.

There was no precedent within the venture business for providing an outsider such access. I suspect that the Benchmark partners thought that something ballsy like this, which was sure to make the graybeards of the guild squirm, must, ipso facto, be a good thing.

And they bet that an author who lived among them would see what they believed set them apart from the incumbents—their team ethos, eschewing individual stars. John Doerr, for example, excelled at promoting the visibility of John Doerr, but he evinced no ability (or wish) to raise up his partners to the same prominence he enjoyed. (And after hearing so much about Doerr, what entrepreneur who approached his firm, Kleiner Perkins, wanted to be deflected to one of the other partners, an unknown not-Doerr?)

Benchmark partners had selected one another on the basis of perceived ability to subordinate individual ego to the larger interests of the collective. It was a self-acknowledged experiment, but they were hopeful that the merits of their alternative model—a partnership of equals—would, in the end, outshine Kleiner Perkins's heliocentric system that revolved around Doerr. The industry held that it took five years before anyone could tell whether a new venture capitalist was going to be successful, and ten years for a single venture fund to fully mature and do its final accounting, so it would be many years, at best, before Benchmark would be in a position to place its record next to Kleiner's.

So I assumed. I began work in the fall of 1997, spending a majority of my time at Benchmark's office but also trying to capture life within as many of the portfolio companies I could persuade to accept my presence on the same terms as Benchmark had. One small, thirty-employee company was especially cooperative and open—eBay. I was glad for the welcome but could not help but think that this was one of those good *little* businesses. When I began, I couldn't understand how the partners at Benchmark could speak so enthusiastically about eBay's prospects. Early in 1998, long before eBay's initial public offering (IPO) was on the horizon, the partner who served as an eBay director told a business acquaintance with dead seriousness that "I wouldn't take half of Yahoo's stock for eBay right now"—and Yahoo's market cap was $5 billion at the time. He foresaw; I did not.

What he did not foresee—nor did his partners, nor (again) did I— was the way in which the Benchmark partners' engagement in backing start-ups in this particularly receptive historical moment would create extraordinary wealth. The partners who came together in 1995 to form Benchmark had already individually made considerable sums of money, either in venture capital or as entrepreneurs themselves. Two had a net worth of approximately $15 million each; the two others were single-digit millionaires. Initially, their joint efforts went well enough, but in 1998 results began to come in not just from eBay but from an overflowing basketful of others that increased their paper wealth from the considerable to the unimaginable. By 1999, the net worth on paper of all of the founding partners had increased by approximately $350 million—individually.

■

I was the writer in residence at Benchmark for two years, from the fall of 1997 to the fall of 1999. By the end, I was buried beneath a mass of material encompassing more than seventy portfolio companies and dozens of narrative threads that interwove ambition, personalities, and business experimentation. To create from this a single coherent story, I had to winnow the significant elements of many stories.

I decided first to introduce two of the five partners at the time: Dave Beirne (pronounced "burn"), who joined Benchmark just before I began my research and who provides the perspective of a newcomer to the venture capital business; and Bob Kagle, whose investment interests included companies like eBay that did broad consumer marketing.

When selecting which companies to include in this chronicle, I favored those whose products or services were aimed at a mass customer base (for example, new watches sold via the Web), rather than those aimed for information-technology professionals (like chip sets for network-equipment manufacturers). I also was drawn to companies that experienced trials, challenges, setbacks—those that went sideways—over those that did not because companies, like people, that live a charmed existence wholly free of travails are less interesting than those acquainted with life's complications.

■

It is a wee bit eerie to see, in hindsight, how the Benchmark boys' original notion of a partnership of equals turned out to have been echoed in impersonal performance statistics. Even the partners themselves would never have guessed in advance that four and a half years after Benchmark's founding, of the five investments that were the firm's all-time biggest hits to date, no two had been discovered and directed by the same partner: five hits, five partners.

One of those top five was an investment made in Critical Path, a company that provided e-mail services for large corporations and Internet-service providers. In the fall of 1997 Critical Path's entrepreneur had first invited Kleiner Perkins to invest in his company, which had just launched its service. The deal bounced to partner Will Hearst, a scion of the publishing family—and one of Kleiner Perkins's numerous not-Doerrs. Hearst professed an immediate liking, but he could not impel Doerr and the other partners to move; one month, two months, three months went by. For the entrepreneur, a wait so long would have been intolerable were it not for the consoling thought that the leading venture capital firm in the galaxy was saying it might invest in his company.

By the time Kleiner Perkins finally got around to tendering an offer, the entrepreneur had been wooed by another venerable Sand Hill Road firm, Mohr Davidow Ventures, founded in 1983. Seeing the entrepreneur hesitate in accepting Kleiner Perkins's offer, Mohr Davidow, in turn, contacted two other venture firms to see if either would be willing to be a co-investor. One was Benchmark, founded fewer than three years previously and chosen because Mohr Davidow viewed the Benchmark partners as a hardworking, aggressive group that would love nothing more than the opportunity to beat Kleiner Perkins in winning over the entrepreneur.

While the other prospective co-investor failed to respond, the Benchmark partner who got the first call, on a Monday, set his partners scrambling into immediate action. Two met with the entrepreneur that night; the others met with him the next day. At the end of day two Benchmark and Mohr Davidow made an offer, which on its face was less attractive to the entrepreneur, as it was based on a lower valuation of the company than KP had tendered. But the entrepreneur liked the combination of technical and business acumen and hustle he saw in the challengers. He liked their style, too. On Thursday, only four days after first showing the deal to Benchmark, the entrepreneur decided to go with Benchmark and Mohr Davidow.

There was one awkward moment, when a Benchmark partner, a Mohr Davidow partner, and the entrepreneur were sealing the deal with handshakes in a glass-walled conference room in Critical Path's offices. Who should walk in but Will Hearst, who, after doing a double take, could do nothing but take a seat outside the room and do a little bit of waiting himself. He had been aware of Mohr Davidow's presence in the picture, but the Benchmark factor apparently was news to him.

Obtaining the opportunity to invest in a cash-burning company that had only just launched its service and had yet to sign a single significant customer was not an instant win for Benchmark. (One partner summed up the situation: "The good news is, we won. The bad news is, we won.") Recruiting a new CEO, a new management team, a number of heavyweights for the board of directors, and then bankers for the IPO—these things lay ahead. But in November 1999, eighteen months after Benchmark invested and seven months after Critical Path's IPO, its trading price gave it a market capitalization of $2.9 billion. Benchmark's investment was now worth eighty-seven times the original sum.

That Benchmark was a participant in the story at all was a testament to the power of its team sales effort—the Benchmark bear hug. When competing for deals, nothing was sweeter than this, having an entrepreneur walk right out of Kleiner's clutches of his own free will. It seemed to indicate that the partnership was making a mark far faster than its partners had thought possible.

eBoys

1. The Right Answer

The guy. No special emphasis on either *the* or *guy*, but no intervening pause, either. *TheGuy*.

That's the person needed to head a start-up once it has grown beyond a seed. To wit, a stud, ideally, a big honkin' stud or a total fuckin' stud. He (or, yes, she) will not lack for balls, at least in one sense, but in another will work his nuts off, or his ass off (these being valuable pieces of anatomical real estate; you never hear "works his index finger off"). A high-hustle guy. A total can-do guy. A winner. Smart. Someone with integrity-off-the-charts. Scrappy. A kick-ass dude, a nail-eatin', nut-crushin' (that trope again!) decision maker, a competitor with killer instincts. Someone who attracts and hires A's, unafraid to hire above himself. A player. A hitter.

Finding TheGuy—finding the Right Answer—for companies in need was Dave Beirne's world for ten years.

Thanks to happenstance, Beirne's career as a search guy had begun at the age of twenty-two in cold-call hell. Freshly graduated in 1985 from a small school, Bryant College, with a business degree, he had an appetite for work. During his last two years of college, he had taken a full course load, worked at IBM virtually full-time as a marketing assistant, captained the lacrosse team, and led buddies in sundry intramural sports—and in what in the 1980s was defined as the back half of work-hard/play-hard (the lock-and-load party, for example: the dorm door was locked, and a concoction of liquor and

Kool-Aid that filled a giant garbage can in the room's center was drunk until every person was loaded).

He had his coterie of mates, to whom he was fiercely loyal. But outside that circle, he was not a gregarious person. In fact, he was unable to mix without putting many on the defensive. He walked with a chip on his shoulder that he took no pains to disguise. He had a particular aversion to anyone whose status derived from inherited privilege. A college friend would later liken his attitude to that of a ghetto-hardened tough: If it was given to ya, don't think you're better than me.

His own family had prospered from blue-collar roots, working for General Motors. His grandfather was a union leader who worked forty-two years on the assembly line at the Tarrytown, New York, plant, and his father, Gus, had followed, directly out of high school, hanging doors on the line. While Dave Beirne was growing up, his father worked the swing shift. But eventually, Gus was able to make the jump to line management, and when Dave was in high school his father moved into the upper reaches and eventually would oversee fifty thousand people at his career's peak before retiring. The ascendance of this high school graduate happened too late for his son Dave to think as ambitiously as he might have about where to take strong grades when applying to college, and too late for Dave to change his own sense of class status. At Bryant he all but shouted: Don't think anything was handed to my dad or to me.

Graduating from a small school without the national reputation of an Ivy, he was at a disadvantage for entrée to the most promising career tracks in business. Resolved to gather the experience and money he would need in order to obtain a Harvard MBA, the instrument that would give him parity, he spoke with anyone he could think of about entry-level positions. He was introduced to Chuck Ramsey, an executive recruiter at Sales Consultants who worked with technology companies; Ramsey was willing to overlook the fact that the kid did not even know what a recruiter did and give him a try.

Hiring Dave Beirne was not an especially expensive risk; the only pay was the commission earned when a candidate was successfully placed, and it was up to the "account executive," as Beirne was grandly titled, to obtain the recruiting assignment from an employer willing to pay a contingency fee when hiring a recommended candidate. Beirne was given a phone, a desk, Yellow Pages, and training that consisted of a simple injunction: Have at it.

It was not clear why either a prospective client or candidate would take Dave Beirne seriously. He was young, and looked even younger than he was; his job experience at that point—summer work on the assembly line and the IBM assistantship as essentially a gofer—had not provided a tour of the upper floors of power. He had no list of successful placements. Why would anyone look at him and sign on?

The answer: No one did look at him. The business of placing low- and midlevel sales people was conducted entirely on the phone. What prospective employers and employees heard was a baritone that conferred the authority of someone twice his age. He was a quick study, put in more hours than anyone else, talked his way into assignments, and found recruits.

Because debt was anathema to him, he had started with the intention of first saving up enough to pay for business school, and only then applying. But commissions rolled in, almost instantly. (After only six weeks on the job, the kid had suggested to Ramsey, twenty-one years his senior, that the two should leave their employer and start their own firm; Ramsey demurred.) Beirne did sensationally, and the savings were in place in months, not years. He had simply leaped over the stepping-stone of business school to the other shore.

A little more than a year later, Beirne finally persuaded Ramsey to join him and start their own search firm, which would exclusively serve clients in high-tech businesses. Late afternoon on day one in their new office in Ossining, New York—with no clients, no candidates, no furniture yet, but a new phone system in place—Beirne got a call from his wife, who informed him, "Market's down five hundred points and still going. You couldn't have picked a worse time to do this." It was October 19, 1987. Perhaps he should have gone to biz school after all, she couldn't suppress saying.

We'll be fine, he reassured her. Then he took immediate action. He purchased a couple of six-packs of Budweiser and sat on the floor with Ramsey, making outlandish predictions about the certain future success of Ramsey Beirne.

When narrated by Beirne, the firm's beginning on that forlorn day in October 1987 was the low point, and Ramsey Beirne's conquests, with ever higher-profile search assignments, were a string of triumphs comprising an ascending slope. Ten years later *Vanity Fair* likened him to Tom Cruise's Jerry Maguire (for the search for Microsoft's chief operating officer he "placed 400 calls, put 79 candidates on his long list, conducted 29 face-to-face interviews, and showed 5 people to Gates") and wrote that he had "almost single-handedly turned headhunting into as quasi-glamorous a field as Hollywood agenting." A *New York Times* piece highlighted Beirne's aggressiveness. "We have no fear," he had declared. "If we could find God's phone number, we'd call Him."

His six-foot-six physical presence enhanced the persona, too. A profile in *Fortune* carried a photograph of Beirne posed like a celebrity for Titleist, in sweater and chinos, standing on a green and leaning on a driver. He was identified above the photo as "The Head-hunter."

When it was Beirne himself telling the Ramsey Beirne story, he spun it as a seamless narrative of collective effort, a football team that started on its own goal line but then scored, scored, scored. What he left out in the telling were the complicating parts that made it interesting, the ways at several junctures he badgered his partners to undertake risks, jeopardizing modest success for the chance to move to the top. He also left out the way he and his colleagues had to project an aura of success for years before it actually existed, the way credit card debt and second mortgages had to tide the business over in the interim, the way the lack of personal contacts within the Establishment meant that Ramsey Beirne Associates advanced by dint of brute-force will.

To begin with, Ramsey and Beirne decided to serve only high-tech businesses, and focus on start-up companies as their clients. Yet, for family reasons, they were determined to set up shop in Ossining, far from Silicon Valley, where most of their prospective clients would be. Erasing that geographic distance meant they would have to be that much better than the competition that enjoyed the benefits of proximity to clients. It also meant that Ramsey Beirne Associates would have to be willing to travel all the time—"living in the tube," as Beirne would refer to the weekly or twice-weekly red-eyes across the continent.

Dave Beirne's pitch to the first prospective client was to ask for one shot, an opportunity to show what his brand of service was like, and once he had the chance, he *went maniacal* on it, *out-testosteroned* everybody, he'd say.

The regimen of interviews and travel was self-consciously macho, that is to say, not only heedless of physical well-being, but proudly so. His clients could say of him that he never said no, never deflected a request, never took an easy way out. At one point, he personally had twenty-seven separate searches under way—twenty-seven plates spinning on poles, all needing attention simultaneously. If he felt in danger of coming up short, he ordered his endocrine system to step up the pace.

Extraordinary expenditure of effort was not for naught, but it failed to produce extraordinary income. In their first year of business, the average fee Ramsey Beirne collected per placement—which took an average of three months to complete—was a dismal $5,000, a statistic that meant the business was barely alive. Such fees were an affront to the effort—double that of the competition, they felt—that was poured into each search.

In year two, Beirne convinced Ramsey and their first associate, Alan Seiler, to abandon the low-rent contingency-fee model and instead adopt a high-rent retainer-fee model, the one that only the elite search firms used. Clients would now be asked to pay up front, in order to obtain Ramsey Beirne's attention—and the fee would be collected whether Ramsey Beirne delivered candidates that the client decided to hire or not. To be a success, one must act the part, and a retainer fee was the way to communicate that one's services were in demand.

That was the theory. It was not easy, however, to remain confident when Ramsey Beirne's revenue immediately dropped to zero—and remained there. Beirne was barely able to keep his colleagues from abandoning the experiment as the months went by and their personal savings evaporated. Finally, six months later, they got their first retainer, from Xywrite, a small software publisher, which paid Ramsey Beirne $42,000 to undertake a search.

It was a milestone, but it did not turn out to be the harbinger of merry times. More business dribbled in, and each engagement made it a little easier to get the next one, but even after five years in business, Ramsey Beirne was barely eking out an existence. By then, the three principals were heavily in debt, and spouses were wondering how much longer they would be asked to wait for the experiment to prove itself.

The pain of the hard times was shared by all in the firm, which had instituted profit sharing as the principal form of compensation. To reinforce a team ethos, Ramsey Beirne's organization was flat: no managing directors, no bosses. Virtually no underlings, either. Even when it had grown to twenty associates, there was only one assistant serving the entire office ("I was cheap," Beirne said), so if something needed doing, you did it yourself. Service to clients with a personal touch was also to be a hallmark, and the founders held off installing voice mail. The phone was to be answered, promptly, by a human— even in the after hours. So when a client in Woodside, California, pacing the den at midnight, Pacific time, decided to call Ramsey Beirne, three o'clock New York time, the call would be forwarded, and when the associate groggily made out the question, "Were you asleep?" he was to answer brightly, "Oh, no, I was just going through some papers when you called. What's up?"

Professionals exude success, and that was all the outside world saw, if it noticed Ramsey Beirne at all. Beirne would direct that a cold call open with, "Hi, we're Ramsey Beirne, the leading retained executive search firm in high technology."

His colleagues thought this was a bit much. "Well, Dave, couldn't one argue that—"

"We *are*. Go."

If said to a client with sufficient force, it would not be questioned. And if a prospect laughed at the audacity of this little firm in Ossining and said, "So, let me ask you a question—how can you guys call yourself the leading firm?" Beirne and his colleagues would reply, "We brought in the COO of Central Point. We built the whole management team." The prospect probably had never heard of Central Point Software, either, but Central Point must have been an important client for Ramsey Beirne to lay claim to it in the way that it did.

If, when dialing for dollars, Seiler lucked upon a company in Boston that was about to launch a search and would be willing to hear a pitch from Ramsey Beirne at a breakfast meeting the next morning at 8:30, then Beirne would call back and ask that it be moved to 7:30, just to show that his blood was Type A—and he and Chuck Ramsey would set off for Boston by car at 2:30 A.M.

Once liberated from the telephone and actually in the door, Dave Beirne could really go to work, selling by not selling. No backslapping bonhomie, no inane chitchat, no annoying repetition of your first name, no clumsy paraphrasing of what you'd just told him.

"I have nothing to sell you today—let's take that off the table and just talk," he would say. "My goal is to earn the right to have a relationship with you, and I know it's my responsibility to earn the right." He'd vacuum up information about the candidate's command of the business, but also about intellect, ethics, leadership, energy. Beirne likened it to digging into someone's soul, then showing the person a portrait.

He had removed anything uncouth in his appearance that would provide an excuse for him to be turned away. There wasn't a hint of New Yawk in his voice, and you would never see him when his hair wasn't freshly cut, gelled, combed, and parted, when his white dress shirts did not consist more of starch than cotton.

Once he got in, he could get individuals who were ten, twenty, thirty years his senior to open up. His voice was measured and controlled; his sentences were well composed—they never began, then aborted and restarted; his manner was free of tics that would betray impatience. Most important, he didn't display the know-it-all arrogance seen in many who have coasted through the most selective colleges, nor was he handicapped by a parvenu's tendency to try to bluster his way to status parity by talking incessantly. He instead used his smarts in the employ of listening. His prospective clients and candidates discovered he was a paragon of the quick study, who when asked to restate what he'd been told got it right, absolutely right, and followed with questions that showed strategic instincts about how to make the business or career grow. Respect, trust, and confiding followed.

He conceived of Ramsey Beirne Associates as a sports team—new associates were hired, in part, on the basis of athleticism. But within the team, an internal dialectic was at work. There was Beirne, who saw himself as merely a team member, and then there was everyone else, who collectively created in their minds a second Beirne, a legend of outsized proportions who was the personification of power-through-sheer-will. The real Dave Beirne prided himself on his ability to accord all of the firm's clients unstinting service and politeness.

His colleagues, however, lovingly passed on tales, likely apocryphal, of another mythic Dave Beirne that left the real one aghast.

One legend, for example, concerned the day Beirne got irate about a client's failure to pay. The client had hired the person that Ramsey Beirne had recommended and had declared that it was happy with the choice. But it was dragging its feet in accounts payable to ease its own cash-flow problems.

A happy client was an asset that Ramsey Beirne was in no position at that point to antagonize. But Beirne called the company's CEO and was put into voice mail. Office lore had Beirne saying, "Joe. David Beirne. Here's the deal. I want my fuckin' money Federal Expressed over-fuckin'-night, right now. This is the most unprofessional bullshit thing I've ever heard, goddamn it. You're better than that, and you know you're better than that. So stop playing this fuckin' game and just get it done."

Later, when the story was recounted, Beirne said he never would have used profanity when speaking with a client. But to his colleagues who told it, the story's principal point was not the language, but rather how the rest of the story permitted a new Dave Beirne, a kinder, gentler one, to appear. After he hung up, the story went, he looked over at his colleagues, whose mouths were agape, and said, "That was the right thing to do, right, guys? I mean, this guy owes us money." The others reassured him but steeled themselves for the repercussions when Beirne's message was picked up.

The CEO called back. "David, I wanted to turn that into a tape. That's an unbelievable message." He said he had transferred Beirne's message to his own collections department, saying, "This guy is how we should be collecting our friggin' money." And to Beirne he added, "By the way, your check's on the way." It arrived as promised, via FedEx.

The large gamble, doing only retained searches for high-tech startups, had still failed to pay off in a big way, which was the only way that would be satisfactory to Beirne. The search projects remained smallish.

When the firm was started, Beirne had devoured every business book on sales that he could find, and all of them said you should sell only to the decision maker. He thought he had done just that when he eschewed human-resources departments and focused on cold-calling the CEO's of companies he wanted to be retained by. Over time, a pattern emerged: The CEO would listen to a Ramsey Beirne pitch to take on a search assignment, say he would consider it, then disappear for a few days before returning with an answer. The CEO's of these small companies were consulting someone else, and that someone else, upon investigation, turned out to be the venture capitalist who sat on the company's board of directors.

The reason for this cannot be understood by looking at venture capitalists as financiers. If their function in the economy is that of bankers, then they would not be asked by the CEO what search firm they recommend. The venture capitalists qua bankers would make their investment, putting up capital in exchange for a minority stake in the fledgling enterprise, and if things went well, that would be the last one would hear of them until their exit with the sale of the company or after an IPO.

That's the role of "investors," venture capitalists would say, pronouncing the word with disdain; *investor* is a euphemism for gambler. The role that they preferred, or at least said they preferred, was that of "company builder," which meant serving as an active board member and as informal consultant to the CEO in between board meetings. With a noncontrolling minority stake, the venture capitalist was not a puppeteer who could pull the strings of a CEO marionette at will. Any informal role depended instead on the personal relationship between the venture capitalist and the entrepreneur, on whether the latter respected the judgment of the former—and the former was actually willing to provide the time to work with the latter.

In Silicon Valley, where venture capitalists were more familiar than elsewhere, their public reputation was not a particularly positive one; they were seen by many as the heartless power mongers who reaped the fattest profits from the toil of entrepreneurial serfs, the brutes who with a snap of their fingers vaporized those who lost their favor. This reputation did not square with the anecdotal testimony of actual entrepreneurs who had venture backing. The entrepreneurs' biggest complaint with venture capitalists was not that they were too meddlesome but that they were not meddlesome enough—once they had invested, they didn't return phone calls. From this perspective, venture capitalists were more like bankers than they realized.

What a venture capitalist and his partners possessed was the fund of knowledge about strategy and operations that was built upon experience with dozens, even hundreds, of companies. It was the venture guys who also knew the best among public relations firms, attorneys, accountants, investment bankers—and executive search firms. They helped on searches by suggesting names, interviewing candidates, recommending some and not others, and judging the search firm's performance during the process. This knowledge was important not just for hiring the VP's of marketing or engineering that were routinely needed in a portfolio company, but also for when the CEO turned out not to be TheGuy, and the Right Answer had to be found.

Once Dave Beirne understood whom his prospective clients were consulting—the CEO's of start-ups—he knew to whom he should be selling the services of Ramsey Beirne Associates. However, by virtue of the defensive bulwarks that venture capitalists erected against strangers, they were as inaccessible to him as they were to an unknown entrepreneur. In a way, Beirne had landed right back where he started, which is to say that lacking access to back doors or old-school ties, he had only elemental resources: the Yellow Pages, a phone, and a stomach that was protectively lined for cold calls.

The break came in 1990, when his dialing finger took him up to TA Associates in Boston, where Brian Conway, a junior partner himself only a few years out of Stanford business school, agreed to a meeting. Upon arrival, Beirne cast aside his customary persona of the Quiet Therapist and instead appeared as Conan the Eager Barbarian—Chuck Ramsey practically had to hold on to Beirne to keep him from leaping across the table. Conway figured he could toss Beirne a bone and see what happened. The bone was returned, the search completed successfully. Another search, another success. As improbable as it seemed for a guy who looked young enough to still be chug-a-lugging at a lock-and-load party, Dave Beirne got the job done. Word quickly spread within the incestuous world of the venture guys, who shared board seats and traded notes, and Ramsey Beirne began to get the choice assignments that had eluded the firm until then.

John Doerr, of Kleiner Perkins, took a particular liking to Dave Beirne's work. It was Doerr who chose Beirne to work on the highest-profile assignments, to find the CEO's of the companies that would bring Doerr wide fame: Netscape, Excite, @Home, Healtheon. Bill Gates called: Could Ramsey Beirne take over a search for Microsoft's chief operating officer? Yes (that was the one where Beirne would personally interview everyone on his shortlist of twenty-nine). Xerox called, seeking help in its search for a new president. The retainer was a crisp million dollars—something of an improvement over the $5,000-a-pop contingency-fee business where he'd begun.

At the same time that Ramsey Beirne's business was flourishing, a group of three young venture capitalists in Menlo Park—Bruce Dunlevie, Bob Kagle, and Andy Rachleff—decided to step free of their old firms, and with software entrepreneur Kevin Harvey they set up Benchmark Capital. In the spring of 1997 Bruce Dunlevie, whom Dave Beirne had come to know in the course of search assignments, dropped by the Ramsey Beirne office in New York, ostensibly to meet the newly hired Ramsey Beirne associates. At the end of his visit, Dunlevie asked to speak with Beirne alone. I've got a bit of a curveball for you, Dunlevie began. Would Beirne be willing to join Benchmark as a partner? There's only one guy we want, he said, and it's you.

At first Beirne laughed, thinking Dunlevie wasn't serious. Then he protested that there was no way he could consider leaving his own firm. But once Dunlevie had extended the invitation to change careers, Beirne could no longer look at the search business in the same way as before. When you demand a million dollars for your attention and get it, what can you do for an encore? He decided he liked to climb more than having climbed. And now he could see that the venture guys reaped greater rewards—financially and psychically—than did search guys because their relationship with the fastest-growing companies was not like his, with its intense but short-lived engagements for particular assignments. If he was going to make the change, Benchmark was the group to hook up with. Their immodest ambition (as their chosen name suggests) was to reinvent the venture business—an anthem he had used in the search business. The Benchmark partners had an esprit de corps that also felt comfortably familiar; they were tall, six feet two to six-four, and a young group for the venture capital world, ranging in age from thirty-three to forty-one. The Benchmark boys would make his career transition instantaneous. They believed in equal partnerships and were not going to ask him to go through a let's-get-better-acquainted probationary trial. He would be a fully enfranchised partner, with an equal share, on his first day.

But a share of what? So young that it had not even finished investing its first fund, Benchmark was the unproven upstart in a feudal, hierarchical guild. Looming over it was Doerr's firm, venerable Kleiner Perkins, in its twenty-fifth year, snugly—and not a little smugly—ensconced on a throne at the summit. When Beirne told Doerr of his plans to join Benchmark, Doerr tried to persuade him to join Kleiner Perkins instead. Doerr said he would personally champion Beirne's candidacy. If you were willing to abide complacency for security, Kleiner Perkins was the place to go. But if you liked the climb, if you liked the way partners put team interests foremost, if you liked the idealism of changing the rules of the venture capital game by trying to provide entrepreneurs a level of service that even Dave Beirne would approvingly call maniacal, then Benchmark was the place to be.

2. Good People

Beige and white, constructed of glass, wood, stucco, and more glass, perched on a hillside amid sheltering oak and eucalyptus, the small office building in which Benchmark resides would look quite at home at Pebble Beach. Two stories, each flanked with flower-edged terraces on the sides and rear, create a Mediterranean effect, undisturbed by the lower parking level, which is hidden at the rear of the hill.

By the late 1990s, these offices and the others like it along Sand Hill Road commanded the highest commercial rents in the country. The first venture capital firm to take up residency in that stretch had been Kleiner Perkins, in 1972, when Interstate 280 was newly opened and the nearby land behind Stanford University was still undeveloped. Since then it had become exceedingly valuable as elsewhere the last remaining orchards of Silicon Valley gave way to condominiums, offices, and strip malls.

Benchmark's building was part of an office park that had been the corporate headquarters of Saga Corporation, a food-services company that prospered by operating college cafeterias. By the time Marriott bought the company, the buildings resembled an alpine retreat, high above the megalopolis, complete with its own conference center.

Marriott did not wish to run an office park, so it sold the property. The buyer, seeking a real estate investment with prospects for excellent returns, was not a real estate baron but a nonprofit, the Henry J. Kaiser Family Foundation. The same impulse that had led it and other foundations to diversify their portfolios into what was called "alternative investing," like venture capital funds, also led to diversification in real estate. A Marxist critique of "late capitalism" would have difficulty disentangling the interests of the for-profits from those of the nonprofits. Not only was Benchmark working, in part, "for" the nonprofits that supplied its capital, but its landlord also happened to be a nonprofit, too.

A visitor entering the Benchmark office foyer would notice foremost the two walls of plaques, each commemorating the initial public offering or sale of companies that the individual partners had overseen in their relatively short venture capital careers. They were displayed to reassure the visiting entrepreneurs that the Benchmark partners' youth should not be read as inexperience.

Though the plaques did not mention the fact, the commemorated companies were from past portfolios when two of the partners were at Merrill Pickard, which had occupied the floor that Benchmark now took up, and another partner had been at Technology Venture Investors (TVI), which had been on the floor below. The founders of both these firms had decided to retire at about the same time, so the less senior partners had been faced with the decision whether to inherit the mantle and carry on, or set up a new firm, with a new configuration of partners, new limited partners who would provide the capital—and an opportunity to define their own organizational culture. Benchmark's formation in 1995 could be interpreted either as the creation of a new household in the natural life cycle of a family or as polite patricide.

Benchmark's Bob Kagle was thirty-nine at the time of the firm's founding. In a photograph taken at the time, he looks like an older student-council president, with his short wavy hair brushed up and back in an earnest fashion. The photo does not capture Kagle's kinetic energy; in person, he communicates with his whole body, shifting weight from foot to foot, popping the top of a closed fist with an open palm, rising up and down on tiptoes as he talks, leaning in and then out, always in motion. When he laughs, which he does readily, it is a chuckle that comes from deep in the gut.

While Dave Beirne projects power, Bob Kagle projects empathy. From his previous experience as a venture capitalist, he was at Benchmark's formation already extremely wealthy, but material success was a garment he refused to wear. He was determined to remain unchanged, as hungry to learn, to connect with *you,* as he'd ever been.

Benchmark's mahogany-and-art-appointed office on Sand Hill Road was an unlikely destination for a working-class student from a single-parent household in Flint, Michigan. Like Beirne's family in New York, Kagle's relatives in every direction were employed by General Motors, but their careers lacked the happy ending. Kagle's great-grandfather was killed at the age of thirty-eight in the great 1937 Buick sit-down strike. For the family's later generations, the comforts enjoyed by other members of the unionized working class were scant. His mother struggled to support her elderly parents as well as three children and faced occasional brushes with eviction. As a teenager, Kagle picked up a hobby of reading books on the Depression, and the family's experiences produced in the adult Bob Kagle an uncommonly strong need for wholly unencumbered security: no mortgages, no credit cards, everything owned free and clear, safely beyond the reach of creditors.

Though he was salutatorian of his high school class and an active leader in student government, it was one fortuitous event, not the hydraulic workings of a meritocracy, that ultimately delivered Kagle to a college campus, the first person in his family to make it there. He first needed one big break.

The only college he was aware of that offered full scholarships was a local engineering school, General Motors Institute. Its name was not just a polite nod to an institutional benefactor; the college was literally owned by General Motors. Faculty members were hired and fired by the corporation, received paychecks from the same source, were given the same health benefits—and the same employee discounts on GM cars—as were the assembly-line workers. The students received stipends from the same giant corporation.

A GMI education took five years and consisted of alternating six-week stints in the classroom and in the workplace, in actual GM plants. The students were paid for the work, thus covering their living expenses; they also began accumulating credits toward the ultimate prize: a pension, the cynosure of everyone—even teenagers—in working-class Flint.

It was an attractive package, but there was a catch: GMI would not even accept an application until a prospective student had first secured a sponsorship from a General Motors unit, whose budget would supply the wages paid during the working half of the program. Kagle had applied to every car division in town and had been turned down by all. The number of slots was small, and the number of college-bound sons and daughters of plant managers large, so the politically unconnected had a difficult time squeezing in. The contingent event that changed his life, Kagle said in retrospect, was when his mother gathered all of her oldest son's report cards, placed them in a shoe box, screwed up her courage, and approached the education czar in her own division, AC Spark Plug, which Kagle had not applied to, and asked that her son's case be considered on its merits. He got a hearing, and then a sponsorship.

A working-class background did not make one automatically appreciative of the college experience. GMI students were all working-class, and yet they, like students anywhere, had a tradition of denigrating their school. But Bob Kagle stood apart. During his senior year, in an article in the school newspaper, the *Technician,* he railed at his classmates who were relentlessly negative. "I want to be able to say to classmates 'I'm proud to be at GMI' without them thinking that I'm in dire need of psychiatric attention," but he was not afraid to declare in print: "I appreciate this school."

GMI's compact campus was too small to constitute a world unto itself. In Kagle's student days, one border of the campus was occupied by Chevrolet's blocks-long Happy Valley assembly plant, whose workers shared the same parking garage as the students. Then the college's world was bounded by GM in all respects. This was brought home forcefully after Kagle's freshman year, when GM's corporate fortunes hit a downdraft. All divisions were ordered to cut budgets, and students' paid internships were a tempting target of cost-cutters. When the internships disappeared, the students did, too. It was happenstance that Kagle's work-study internship was spared. The college had to fulfill budget-cutting goals itself; over the course of one summer, a third of the faculty was dismissed. (In 1982, after Kagle's grad-

uation, General Motors spun the school off when the parent corporation experienced deep financial losses.)

The yaws of General Motors were unsettling, but for Kagle it was
impossible to imagine life beyond. He and his closest friend, Curt
Wozniak, spent many hours talking about future career plans, and
when they spun their wildest dreams, it was to imagine becoming—
someday, in an impossibly far-off future—a general manager of a division of General Motors.

Wozniak, like Bob Kagle, was doing well in his classes and like his
friend was depressed to see the low morale of GM's white-collar employees during the off-campus work stints. When Kagle proposed
that the two apply to the same graduate schools—Kagle had done the
research and determined that Stanford's business school was the
best—Wozniak acquiesced. Stanford was unsure about whether to
take GMI seriously, owned, as it was, by a corporation. From afar it
appeared to be some unfamiliar form of trade school. But Kagle and
Wozniak were admitted, becoming two of the first students from
GMI. And thanks to General Motors, they could take along full graduate fellowships, which the company awarded to a handful of students that it regarded as future executive material. Paradoxically, they
arrived in California in better financial shape than their middle-class
peers who had to take out major student loans.

It was 1978, and Kagle thought he would be able to sell his new
gold Trans Am—emblazoned with what he thought was a most attractive feature, an eagle on the hood—for a tidy profit when he arrived in Palo Alto. The plan failed; Stanford students were not
interested in eagle-adorned muscle cars. Transplanted to California,
Kagle and Wozniak felt unsophisticated. Unlike most of their new
business-school classmates, who had worked for several years after
graduation and were still unmarried, the two from Michigan came directly from their undergraduate school and were already married.

No one had heard of their college, but while their Stanford classmates found the heavily quantitative material of the first semester's
courses a challenge, the two engineers yawned. Their work experience also stood them in good stead. Kagle took a manufacturing
course and impressed the second-year students, including one who
would later invite him to join his venture capital firm. Kagle and Wozniak befriended two others who also came from the Motor City area:

Steve Ballmer (future president of Microsoft) and Scott McNealy (cofounder and longtime CEO of Sun Microsystems).

General Motors had sent Bob Kagle to graduate school, and it was understood that it was to General Motors that he was to return. But as graduation neared and he negotiated the details of where he would be working, he was dismayed that the company was going to send him to lonely exile: the finance group in New York, preparing reports for the board.

Meanwhile, management consulting firms were recruiting him, too. Even after two years at Stanford, however, the blue-collar need for security, what Kagle later would call "the psychology of the Midwest," remained strong. "I'll be giving up five years' credit toward my retirement if I leave GM now," he worried. But when he told a career manager at a GM plant he was visiting about his frustration that the company would not return him to a factory, he received surprising advice to consider the opportunities offered by other firms: It's a big world out there—go for it! (Three weeks later this same manager left GM himself.) Feeling as if he had been granted emancipation papers, Kagle joined Boston Consulting Group in 1980 and three years later was recruited by Dave Marquardt to join Technology Venture Investors. He was able to repay his alma mater with a grant of Microsoft stock—Marquardt, thanks to the Stanford business-school connection to Steve Ballmer, had been the sole venture capitalist permitted to invest in Microsoft.

Kagle learned the nuts and bolts of venture capital investing at a desk set up in the office of TVI's avuncular founder, Burt McMurtry. In retrospect the moment of his joining turned out to have been the last of the 1980s go-go days for investments in early-stage companies. By mid-1984, the technology sector was in a major slump, and so too was venture capital. There were lessons to be learned from the abrupt end of a time of investor euphoria, overpriced valuations, and me-too companies, and no one was more constitutionally ready to learn than Depression buff Bob Kagle. What he was witnessing was what he had always feared: Good times disappear in a blink.

Years later Kagle would walk into a partners' meeting at Benchmark and say, "Who'd I tell the RCA story to? When you guys hear this one, it's going to kill ya. In 1929 RCA was trading at five hundred dollars a share—"

A Benchmark partner, egging him on, would mockingly play the innocent foil: "Oh, my God! *Then* what happened?"

"Went to five dollars a share. *And* it was still in the Fortune Fifty when it was at five bucks!"

Kagle had a credibility problem, the other partner would remind everyone with a laugh. "Bob will say, 'I entered venture capital just as things went bad. It was hellish!' Then I say, 'How bad was it, Bob?' 'We did Microsoft, Compaq, and Sun, granted, but, oh, it was bad.' "

Not so bad that the junior associate didn't have some early successes himself. The firm had seen in him a well-trained engineer with the general business education of an MBA, and one of his first investment hits, Synopsys, seemed to be in his natural power alley: electronic design automation software used for integrated circuits. And yet being a technology investor—finding proprietary intellectual property and exploiting it—was not what he liked to do most. The engineering degree was his passport out of Flint, but what he secretly wanted to do was "consumer investing," that is, working with businesses that sold directly to the broad public and whose fate would be determined by marketing, positioning, segment leadership, and branding. In short, businesses based on mastering consumer psychology.

In the venture world, real men did tech deals and only tech deals; at TVI, Kagle had to keep his consumer inclinations hidden. He'd brought in Starbucks as a prospective early-stage investment, but his partners could not get comfortable with "a coffee deal." They did indulge him by approving an investment in a Dutch food company that tried unsuccessfully to introduce to American palates a pudding similar to yogurt called Tootje.

The ideal company for Kagle would be one that combined his strength in technology and his interest in consumer marketing, but such a hybrid was impossible to find. The closest he got was the day he came out of a breakfast meeting in the Town & Country shopping center across from Stanford and saw an improbably long line snaking out of the tiny, adjacent restaurant, a newly opened place called Juice Club. He canceled his appointments for the morning, interviewed customers and employees on the spot, tracked down the owner, who lived in San Luis Obispo in central California, and lobbied for a hearing. He flew down and persuaded the twenty-seven-year-old to abandon a franchise strategy and instead use venture capital to expand his business. They would soon relaunch the business as Jamba Juice. But is a countertop filled with blenders a high-tech deal?

In Kagle's first two years at Benchmark—when he was newly unencumbered by the straitjacket of a prescribed role—he made investments in technology or consumer marketing. He persuaded his partners to put more money into Jamba Juice, and he oversaw the incubation within Benchmark's office of Ariba, whose software systems made it easy for businesses to order supplies online. But he had still not found the opportunity to work on a project that would meld his twin interests. Until eBay.

■

It was late 1996, and eBay's online auction business had been solidly profitable since it was launched; the company did not need a cent. But Pierre Omidyar, twenty-nine, the original founder, and his new partner, Jeff Skoll, thirty-one, were the rare entrepreneurs who knew they needed to hire a CEO and other seasoned executives with skills they lacked. It appeared to them that the only way they would be able to attract people with deeper management experience than they had was by obtaining the imprimatur of a well-regarded venture capital firm. Selling a minority share of their equity to venture capitalists was the intermediate step they had to take to get the good people they sought.

When choosing which venture capital firms to approach, entrepreneurs had little hard data about a given firm's past performance. The firms did not publicly release data about their funds' performance, and the very nature of the investments made it difficult, or premature, to assign an interim value to recent investments before the market objectively monetized them. That is why it is a form of investment called private equity—there are no public markets to assign prices, no publicly released quarterly reports, no helpful market analysts to comb through the data and issue public estimates of future earnings.

It is an illiquid form of investment, too, quite different from a mutual fund. Once a venture capital firm puts cash in, there is no way to get cash back out before the company is sold to another or goes public. The payback, if the venture is successful, will be a distribution of stock—either the company's own or the stock of an acquiring company—and it may take as long as ten years, the life of a single venture capital fund's partnership, before the invested capital is returned.

Unlike mutual funds, whose performance must be publicly disclosed, a venture capital fund reports only to its own extremely small constituency of investors. In Benchmark's first fund, it reported to only thirteen limited partners (including six charitable foundations: Ford, Hewlett, Mott, Wellcome, Searle, and Knight). But even if Omidyar could have seen Benchmark's most recent quarterly report, it was far too early in the firm's life to learn anything useful. Only $15.8 million had been invested across nine companies. The value of the portfolio was currently placed at $19.6 million, bumped modestly up by the higher valuation of one company during a second round of financing.

To an entrepreneur, a venture firm's portfolio is of interest only if it has a marquee name, a franchise company that dominates its industry the way a seven-foot-four center who can score will dominate on the basketball court. Among the nine companies in Benchmark's portfolio, none was such a franchise.

Omidyar, a software engineer, knew of Benchmark because of past entrepreneurial experience. He had been one of four cofounders of a pen-computing software company called Ink Development. Bruce Dunlevie, who was at Merrill Pickard before joining with Kagle to organize Benchmark, had invested in the company, and Omidyar had liked working with him.

Dunlevie, who had grown up in Dallas, Texas, and played quarterback on his high school football team, was trim, lacking the middle-age heft of a former football player. He carried his six-foot-four body in a way that seemed intended to make it inconspicuous, which made his bone-pulverizing handshake all the more jarring to the victim. He had thin, blond-brown receding hair kept extremely short; his face, too, lacked features that demanded attention, almost as if he had custom-ordered his own physiognomy to match his desire for public invisibility. He had gone to Rice and spent his junior year studying history at Cambridge University; he remained an omnivorous reader but kept unadvertised his great love, the nineteenth-century English novel. Intellectually peripatetic, he had hopped after graduation from computer programming to investment banking to managing a computer factory, before becoming a venture capitalist.

Pierre Omidyar had abundant reasons to be impressed with Dunlevie's track record as a venture guy. It was Dunlevie who had helped arrange a way for Ink, which had evolved into another company, eShop, to do something that few pen-computing companies in the early 1990s were able to accomplish: make money. EShop was sold to Microsoft. (Dunlevie was 3 for 3 in his pen-computing investments; another company that he backed was Palm, whose PalmPilot several years later would be a broadly recognized brand but had not yet become the franchise it would be later for 3Com.)

After eShop's sale, Omidyar had periodically phoned Dunlevie, telling him of progress in his newest venture. "I've got this e-commerce site called eBay. It's gathering steam," Omidyar had said when he called in late 1996.

Dunlevie had not mustered interest, however, in the base concept—garage sales and flea markets. "It sounds great. Why don't you send me a business plan?"

"I don't really have one."

"Sounds fascinating. Why don't you call me back in the new year."

In early 1997 Omidyar got back in touch. Dunlevie again politely declared the concept fascinating and asked for the plan; again Omidyar said he didn't have one, and Dunlevie once again said, "Why don't you—"

But before Dunlevie could brush him off again, Omidyar had countered: "Why don't we get together? Old times' sake." So Dunlevie acquiesced and put him on the calendar.

■

In securing that meeting, Omidyar was already far ahead of most. He was one of fifteen hundred entrepreneurs who would pop a plan—or in his case, not pop a plan—into Benchmark Capital's in box in 1997. Only nine would be funded that year.

In a way, venture capitalists and book publishers are similar, in that their job description requires an ability to say no often. Actually, publishers have off-loaded to literary agents the task of sifting through manuscripts from unknowns. But there is no professional equivalent to agents in the world of venture capital funding. So venture capitalists deputize other entrepreneurs, executives, attorneys, and friends whose judgment they trust to do the preliminary screening. The business plan that comes in from a complete stranger, either without the blessing of someone the venture capital firm knows well or without professional accomplishments that render an introduction superfluous is all but certain not to make the cut. In fact, knowing that this is the case becomes a tacit requirement from the perspective of a venture guy: Anyone whom I don't know who approaches me directly with a business plan shows me they haven't passed Entrepreneurship 101.

Of the fifteen hundred proposals that came in, perhaps one third were from unknown entrepreneurs; their fate was determined before the entrepreneur even affixed the stamp or pressed the e-mail send button. The ones that received attention at Benchmark were the remaining thousand or so involving people who, like Omidyar, were professionally or personally known to one of the partners or had an accompanying recommendation from an authority close to the firm. About five hundred of those seemed interesting enough to warrant a meeting with one partner. Two hundred won second meetings, and half of those received additional review.

The arithmetic at this late stage may seem dismaying—one hundred serious contenders vying for nine slots—but it is mitigated to the extent that other venture firms choose the same hundred as their most serious candidates for funding, too. Anecdotally, it seemed as if all the companies that come close but fail to be chosen by their first-choice venture firm get picked up by another. In 1997 it appeared that the odds of being funded by what the industry regards as a top-tier firm were both better, and worse, than 1 in 150. For the deals that, for whatever reasons, were regarded as hot, the odds of being funded were excellent, and for everyone else, they were essentially nil.

Adjusting the numbers accordingly, the distribution of power between entrepreneurs and prospective investors was not as out-of-balance as it may at first appear. With several firms vying for an attractive deal, it was the venture capitalists who had to do more of the selling, and the entrepreneur who did the choosing. This was true in eBay's case: Omidyar had a shortlist of four firms including Benchmark. But the less experienced entrepreneur often forgot the power that he possessed when he made the climb up the hill to the venture firm's office as supplicant.

■

The picture framed by the floor-to-ceiling windows lining Benchmark's offices was a composition of sun-drenched sweetness; a wag, unaffiliated with Benchmark, had once declared aptly, "Heaven is but a local call." Inside, Benchmark's furnishings had been inherited from the previous occupant, Merrill Pickard, and had passed from posh to once posh—lacking the ostentation of the *Architectural Digest* showplace up the road at Kleiner Perkins but more showy than the ostentatiously Spartan quarters of another neighbor on Sand Hill Road, Sequoia Capital. The gradations that placed its décor in a middling range among venture capital firms were not necessarily visible to the visiting entrepreneur, who most often arrived for a first visit in a state of nervous agitation, fighting back stage fright.

Different venture capital firms have different traditions, seeking to either maximize the entrepreneur's performance anxiety or ameliorate it. Benchmark's partners took pains to set an informal mood and remove the notion that the visit involved a command performance. On the day of Omidyar's appointment, Bruce Dunlevie had roped Bob Kagle into the meeting in the conference room by mentioning to Kagle the one salient, if improbable, datum that blunted the stigma of a flea-market deal with twenty employees and only sixty thousand listings: EBay was a profitable Internet company. Dunlevie hoped that Kagle would take an interest in the project and assume responsibility, either taking the advocate's role or turning it down.

Pierre Omidyar arrived. He had dark brown hair pulled into a ponytail, a Vandyke beard, glasses, and a thoughtful mien. His body language never got more aggressive than looking someone directly in the eyes. He did not raise his voice in anger; when provoked beyond his high threshold of tolerance, he would merely drop his chin, look downward, and shake his head in disappointment. His core belief system, revolving around trust that people will act honorably, seemed ill-suited for the rough-and-tumble of the real world. Piloted by Omidyar, eBay resembled a silent-movie comedian walking through a construction site unharmed, while on either side other start-ups were bonked by collapsing ladders and falling paint cans.

Omidyar had not brought his own laptop, as most visitors do. Instead, he used whatever Benchmark had to offer. Having arrived without PowerPoint slides, without handouts or plan, Omidyar talked extemporaneously, planning to rely on the ultimate ace: a website that was not only up and running but making money. But when he tried to show off the site to Kagle and Dunlevie, he couldn't get the home page to come up. EBay's server had gone down, a not-uncommon occurrence.

Dunlevie hurriedly spoke up, pretending that he didn't know what had happened: "Our Internet connection is flaky—I apologize."

Embarrassed by being unable to demo his site, Omidyar was grateful for Dunlevie's gesture. And the visit had provided him with a chance to meet Bob Kagle for the first time. Omidyar had quickly arrived at a judgment: Kagle would be a perfect director for eBay.

On his part, Kagle left the meeting far from sold. Later, when he sat down at his PC and reached eBay's resuscitated site to have a look, he found its appearance surprisingly crude. Courier typeface, no color, monotonous lines of listings. The branding was confusing, too; one typed in "www.ebay.com" but then landed in something called Auction Web. And Omidyar himself was an enigma, hard to evaluate.

Kagle's partners were convinced, however, that this was a deal that had Kagle's name on it. To pass a deal on to another partner, one did not extol the virtues of the company. The proselytizing instead worked this way: One partner would poke his head into Kagle's office and ask innocently, "Bob, what's doing with eBay?" A bit later, another would drop by and ask for an update. So the day would go. Kagle was amenable to these visits, taking in their message, which was: Spend more time with this one before you make a decision.

It was a fishing lure that hooked Kagle. He was a collector of hand-carved fish decoys, and when he went to eBay's site, he was surprised to discover many for sale, including one rare item that had been made by a famed carver from Flint, Kagle's hometown. Kagle bid—and lost—but the experience pulled him into eBay's world. Over the next two weeks, he met with Omidyar outside of Benchmark's office and discovered that he was an anomalous kind of engineer, one who was consumed by the idea of community—every other sentence, he spoke about the eBay *community,* building the *community,* learning from the *community,* protecting the *community.* It was a passion similar to what, in Bob-speak, Kagle had for deals that brought out *the humanity;* that's what Kagle liked most of all, *the humanity.* The more Omidyar talked about his community vision, the more Kagle, as he put it, was "lovin' him—this guy is *good people."* And Omidyar felt the same way about Kagle.

Omidyar and partner Jeff Skoll faced a decision that boiled down to taking one of two offers. The heart of an offer is the monetary valuation of the company that will receive the investment. All other things being equal, the higher the valuation, the better for the entrepreneur. For example, if in case A one venture firm offers to invest $5 million and appraises the value of the company, in its present form, at $20 million, and in case B another venture firm also offers to invest $5 million but appraises the company's current value at $45 million, the entrepreneur would naturally view the second offer as much more attractive, because the same amount of capital received would buy a smaller percentage of his company.

To illustrate the jargon used in venture capital, hypothetical Firm A's offer to invest $5 million in a company assigned a value of $20 million would be expressed in terse shorthand: 5 at 20. The phrasing does not spell out what percentage of equity the investment would purchase, as that is easily calculated by the two numbers provided: the amount to be invested and the value of the company before the investment is made, or the "pre-money valuation." Add the $5 million of capital invested to the $20 million pre-money valuation (most commonly shortened simply to "pre-," as in, "We did the deal, five at twenty pre-"), and the resulting number, $25 million, is the "post-money valuation" and is the basis for determining how much equity is purchased. A $5 million investment in a company that will, upon completion of the deal, be nominally worth $25 million buys a 20 percent share of equity. So in case A the entrepreneur would have to give up 20 percent of his equity in the company for $5 million.

In case B, however, where a hypothetical venture capital firm offers 5 at 45 pre-, the arithmetic is much more favorable to the entrepreneur. Here a $5 million investment in a $45 million company that will be worth $50 million "post-" will only buy a 10 percent share of the equity, which would mean the entrepreneur would receive the same amount of capital but only have to relinquish half as much equity in order to secure the investment. It is those differences that put the interests of the entrepreneur and the venture capital firm in conflict at the time of negotiations. The entrepreneur wants the pre-money valuation to be as high as possible; the venture firm wants it as low as possible. There is no independent authority to set the valuations; it is settled solely through negotiation.

Of the two offers that the eBay entrepreneurs received, Benchmark's was on its face the least attractive. It appraised eBay's present value at approximately $20 million, and was, uncannily, only a tad below what Skoll had conservatively calculated the value of the company to be. (How did Benchmark do that, Omidyar wanted to know. Amazing!) The other offer, from Knight Ridder, was based on a valuation of $50 million.

If the investment was about the money, Omidyar should have taken the stack of green from Knight Ridder and run. It wasn't, and he didn't. The Knight Ridder offer meant selling the company in its entirety; the Benchmark offer, by contrast, meant selling only about 20 percent of the company and working with Kagle, recruiting a new CEO, and remaining in residence, with a role in future growth of the eBay community. Omidyar chose Benchmark.

EBay was an anomaly: a profitable company that was able to self-fund its growth and that turned to venture capital solely for contacts and counsel. No larger lesson can be drawn. When Benchmark wired the first millions to eBay's bank account, the figurative check was tossed into the vault—and there it would sit, unneeded and undisturbed.

3. Go Big or Go Home

Venture capitalists are not in the idea-generating end of business—that is a gift they neither have nor need. The venture guy's job is to refine his powers of evaluation, to hone the ability to see the outline of one good idea among the thousand brought in by entrepreneurs that are too small or me-too.

Dave Beirne did not know this, however. He arrived at Benchmark with ambitions to contribute to the partnership, fast, in any way he could, and he had some ideas for new businesses for which he hoped he could find entrepreneurs. One of the concepts that kept nagging him was an e-commerce business that he called MyStore, which would sell online everything for everyday needs. Start with groceries and move toward an online Wal-Mart.

"Well, shit," Bruce Dunlevie said when Beirne told him his idea as the two sat in Dunlevie's office, "have I got the plan for you." The five partners' individual offices were arranged along the rear and were rarely used for visitors, who were met in conference rooms at the front; within their sphere of private space, the partners dropped in to one another's offices throughout the day for informal consultations like this one. Dunlevie reached into a stack of papers and pulled out a business plan called Oasis. He tossed it to Beirne, explaining that he and the other partners lacked the balls to do it. Would Beirne be willing to get together with the guy?

What caught the eye immediately was the name of the entrepreneur: Louis Borders, the cofounder of Borders Books and Music. The company had grown from unlikely beginnings as a used-book store Borders and his brother Tom had opened in 1971 in the small town of Ann Arbor, on the edge of the University of Michigan campus, where Louis had earned a degree in mathematics. When they started the store Louis was twenty-three years old. Two years later, they added new books and subsequently developed a well-stocked-and-damn-the-accountants identity. In fact, Louis Borders had applied a talent for developing computer systems; he created artificial-intelligence software designed expressly for managing the inventory of a very large bookstore.

Initially, Borders used the systems as the basis for a separate business, serving other bookstores, but eventually—fifteen years after opening the first store—a second store was added. With the software, Borders Books pioneered in opening bookstores with a much larger stock—150,000 to 200,000 titles—than the typical 40,000 titles carried by the chain bookstores in malls. In 1992, on the eve of an IPO that would have valued the company, then consisting of twenty-one stores, at $180 million, the Borders brothers sold the company to Kmart for an undisclosed sum that presumably matched the IPO price and added a premium for the cession of independence.

The hyperexpansion of the chain would come later, after Borders no longer was associated with the company—and after Kmart spun the unit off in 1995 to become a wholly publicly owned company. To an onlooker in 1997, the ubiquity of a chain of 175 stores may have seemed the embodiment of the eponymous founder's will to expand, but in fact, that was not the case. Not surprisingly, after the sale of the company, Louis Borders had not felt a residual fever. Already living in the Bay Area, he spent his time looking at business plans as a potential "angel" investor and staying fit by playing a lot of basketball. He was not like Tom Wolfe's Charlie Croker, someone who tried to physically commandeer as much personal space as possible. Of medium height, with black hair and slightly protuberant eyes, he had a deliberately slow, quiet manner of speech tinged with a hard-to-place accent from boyhood (Louisville, Kentucky) and literary tastes that other mathematicians may not have shared (Nadine Gordimer was a particular favorite).

What interrupted this placid semiretirement was the arrival of the

Web, which had brought in its wake, unbidden, the Vision—of Oasis. He had approached Bruce Dunlevie the year before about his intention to start a new business that would sell and deliver to the home . . . everything. Soup to nuts, literally, but much more. Fresh fish, high-end consumer electronics equipment, CDs not to be found anywhere else, men's clothing, you name it. Three million separate stock-keeping units, or SKUs. When he had been in the book business, he had added far too many book titles, at least according to conventional wisdom, and it had worked out well; why not proceed on the same assumption here? The plans also included neighborhood stores, complete with kiosks providing a PC and connection to the Web, for those who wished to place their orders from the store instead of from home.

Earlier that year, after Borders had left the Benchmark office following a presentation to the partners, Bob Kagle had laughingly confessed to Dunlevie his lack of enthusiasm for Borders's grandiosity: "Fresh fish to washing machines? I'm just thinking too small." But Dunlevie had kept in touch with Borders, trying to persuade him to narrow the number of SKUs that he'd start out with from three million to one million, and to drop the idea of retail stores. It was a campaign waged at a low level of intensity. Borders was stubborn, progress was slow, and after these episodic discussions had rattled on for almost a year, there was still no deal in the offing.

Borders's ideas, as laid out in the current plan that Beirne opened, were dangerously unconventional and quaintly nostalgic at the same time. Louis Borders was forty-nine, not old enough to personally remember the halcyon days of home-delivery services, but old enough to remember older people remembering them. "In the old days, life was easier. When Mom needed groceries she would call the neighborhood market and it would deliver groceries in an hour or so. The dry cleaners picked up and delivered on Thursdays. The milkman came on Tuesdays and Fridays." He wrote longingly, too, of the way that neighborhood stores used to be small and the clerks knew their customers personally. Malls and superstores greatly increased selection but at the price of destroying the personal touches of a retail system that used to deliver to the home. Now, Borders believed, advances in technology made it possible to restore what had been lost. "Logistics and materials handling technology create new possi-

bilities for automated distribution. Expert systems and other artificial-intelligence systems enable the customization of inventory to
precisely fit a neighborhood store or an Internet customer."

Borders took the capabilities of such systems for granted, and lav-
ished his attention on the neighborhood store, which he conceived of
as a combination café and retail store whose intellectual parentage
could easily be traced back to Borders Books. "In contrast to malls
and superstores," Borders wrote, the Oasis Store would "retain the
comfortable ambience of a neighborhood meeting place."

Dunlevie had finally succeeded in getting Borders to pare the
SKUs down to one million, but even that number struck Beirne as
being essentially infinite. Borders still envisioned Oasis offering not
only groceries and home-meal replacements but the retail merchandise of a "modern general store," including books, music, consumer
electronics, housewares, toys, and sportswear. Borders matter-of-
factly defined his chosen corner of the market as "the U.S. retail market," which happened to be $2.3 trillion as of 1995.

When he joined Benchmark, Beirne had said he wanted to pursue
a go-big strategy, and this one certainly qualified. But he did not accept the whole vision. He wanted instead to start with groceries only,
use Borders's ideas about hub-and-spokes with an automated warehouse and neighborhood depots to replenish local delivery vans, but
drop the idea of retail storefronts, which entailed unnecessary cost
and complexity. Would Borders accept a less ambitious vision for this
new company's start?

When Dave Beirne met with Borders for the first time, he shared
his own thinking about MyStore, with conviction and details that
showed it was not something he had cooked up to pander to Borders.
But like a surgical resident facing a prospective first patient, any new
venture capitalist will have difficulty signing up entrepreneurs; nobody wants to be first. In Beirne's case, however, he had been offering advice about business strategy to clients for a long while; it was
part of what differentiated Ramsey Beirne from other executive
search firms. Borders took to Beirne and, at Benchmark's prodding,
agreed to drop the idea of the retail stores.

Even so, this was a deal that was going to require an enormous
amount of capital: $35 million, perhaps, to get Oasis, rechristened
Webvan, up and running in a single city, and another $25 million for

each additional city. Webvan's capital needs would have seemed to make it a deal unsuitable for an early-stage venture capital fund, but Webvan was only going to raise about $10 million initially. After planning advanced further, another round of financing would rely on OPM—Other People's Money—which would come in when Webvan commanded a much higher valuation. Presently, the Webvan deal was 9 pre-, that is, valued at $9 million before it received the infusion of capital. The company then consisted of Louis Borders, a handful of senior managers he had hired from the grocery business, and an office in Foster City, California, that he had set up under the purposely unrevealing name of Intelligent Systems for Retail.

Having worked closely with Jim Clark in building Netscape before joining Benchmark, Beirne knew that the past success of a name-brand entrepreneur was an asset that would allow him to paint a picture of future success, which in turn would attract more capital and more good people. The identical business concept in the hands of an unknown entrepreneur, however, would starve for lack of nourishment.

Entrepreneurs who sought venture funding usually did not need to invest any more personal money into the venture than they had already spent to bring it to life. But some venture capitalists did demand more. Arthur Rock, the senior dean of American venture capitalists and an early investor in Intel, always insisted whenever his venture firm put money into a start-up that the entrepreneur co-invest one third of his total net worth, whether it be large or small. If the entrepreneur was extremely wealthy, the venture firm had higher expectations about his co-investing. The venture guys didn't want the high-net-worth entrepreneur to regard the start-up as a hobby. To prove commitment, he was asked to have skin in the game, and that was what Beirne asked of Borders, whose net worth Beirne assumed to be around $100 million. Borders put in $3.5 million, along with Benchmark's $3.5 million, and $3.5 million was sought from another venture firm, not to spread financial risk—the amount involved was too small relatively for that to be a pressing issue—but in order to tap the other firm's access to capital markets—more OPM—which would be needed.

Beirne sent Borders over to pitch Kleiner's John Doerr. This, a deal that could redefine a huge swath of the economy, was sure to excite Doerr. And it appeared that he had taken graciously Beirne's decision to join Benchmark instead of Kleiner, saying at the time he would like to work jointly on a project with Beirne.

Borders's presentation at Kleiner Perkins did not go well, however. He spent most of his time talking about the bricks and mortar and the trucks. And he backpedaled; the neighborhood depots, he said, could be retail stores, too. So he had not given up on his original concept after all.

It mattered not a bit. Doerr appeared to be uncharacteristically exhausted during the presentation, and Borders was not impressed. And it dawned on Beirne that Doerr, notwithstanding his polite offer of wanting to work together, might not really be interested in doing so, and might actually wish for him to fail in a satisfyingly spectacular way—a scenario that this deal, with its outsized ambitions, seemed well-suited to bring about. Kleiner was out.

Beirne next turned to Sequoia Capital, which, like Kleiner Perkins, was founded in 1972, and whose partner Mike Moritz had backed Yahoo, a connection that Beirne thought would be valuable in sending online customers to Webvan. The presentation went well. Don Valentine, Sequoia's crusty founder, who was known to ask a visiting supplicant, "Who cares?" (or, in a more vulgar rendering when impressions of Valentine were performed, "Why the fuck should we give you our money?"), seemed pleased. He had no compunction about asking the question that everyone else in the room had to have been wondering about but hadn't asked: Louis, your family alone could fund this. Why the hell are you talking to us?

"When I came out here ten years ago," Borders said, "I had a cynical view of venture capital—vulture capital." But he had subsequently seen that "in order to be able to attract the best people, you need to have the backing of winners. It's not the money"—he did not realize that that was the exact phrase eBay's Pierre Omidyar had just used when he'd gone to Benchmark—"it's the Rolodex, it's being backed by the venture firms that have a record of knocking it out of the park."

Valentine beamed. Sequoia was in, and Mike Moritz joined Beirne on the Webvan board.

Borders now had two venture guys who were telling him the same thing: Don't even think about restoring the original idea of retail storefronts. Stick to online ordering and home delivery. Cut out everything initially but groceries, on which the average household spends $5,000 a year—a considerably larger figure than the annual household expenditures on books. And, Louis, you've got to reduce the number of SKUs for your launch.

Slowly, slowly, Borders backed down. From one million SKUs, to 500,000, 200,000, 100,000, 50,000, then down to 30,000, only 50 percent more items than a huge Safeway carried.

■

Each Monday morning the Benchmark partners held a free-form partners' meeting. No one held a particular place around the table, but what each partner typically brought with him to the meeting revealed some differences in personality.

As the venture guy behind the PalmPilot, Bruce Dunlevie not surprisingly used a Pilot to make appointments and look up phone numbers for other partners during the meeting, but he also brought along a tall messy stack of legal pads, each reserved for a separate pending deal, with many pages filled in and the top pages folded over; interspersed were clippings from the computer-industry trade press, which he would pull out and send flying across the table, like paper Frisbees, to the partner who may have missed the item.

Dunlevie's investments were perhaps the most eclectic among the Benchmark partners, spanning hardware and software, companies marketing to business customers and those marketing to consumers, but if his interests had to be pigeonholed, he would be labeled the hardware guy. If a single specialty category had to be assigned to the others, Andy Rachleff would be the network equipment and telecommunications guy. He too consulted his Pilot frequently during meetings to check on appointments, but he did not use it for his list of calls to make. In the venture capital business, telephone calls form the heart of every workday, and Rachleff, a person who approached his work with methodical care, brought with him a one-page printout of his to-do list that he kept in an Excel spreadsheet; he would annotate or remove items from the printout as the meeting proceeded and update his file on his office computer later. The list was not legible to anyone sitting by his side; he employed the very smallest font in order to shrink the many dozens of entries down to one page.

Having come to venture capital from his prior career as a software entrepreneur, Kevin Harvey would have been the one most likely to use the most up-to-date gadgetry and software to organize his professional life, but he did not. His style was a radical minimalism: an empty legal pad or, often, nothing in his hands at all. He explained his positions on close votes within the partnership with the same spareness, a trait that he was the first to lampoon.

Among the group were those who clung stubbornly to throwback instruments born long before Silicon Valley came into being. Though trained as an electrical and mechanical engineer, though he was an investor in the most advanced electronic design automation software, Bob Kagle used a low-tech device: a dime-store datebook so small that when he held it in both hands, flipping its tiny pages to locate a given day's schedule, it almost looked like a dollhouse miniature. The most conspicuous anachronism in the room, however, would have fit well in a nineteenth-century counting room (yet had an instant-on feature faster than even the Pilot's): a leather-bound journal that Dave Beirne brought to the meeting to jot down the occasional note about a call to be made. He had used the same kind of journal while at Ramsey Beirne—a new one put into service with the arrival of each new year—and as he was a newly arrived Silicon Valley resident, it was too early to know whether over time he would hold to the journal or put it aside for a recording medium of more recent provenance.

No one knew in advance of the Monday partners' meeting which topics would end up occupying the bulk of the group's attention. During the rest of the week, conversations between partners in every possible pairing kept everyone informed about most prospective deals under someone's consideration, so the gathering of the partners was the time for going deeper into discussion of a deal, or for bouncing ideas off the group and picking up warning signals from others about generic problems in a portfolio company that one could not see on one's own.

On a Monday morning in December 1997, two months after the close of Webvan's first round of financing, Dave Beirne brought to the group a brief report on work that had already begun on that venture's second round. Benchmark and Sequoia would not be putting additional money in; other investors would come in, and the size of equity owned by the original two backers would shrink.

As was his style at the partners' meeting, Beirne wasted no time with preamble or throat clearing. "We need to raise thirty-three million for Louis Borders," he said. He looked over to Kevin Harvey. "So if you'd open your checkbook, Kev." In a serious vein, he explained that the company needed to have $18.5 million immediately in order to get the first distribution center leased and equipped.

"For one?" Kevin Harvey wanted to know. "Ooooooh!"

Andy Rachleff answered for Beirne: "Yes, one!" He found this amusing.

Harvey didn't join in Rachleff's laughter. "Only one?" he tried again.

"Only one," Beirne said. "And we need for the real estate, fifteen million."

Beirne itemized what the money was needed for. "This is everything—vehicles, trays and totes, the office space, kitchen equipment, material-handling equipment. All the conveyors and carousels, software for the conveyors and carousels, all the hardware."

For chief financial officer, Harvey said to Beirne, "You're going to need to find a guy of just untold proportions."

"I know that."

Rachleff suggested the name of someone he had worked with before who would love the challenge. "Really well regarded on Wall Street. I could call him up."

"Please."

Rachleff also had a suggestion for a potential funding source for this round, a bank on the East Coast. He had a buddy there he could run the idea by. "They don't want to be involved in start-ups 'cause you can't put enough capital to work but"—he laughed—"that won't be a problem here."

"Please."

Rachleff reflected, "A lot of this stuff—vans and things—those are real assets. They're not like what we usually finance."

"Damn straight," said Beirne.

Kagle, who when he was growing up had watched GM embrace automation in a notoriously expensive and ineffective way, had been listening silently but could not hold back any longer. "That automation shit is going to kill you here." He shook his head. "That just eats my gut out that he's going to put so much money into that up front when you're just shaking the thing down. It just seems like there's a time and place for that. Dave, has anything changed in the company other than refining the concept since the investment?"

"No. The concept is what we funded."

Kevin Harvey, who was one of the most optimistic bulls in the partnership, was also one of the most skeptical reviewers of a given deal. He shared Kagle's concern. "There's no demonstration of anything other than it's more refined?"

"Correct."

Beirne had been persuaded by Borders that the current plan was the right one.

"You have to have the warehouse," he reasoned. "You can say, 'Okay, get a slightly smaller warehouse.' The differences aren't that great. You have to have that in place. You have to have a certain number of trucks to do the delivery. It's not inventory—that's not your cost. So scaling the plan back slightly is scaling the plan back dramatically. You either do it, or you don't. I think we'll know this time next year whether this company is going to happen or not."

"It doesn't have to be that way," Kagle persisted.

"That's how the game is being played. I tried to get him to think smaller. He's not thinking smaller. He's thinking big. This is a big bang. It's his ego and his money on the line, guys, and he's got his heart and soul into it."

"That's what we were signing up for on that," Bruce Dunlevie said with equanimity.

"It's a big bang deal," Harvey conceded, "but if he's raising more money, hasn't hired a VP of engineering, the plan's evolved in his *head,* but nothing's happened, nothing's done, no progress."

"A lot of progress has happened. Everything is architected. He believes the system will be done."

Beirne wound up his report. "That's where we are. Louis is very thoughtful. I think he is a perfectionist. He is totally confident that we're going to be able to do a hundred million in revenue with him as CEO before we even bring in the other CEO, and he still says we're bringing in the other CEO. He's doing all the right things."

Beirne was silent for a few moments, then continued. "The beauty of this business is—I don't think this is a four-round financing. There is not another venture round."

"And it's not our money," Rachleff added.

"We need so much money . . ." Beirne paused. "Either raise the money or it's fucking over."

■

Later that morning Dave Beirne made a vow that took the form of a confession. "My goal," he said, "is to be either a really successful venture capitalist quick, or be out of the business in a hurry." He did not smile.

Bob Kagle said, too quickly, "You're on that game plan, Dave." He laughed quickly to try to soften the comment.

Beirne did not back off. "It will be one of the two." He slowly nodded his head.

■

Kagle could not convince Borders, through Beirne, to try a less capital-intensive, smaller-scale approach, but a little business in Los Angeles, named Pink Dot, caught his eye because it seemed to be a low-cost home-delivery service that was already thriving. He took Beirne along to L.A. for a visit. Both were impressed with what they saw.

After returning home, Kagle told the others with characteristic animation: "Just strictly 7-Eleven on wheels. Only the convenience-store products. They're up to north of twelve million dollars annualized run rate in sales. The two new stores are positive comps already."

"I think it's a great business," Beirne chimed in.

"Yeah, fifty-five hundred SKUs." The delivery charge was $1.99 for the first thirty days; then it went to $2.99. It was impulse purchases, Kagle explained. "It's all people that decide at the last minute they wanted something. So it's *not* somebody's weekly grocery shopping. It's not something that's likely to compete that directly with Louis for that part of the market. So that's the big question I'd like us to wrestle with before we bring this guy up here and think about it." A venture firm would not invest in a company whose business directly overlapped with another's in the portfolio.

Beirne added more details about what they saw on their visit:

"Watching this girl on the phone in their mini–call center—the ability to do the McDonald's 'So would you like fries with that?'—the ability to add on to someone's bill—'Yes, yes, yes, yes'—the next thing you know, you've got a twenty-dollar order and away you go, and 'I just called for milk!' She gets an order, she just flew." The woman in the call center worked by prompts from the system. "Barely spoke English, but didn't need to. I'm serious. It's so cool."

At Beirne's mention that the call-center people probably didn't earn more than the minimum wage, Kagle broke in: "This *is* an entrepreneurial company, and a lot of this has been done without a lot of capital, so there's a big need to professionalize it."

He was impressed, though, by how successfully the company had acquired customers with a very limited marketing budget. "They do bus benches and billboards on sides of buses, just little things, and drive these small blue-and-pink VW bugs around. Pink Dot. This thing has eyes on it—it's absolutely hysterical."

Dunlevie asked, "Is there likely Web orientation to Pink Dot? Not in our minds, in *their* minds?"

The company had a website but did less than 10 percent of its volume through it. "I think this is a big insight on their part," Kagle enthused. "They said, 'Hey, look, all the volume is on the phone today!'" Here was a company that was using no more technology than what was needed.

Beirne thought that most Pink Dot customers would continue to order over the phone instead of on the Web. "You're not going to boot up your computer just to go order milk and a six-pack of Budweiser. A majority of what they're doing is beer, soda, milk, and cigarettes."

"Do we want to invest in companies who are doing beer and cigarettes?" Dunlevie maintained a deadpan expression.

"You mean, compared to gambling?" Kagle asked, laughing. Benchmark Capital's very first investment in 1995 was as a co-investor, with Kleiner Perkins, in Silicon Gaming, a manufacturer of electronic slot machines.

"Cover all the vices," someone said.

Discussions with Pink Dot progressed a bit further, and the prospective new CEO of the company came up to meet with the partners. But afterward Kagle told his partners that he could not "get comfortable with the entrepreneur," one of his inviolate prerequisites for doing a deal, and the discussions ended. Pink Dot was just one of many dozens of companies that would get far along in the process but not go all the way.

Webvan, in the meantime, did not lack for investor interest. Seven months after Benchmark's financing, the company raised another $33 million. It was still a long way from opening for business, but the premoney valuation of the company on this round had gone up to $200 million.

■

Let's roll.

It was December 1998, a year after Dave Beirne had told the partners about the large checks that Webvan was writing. In the interim, Beirne had developed a close working relationship with Louis Borders, speaking daily by phone, paying visits to Borders's office and the distribution center in Oakland as it was being prepared; meeting with candidates on executive searches; rounding up potential private investors. Webvan was a Silicon Valley baby in gestation, and Beirne would be one of the obstetricians, but one with a heavy emotional investment in the upcoming delivery.

To Beirne's partners, though, Webvan's progress remained an abstraction, the unseen source of Beirne's 2:00 A.M. sweats. They were eager to see the little darling—actually a very big darling, this work-in-progress that would not be open for business for another six months. That Wednesday morning was the appointed time for the other four partners to go to Oakland for a tour of Webvan's not-yet-open-for-business distribution center, but two of the four were still on the phone.

C'mon, c'mon, guys, let's roll.

They let Beirne set the pace, stride, stride, stride, triple time to the stairwell, down and out to the parking level, Beirne jumping into Kevin Harvey's car and the others taking Andy Rachleff's.

The hurry was Beirne's, and not actually necessary. It was compensatory hurry, the combustion of eagerness, frustration, excitement, and concern; he was the new guy, and this deal was not only his most ambitious one, it was the firm's, too. Stepping courageously—or blithely—across the carcasses of other companies that had tried to deliver groceries to the home, Webvan aspired to the revenues of Wal-Mart. Louis Borders was going to pull this off, Beirne believed. The partners needed only to see the new facility taking shape, and they would feel it, too. And they would stop looking at him as a gullible neophyte.

"Louis," Kevin Harvey had said to Borders the year before as they shook hands after agreeing to the investment, offering the most grand of predictions, "this is going to be a billion-dollar company."

"Naw. It's going to be ten billion. Or zero."

That had made an impression on the Benchmark partners in the way a scary prediction that feels right does.

As Harvey's car headed over the San Mateo Bridge, Beirne stared out the side window, into the haze that obscured the southern half of the San Francisco Bay. On the golf course the other day, he said, a friend had floated a theory that leaders, in business or anything else, are driven by demons. The best guys have them—implacable, subterranean demons that are the source of greatness. Harvey, the house critic when at the office, usually could be counted on to take issue with whatever stood as the conventional wisdom du jour, but on this point he peacefully agreed. What about their own demons, Harvey asked. "Oh, yes," Beirne granted. But it was midmorning on a workday, not the time for a personal inventory.

The conversation bounced to the subject of raising kids. How do you protect them from a world of menace, without overprotecting them? It was unanswerable and led only to more questions, offered up without hope of resolution.

The two returned to practical matters—Kleiner Perkins. "Going to the KP Christmas party?" Harvey asked. The haughtiness of aristocrats versus the scrappiness of up-from-the-bottom plebeians; that was how Beirne felt Kleiner Perkins's and Benchmark's cultural values diverged. He remembered how one of Doerr's colleagues "always asked what school you went to. Checking your pedigree."

He grimaced at the thought. "Like dogs sniffing each other." Now he confessed to the absent KP patrician, "Okay, I'm a mutt!"

Beirne offered Harvey a compliment about the new car. More as a gesture of defensiveness than of pride, Harvey ran his hands lightly along the top of the steering wheel. Even though it was a low-end BMW, it remained a BMW after all, so he knew he was brushing awfully close to the sin of ostentation.

"I like it 'cause it doesn't look like a BMW, it looks like a Toyota," he offered.

"Right." Beirne snorted.

Harvey gave as well as he got. "How can you give me shit? What about the Batmobile?" Yes, that one needed explaining. Beirne was consumed by work and family, temperamentally disinclined to pay attention to the world of things. He earned $10 million at Ramsey Beirne the year before he joined Benchmark, so he had the means to spend, but lack of practice and sustained interest meant he committed gaucheries. He also had a tendency to make grand gestures, compounding his susceptibility to his partners' teasing barbs. The others deliberately maintained a lifestyle that was materially muted, at least by Silicon Valley standards. Their cars were family cars, four-door BMW's and Audis. But when Beirne, the new arrival from New York, had decided to get a car suitable, he thought, for the Valley, he walked into a Porsche dealership, announced that whatever he bought he had to be able to drive off the lot right then, and headed home in a two-person black 911 Carrera, a car too small for him to fit in comfortably, let alone his wife and three young kids. That's what Harvey had taken to calling the Batmobile.

No one had more fun pricking any incipient sign of pretension in himself than Harvey. Now, driving toward Oakland, he laughed at the memory of how, after his first company's sale when he was twenty-three, he had gone through his BMW sports car phase, viewing it as the perfect magnet with which "to pick up chicks."

"I bet you didn't do well," Beirne said.

"I didn't."

Beirne, who was already married by that age to the young woman he'd known since he and she were twelve, marveled with a laugh at his own lack of experience.

■

On the drive over, Webvan was not discussed. All Beirne would say was that Harvey and the others would "be blown away" by what they were about to see.

As Beirne and Harvey pulled off an exit just north of the Oakland Coliseum, they entered an industrial world of asphalt, concrete, rail sidings, and grit. It was utilitarian from horizon to horizon, unsoftened by a single green dot of landscaping. And there, sitting across from a drive-in movie theater converted to a flea market, was the future Bay Area Distribution Center of Webvan, a long warehouse painted white, its sides pocked by forty trailer bays. No sign identified the company. A guard shack at the entrance and razor wire along the top of the fence conveyed a message that this was not a retail establishment, but thumbtacked to the shack was an incongruous sign: NOTICE TO SELL ALCOHOLIC BEVERAGES.

The others had already arrived, and as Beirne introduced everyone to the project manager, white hard hats were passed out, a strange accoutrement to the blue dress shirts and khakis that were the Valley uniform. Beirne fell silent, letting the project manager serve as guide. The group stepped inside.

The cavernous dark encompassed 325,000 square feet, an expanse so large that an amusement park of twisting conveyors and motorized racks only partially filled the space, at least until the remaining gear arrived. Brightly colored plastic totes rode atop some of the conveyors, and some nonperishable grocery items zipped by as testing proceeded. Few people were to be seen: a couple of technicians tinkering with the conveyors and some welders working in new rooms in the center, which would house freezers, refrigerated storage, a bakery, and kitchens for preparing the ready-to-heat meals that would be offered along with groceries.

Description had to suffice until the day when the fully loaded system could be demonstrated at work, but the heart of the giant experiment—the place where Borders and Beirne were convinced Webvan would be able to lower costs and escape the notoriously low margins of the grocery business, the spot that all of the security on the outside was intended to keep safely out of view—was the pod. It was a small work area, just large enough for a single worker to be able to swing her arms, where the grocery items came to the picker instead of the picker going to them. Each pod was served by three enormous, motorized racks that traveled in an ellipse—like those at a dry cleaner, only taller, and upon which were hung eight-foot-high towers of bins instead of clothes. The beauty of the system, at least on the blueprints, was that the racks would spin around automatically, so that one worker, standing in one place, would have access to the equivalent inventory of an entire Safeway store. The design eliminated the possibility of human error; when the computer directed that a given bin be positioned near the picker so that the goods could be placed in a tote, a directional arrow lit up, indicating the correct bin. Pick here; now pick here.

Invisible was the system, or rather, systems, which would take in orders submitted via the Web, guide the picking and packing and loading and delivering, keep track of the fifty thousand separate categories of items, do the forecasting and perfect the inventory modeling, and perform a myriad of other functions.

As they toured the facility, the Benchmark partners asked no questions about the systems. They knew that it was Louis Borders's artificial-intelligence-based inventory systems that had modernized book retailing. If problems with Webvan's systems appeared when it went into initial production—if they were solvable—they had the perfect entrepreneur at the helm to find the solutions.

The visitors nodded appreciatively at the spectacle, thanked their guide, returned the hard hats, and stepped outside. The outsized machinery inside had left Beirne vibrating with excitement. As he race-walked to the cars, he said over his shoulder, "My dad was in manufacturing—it's all we talked about." Maybe in the future, he said, "that's what I'll do, go run something like this."

In the car, Beirne called Borders on the car phone and reported on the visit. "Awesome. My partners were blown away."

They were? If so, their visible reaction was restrained. To the others, the visit brought home the challenges that Webvan faced, including the handling of tens of thousands of variously shaped physical goods, with trucks, with employees, with spoilage and traffic jams and unionization headaches. It was a hybrid, Old Economy and New, and the Old part was scary.

And though the other partners shared Beirne's confidence in Borders's abilities to make the infernally complex systems run, they remained uncomfortable about Borders's blind faith in the concept. There were no prelaunch focus groups or surveys planned, no test marketing. Borders was almost pathologically concerned about secrecy, which he believed market testing would compromise. He was convinced that there was no need for research. Build it, and they would come.

Actually, build many. Plans to begin work on distribution centers for other cities had to advance before the first one was open, lest Webvan lose the technological lead. This was in keeping with Beirne's oft-quoted motto: Go big or go home.

4. Accidents Happen

The Entrepreneur is easy to recognize when encountered. This is the person who is afflicted by a monomaniacal fever, who cannot *not* be an entrepreneur.

There are others, though, who do not fit the template, such as Louis Borders, who had left the game, or thought he had, until he was hit with a singular inspiration and could not *not* test the Big Idea. Pierre Omidyar, the founder of eBay, was another nontypical entrepreneur. It was easy to imagine him comfortably disengaged in business, in a fashion that perhaps mirrored the way he was as comfortable living in France, where he was born in 1967 and lived until he was six and where he often returned, as he was living in the United States. With his unaccented English and reticence in divulging private interests, you would not guess that he inhabited a twin world at will.

EBay's creation story did not begin in a garage. Better, for anyone seeking inspiration, it began in Omidyar's apartment and got under way without impinging on his day job. It originally was not even conceived of as a business. In 1995 Omidyar decided on a whim to use the Web pages that came as part of his $30-a-month Internet service to improve upon the online classifieds for selling personal items that were posted on the Net's news groups. With a little code, a simple auction could run that would spare the seller from having to choose among multiple interested buyers. As the code did the work and the space on the Web server came with his account, it cost him nothing out-of-pocket to provide. He conceived of it as a public service, offered free to whoever wished to use it.

Omidyar would later tell feature-story reporters that eBay's origins were the chance result of a conversation with his girlfriend, a collector of Pez dispensers, who asked him one evening at dinner if there was a way he could set up a website for collectors like her. There is a more interesting story that reveals, in microcosm, the combined elements of business and technology that defined that historical moment. Omidyar's apartment, with its dial-up connection to the Internet, theoretically could have been anywhere in the world, but in fact, it indeed mattered that it was situated in Silicon Valley.

Omidyar had not come to the Valley by accident. He grew up near Washington, D.C., and went to Tufts University, near Boston, majoring in computer science. He was so eager to work in the Valley that he couldn't wait for graduation; after his junior year he moved to California to work on a drawing program for the Macintosh. After working a year, he went back to school and finished his degree, then returned to the Valley and worked for Claris as a software engineer. Because he was physically, not virtually, present, he made acquaintances that led him in 1991 to cofound Ink Development, the developer of pen-based software.

The market for pen computing did not materialize, and Ink was headed for oblivion. But one of its the-world-isn't-ready-for-us-yet projects, shopping via electronic pen tablets, involved work that Omidyar, a project manager, oversaw: developing order-processing and accounting systems on the back end to handle the online orders that were to come pouring in via tablets. As Ink was sinking, the work on those back-end database systems was salvaged, and Ink was renamed eShop. Its venture capital backers were Merrill Pickard and Technology Venture Investors, the two firms where Bruce Dunlevie, Andy Rachleff, and Bob Kagle worked pre-Benchmark. Before Microsoft acquired eShop (turning the software into its Merchant Server product), Omidyar left, but tellingly he was fever-free and did not head off to start his own company. He took a job at General Magic, recruiting developers to work with the company's software.

Previously, he had not been a senior executive; General Magic was his first opportunity to get out of his cubicle and away from printouts of code, to develop business relationships with others.

His professional experiences permitted him to see where nascent electronic commerce was headed: businesses selling to other businesses. It was a direction that was not just dull but a threat to the anticommercial gestalt that imbued the Internet, which was still the exclusive domain of academics—professors, students, government researchers. His Internet service provider required all of its customers to sign an "acceptable use" agreement, swearing that they would not use their Internet account for commercial purposes.

Though he thought of himself as having the same "anticommercial mind-set," he wasn't anticommercial so much as he was anti–big business. It maddened him that on Wall Street institutional buyers got newly issued shares in a company's IPO before individuals got a chance. He could not do anything about that, but by combining an online listing service for collectors and garage-sale sellers with a more efficient market-making mechanism, the auction, he could make it easier for individuals to do business with one another—consumer-to-consumer—without the intermediation of big business. First, though, he had to find an Internet service provider that did not require him to renounce commerce of all shape, size, and form.

Silicon Valley had plenty of providers to choose from, and it also had other helpful resources, such as Computer Literacy, a local chain of bookstores that sold nothing but computer books. He loaded up on programming manuals for Perl, a language commonly used with UNIX systems, and designed a Web-based database for his listing service, which he initially called Auction Web.

On Labor Day 1995, he sent an announcement of his free service to the then-center of Webdom, the National Center for Supercomputing Applications's "What's New" Web page. The NCSA's queue was backed up, so it took a month before Auction Web appeared, but once it did, visitors came. And told their friends. Who told *their* friends. Omidyar was pleased to see that by the end of 1995, his little creation was getting a couple of thousand hits a day.

His Internet service provider, Best, was not so pleased. Omidyar's website gobbled a disproportionate share of the computer's resources, as each bid sent in to Auction Web set a separate Perl process in motion. This took Best by surprise; it had not thought to set policies that defined a maximum number of CPU cycles or Web-page hits for an account such as his. Best demanded that Omidyar move his site to a business server, and the monthly charge for his account jumped from $30 a month to $250.

This turn of events forced him to change from a free service to almost free; in February 1996, to try to recoup the charges that Best imposed on him, Omidyar asked sellers to pay a small fee for items sold. There was no charge for listing items, and payment of the fee for items sold relied wholly upon the honesty of the seller to send in the money after the conclusion of a successful auction.

The checks arrived in volume, delivered in the large canvas bags of the U.S. Postal Service. In month one he covered the $250 bill for his Internet service. In month two, $1,000 arrived; month three, $2,000; month four, $5,000; month five, $10,000. He never went into the red, even when he had to install his own server on Best's premises when told that the traffic Auction Web attracted was overwhelming Best's shared business server. Omidyar himself, accidental proprietor of a one-person company that had grown faster than he had ever imagined, was overwhelmed. He was always on duty, even during his regular snowboarding trips to Lake Tahoe; using his laptop there to try to remotely restart systems that had gone down in San Jose was not an ideal arrangement. He desperately needed a full-time UNIX systems expert to oversee the server, but even before that, he needed a helper who did nothing but slice open the envelopes and pull out the checks.

By the middle of 1996, he had to do something: either resign from his day job and try to make a go of this new company, or pull the plug. He was earning more from eBay than from his salary at General Magic, and it may appear that the easy choice would have been to chuck the job. He was twenty-nine years old, without dependents, possessing technical skills and professional experiences that would enable him to work for any employer in the Valley. For such a person, starting a company was not fraught with the risk of lasting professional damage. Moreover, he had already acquired an enviable financial cushion: When eShop was sold to Microsoft in mid-1996,

Omidyar received Microsoft shares by then worth more than a million dollars.

Ah! So that's why Omidyar felt emboldened to jump back into the uncertainty of entrepreneurialism—he had a mattress stuffed with a million dollars of stock to sleep on.

Not so, he later insisted when looking back. That newfound wealth was as likely to have led him to abandon Auction Web—in favor of retirement—as to choose to work on the fledgling company full-time.

"You get a million dollars? When you're twenty-nine?" he asked rhetorically. "Hey, take some time off. Take a *lot* of time off." The retirement option was tempting. Auction Web required constant care and feeding. But when he asked himself the questions "What am I doing this for? Why am I killing myself?" he could rule out the usual answer: money. He came to the realization that he had been having fun and deriving gratification from seeing thousands of people use the service. It was miraculous—"really cool"—how other people had become attached to something he created. Can mere money buy you that?

Omidyar left his day job, but not before finding two others to be partners with him at his newly named company, eBay. He told them to figure out what the value of the company was at that point. Whatever number they told him would be fine; they should split ownership in such a way that the increased value going forward would be split equally three ways.

On the verge of starting, one of the two new partners backed out. He had just started a new job that he liked; it was too good to leave for a flyspeck of a company like eBay, which was going to move from Omidyar's bedroom to an almost equally modest home: the NASA small-business incubator in Mountain View.

The new partner who did take the leap with Omidyar was Jeff Skoll, thirty years old, a Canadian-born engineer who had started two small businesses of his own before going to Stanford to get his MBA. He had graduated the year before and gone to work at Knight Ridder Information, in Mountain View, the division of the large newspaper chain that was charged with figuring out the future of classified ads.

Skoll lived in a house with two friends who had been his classmates at Stanford and had gone to start-ups, and he could not eat a bowl of cereal without hearing his roommates talk nonstop—with the fervor of missionaries—about the Internet and the satisfactions to be derived only at start-ups. One of his housemates introduced him to a few companies, including eBay. When Omidyar, who thought Skoll's analytical skills complemented his own intuitive style of decision making, invited him to join as partner, that was the end of Skoll's dalliance with the large corporation.

By temperament, Skoll could not help but pour himself into the work in a scarily total fashion—once he started at eBay, he worked hundred-hour weeks for the next two and a half years. But he wasn't driven by materialist hungers, and he thought of himself not as a businessperson but as a writer. When their eBay stock had made him and Omidyar paper multibillionaires a mere three years later, the author of a feature story on Skoll's philanthropic activities was surprised to discover that Skoll lived in the same rental house, now with four housemates. Other than buying a new bike and a new car that replaced his ten-year-old Mazda, he hadn't spent anything on himself.

In the fall of 1996, when they moved eBay from the NASA incubator to its first office, it was to a small space in an unassuming three-story building in southwest San Jose, on the edge of Edge City, with modest single-family homes across the street, a condo complex next door, a strip mall nearby.

The partners had to figure out some basic strategic questions: Should eBay try to build a business based on the Auction Web site? Or should it instead try to sell auction-management software to other websites? This was what some prospective angel investors advised them, and with no consumer marketing experience between the two of them, the latter seemed like a more prudent course. But while they deliberated, the number of listings grew organically 40 percent *each month,* without a penny spent in marketing. In the face of vertiginous growth, it was hard to argue forcefully that drastic strategic redirection was needed. They also decided to continue to offer listings in a number of categories, at the risk of spreading coverage too thin, rather than start first with a single category (coins). It was an instinctual call, and a good one.

They discovered that any experienced manager whom they attempted to recruit asked to see that the business had passed the professional vetting of venture guys, had access to their deep pockets and advice and Rolodexes. Steve Westly, a Stanford MBA who was a vice president at another Internet start-up, WhoWhere, was impressed when Jeff Skoll tried to recruit him to eBay as vice president of marketing and he learned that eBay's revenues were $400,000 a month and its expenses $200,000. They had reached the same numbers at WhoWhere, but as at most Internet companies, they were inverted. Still, WhoWhere had venture backing from Venrock, one of the first venture capital firms, and eBay had none. Westly could not bring himself to make the move.

Omidyar and Skoll wanted to recruit an experienced CEO as soon as possible. They wanted someone with not just experience but also the traditional credentials that Wall Street looked for (and who did not harbor anti-big-business inclinations that the analysts might sniff out).

The absence of venture backing that prevented eBay from having any chance of landing the sort of person the eBay founders sought also prevented them from even being able to retain an executive search firm to see what it could find. Omidyar and Skoll were not aware of the existence of such specialized search firms as Ramsey Beirne Associates, but had they been, they would not have gotten their calls returned. A Ramsey Beirne had all the business it could handle, and it did not want to bother executive candidates with an opportunity at a firm that had not passed the screening of venture guys.

That was when Omidyar approached Benchmark. He and Skoll sealed the deal in summer 1997. Afterward, one of the first calls Skoll made, at Bob Kagle's suggestion, was to Ramsey Beirne. The search firm accepted the project, including the provision that the firm could elect in the future to purchase stock at an extremely favorable price.

■

Bob Kagle had Ramsey Beirne's Alan Seiler on the phone. The two had had a number of conversations over the past few weeks.

Kagle was the only one among the other partners at Benchmark who had never used Ramsey Beirne for one of his companies before Dave Beirne joined Benchmark. Kagle's recommendation of Ramsey

Beirne to eBay was a vote of confidence in his new partner, and brought with it an opportunity to learn something indirectly about Beirne by working with his old firm.

There'd been a bit of awkwardness when Kagle had his first chat with Seiler, who had explained that Ramsey Beirne's custom was to do its preliminary work, then present a list of five finalists for the position. What works for me, Kagle had said, would be for me to see the preliminary lists of candidates as you work, and have some discussions about them before we get to the finalists. Seiler had reluctantly agreed and shown Kagle the very first list he'd drawn up, twenty-five names of people that he planned to approach, including the CEO of Sotheby's, the CEO of Marvel Comics, a VP of marketing at Sears, a VP of Hasbro. Kagle had been pleased; it represented good variety and had what he wanted: hitters.

Now Seiler had just sent Kagle the next version of the list, with many names winnowed. As Kagle ran his eyes down the roster, Seiler explained, "I've talked to people and taken out those who are not interested."

"Meg Whitman?" Kagle asked. Whitman was the one at Hasbro; her name had disappeared.

"She's not interested. She declined."

"Go after her," Kagle insisted. "We need to be able to at least talk to her." Small, small world. Kagle had never met Whitman, but he remembered that a good friend of his from business school spoke highly of her; Whitman had succeeded Kagle's friend as head of FTD, the flower-delivery service. A graduate of Princeton, then Harvard Business School, Whitman had been a consultant for eight years at Bain and had moved successfully from consulting into management, first at Procter & Gamble, then at Disney. She could bring brand-building expertise, which eBay sorely needed, as well as the big-picture strategic thinking of a consultant—and she'd overseen the launch of FTD's website.

After hanging up with Seiler, Kagle called his friend to ask about Whitman. The report was highly positive.

Kagle, it turned out, had several other two-degrees-of-separation ties to Meg Whitman; she was regarded as a fellow member of this elite club, composed of players. Beirne actually knew her. The year before, through Intuit's Scott Cook—Cook and Whitman had worked at Bain together—Beirne had persuaded her to come down to Ramsey Beirne and talk to him about her career. She had physical presence—she was six feet tall, wide-shouldered, and blond. She also had a quick wit, a tendency to speak in bursts of single-clause sentences, and no shortage of self-confidence.

Now, in the fall of 1997, Ramsey Beirne called her in Brookline, Massachusetts, to tell her about a great company that happened to be an Internet start-up located in San Jose. Would she be interested in having a look?

She was happy at Hasbro and had been there only a year, too short a time to countenance another job hop. Her husband, a neurosurgeon who directed the brain-tumor program at Massachusetts General, had his own dream job and was not interested in a move. Her two kids were settled in their schools. She told Ramsey Beirne thanks, but no thanks.

Three weeks later Alan Seiler called her back. "I've been talking to Dave Beirne," he said, "and he says you are perfect for this job. Perfect. You owe it to yourself to get on a plane and come out and meet these guys."

She was still not interested, but she realized that now that they had stepped up the pressure, she had to pretend to go along—she needed to humor Dave Beirne and his former associates at Ramsey Beirne, preserve the relationships for that time in the future when she might really need them. For now, she would do as they asked and get on a plane. By being a good trouper, she would show them that she would seriously consider opportunities they brought to her in the future. All it would cost her would be the one day.

The night before she was to leave, she took a look at eBay's website for the first time. She was appalled: electronic classifieds! That was what she was about to fly to California to look at? It was so . . . so . . . so incredibly boring! She'd been foolish to promise to go through the motions. Was there any way she could still wiggle out of the trip and not lose the day? She went to bed, resigned that it was too late to cancel.

Sleep did not come. There had to be more to this than what she had just seen. Dave Beirne would not have her get on a plane to run an electronic-classifieds company. She hopped up, turned her PC back on, and spent two hours wandering around the eBay site. She saw the range of categories and the feedback ratings and got a sense that it was not an exact copy of a newspaper's classified ads. She went back to bed and slept a few hours before flying to California.

Whitman came to the Benchmark office and schmoozed for six hours with Bob Kagle, Pierre Omidyar, and Jeff Skoll. Omidyar kept talking about eBay as an "enabling" business—a curious adjective—that put people together to do business who had had no means to do so before. This was not what she had expected. When she returned home, she called Alan Seiler and said, "Okay, I'll go out again. But this time I need to sit down with someone to go through the financial model."

The Wednesday before Thanksgiving—with forty guests scheduled to arrive at her Brookline home the next day—she was in eBay's new San Jose office, which still had no cubicles. Meeting with eBay's chief financial officer, she learned that unlike online auction pioneer Onsale, unlike Amazon or other e-commerce companies, eBay had no inventory. Nothing to ship. Nothing to warehouse. No carrying costs. No obsolescence. No pick-and-pack. Which meant very good margins. This was good. This was very good. Twenty years of business had taught her a lesson that she illustrated with a simile drawn from football: "Having long gross margins is like starting on the fifty-yard line."

When she returned home, she described eBay to her husband as an Internet company that was growing fast—a string of fourteen months of 40 percent monthly growth, compounded—that she thought had "stumbled onto something that had unbelievable potential." He was amenable to her investigating further. In late December Whitman and her family flew out to California. Over dinner at Kagle's house, her husband met these people Whitman had been talking about: Kagle, Omidyar, and Skoll. Whitman stayed another day, after her family flew home, and at the end of that day Omidyar said, "We'd really like you to join the company." Whitman still was not sure—she'd just learned at dinner that eBay's growth had evaporated in December—going from 40 percent to zero, which gave her pause. She promised Omidyar that she would try to decide quickly.

■

It was Monday morning, and the partners drifted into the conference room. Not Dave Beirne, however—*drifted* is not apt; he came in the only way he knew: emphatically. He dropped his leather-bound journal down on the table with a clap and threw himself backward into his seat, grabbing the chair's two arms at the rear, with his own arms bent, looking as if he were about to propel himself back up onto rings for a gymnastics demonstration. He didn't say a word, but the performance—that's how Kevin Harvey would rib him, insisting that Beirne always put on a performance, even with only his partners present—said, Let's get started.

Before new deals were taken up, Bob Kagle reported on eBay's CEO search.

"We had dinner Saturday night with Meg and her husband. We've been working her through the month of December. I think she's excited."

Bruce Dunlevie didn't know who she was. "Her background is what?"

"She's Disney, FTD, and Playskool, after nine years at Bain. She's running Playskool right now—a six-hundred-million-dollar division of Hasbro. She's very consumer-marketing-savvy. She gets it, whole hog. She's got a great relationship going with Pierre."

Kagle hoped that Whitman would accept the offer. He had made up his mind that she was the right one, a CEO who would be able to work with the founding entrepreneur, when he had driven her to the airport and she'd said to him with genuine concern, "Pierre isn't going anywhere, is he?" But Kagle was a little worried that eBay had offered her only 6 percent equity, lower than the 10 percent that had come to be the Valley standard in recruiting a seasoned CEO. However, he saw eBay's point: That 6 percent was probably worth—and he dropped his voice for emphasis as he told his partners—$9 million today. "That's a pretty big grant to be given," he conceded.

Kagle was being too conservative in valuing the company, Dave Beirne felt. In Beirne's calculations, Whitman would be leaving a $600,000-a-year job at Hasbro to take up a position that would pay her $175,000 a year in salary but with an equity slice already worth $18 million.

"What did her husband object to?" asked Andy Rachleff.

"I think he thought it could be a faddish kind of thing. Here's an interesting statistic for you. They did two million dollars in Beanie Babies in December!" Kagle laughed. "Which, in one point of time, is really exciting"—and, continuing to laugh but with a nervous hiccup—"and another point in time, pretty scary! He was concerned that we might have something here that is sort of a classic consumer cycle."

"Is he qualified to understand?" Harvey asked.

Kagle and Rachleff answered simultaneously: "He's a brain surgeon!" Yes, he was probably smart enough to take this in.

As the laughter subsided, Rachleff asked, "But does he have it in perspective?"

"I think through the course of the dinner we gave him a lot of comfort on a number of these issues. The Beanie Babies is six percent of our business. It's not the kind of thing that's going to move overnight and destroy your business."

"You're going to have every fad go through this," said Beirne.

"Absolutely," Kagle agreed. "We said, 'Perishable consumables. That's our segment.' As long as humans have curiosity, as long as there's interest in these kinds of phenomena, they're going to do it." Whitman's husband had arrived more skeptical than Kagle had anticipated he was going to be, but by the end of his visit, he appeared to have warmed up a bit and was talking about the possibility of getting an appointment at Stanford's medical school. Kagle continued his report: "We're going to be on Meg heavy this week. Her boys were great. We left them a care package at the hotel with Stanford caps and everything. I had them with the right Realtor looking at the right kind of places." Afterward, Whitman had lightheartedly reported that one of her boys thought that thirteen-year-old Kelsey Kagle was rather cute. Summing up, Bob Kagle told his colleagues, "I'm feeling pretty good."

Dave Beirne wanted Kagle to take a more active part in closing Whitman, not leaving it to Omidyar, who didn't have the experience. Kagle said he had coached Omidyar. "I think I did a pretty good job of painting the lay of the land for him. But I didn't want to go outside his comfort zone because I want this relationship between him and Meg to really work, and I think she's gettable."

Beirne remained concerned that the offer would not be sufficient to get Whitman to uproot her family.

Kagle asked Beirne: "Let's say the company goes public in a year. What's the conservative valuation of this company in a year's time?"

That was too far out, Beirne maintained. First we have to get her here.

"How much seasonality do you think there is?" Dunlevie asked.

The number of items listed on the eBay site had fallen dramatically right after Christmas, Kagle said. "We were spooked a little about this before. I think there's probably some. There's not enough so far to track and worry about. January, we're expecting a blowout month. The first five days are unbelievable."

"What do you think the revenues will be in '98?"

"We're thinking it could be thirty million. So wish us luck!"

He remembered something else, a small matter, but the personal touch—surprising Whitman with their attention to something so picayune—could be helpful. He turned to Dave Beirne: "There's something you could help me on. This would be a great, high-class move for us to do. She's got four hundred dollars tied up in a bankruptcy with Nets Inc. that she spent on expenses to fly down there to interview at Ramsey Beirne's encouragement. If we got that to her in the next couple days, that would be such an impressive thing to her."

"I'll write the check," Beirne offered.

"Four hundred dollars?" Dunlevie asked. "*I'll* write the check!"

■

Whitman made up her mind. A company that experienced the growth that eBay had—"organic growth," without marketing—ultimately convinced her that the business potential was unlike anything she was likely to encounter again. Against the advice of her boss, her colleagues, her friends, everyone on the East Coast that she knew, Meg Whitman decided to take the leap and join a thirty-five-person company no one she knew had heard of.

5. Don't Get Screwed

Bruce Dunlevie had just finished meeting with an acquaintance who had founded a new company without first figuring out exactly what it was the new company would make. Dunlevie gave the venture only a one-in-three chance of finding a viable product before the infant company expired.

He told Bob Kagle, "I think all these guys—we're in a social environment where it is so macho to be an entrepreneur, and none of them are product pickers. It's like, 'I'll be an entrepreneur—I don't know what we'll make, I don't even care, but I'll be an entrepreneur.' It's so rah-rah to go out and tell people, 'I'm starting a company.' "

Kagle had another example of the phenomenon: He had paved the way for an entrepreneur and friend to secure a senior position at eBay, only to be told by the friend that he wasn't interested.

Kevin Harvey overheard the story and let out a whistle. The options that came with the eBay position were as certain as anything was to be worth millions of dollars.

"It was like a layup," Kagle said, shaking his head. The wealth on the table was being forsaken for the chance to be a founding CEO of his own venture.

"I think part of this is time," Dunlevie said. "I think this will get cured. But I think he's got to take a run at it."

Kagle actually liked that damn-the-easy-way spirit. "I respect that."

■

To the eyes of Alexis de Tocqueville, the French visitor whose observations of America in the 1830s provide a perennially consulted baseline for comparison with the present, Americans have always appeared comfortable taking business risks. Tocqueville described business in the United States as "a vast lottery" in which a few individuals lost on a daily basis but at the same time the wider society "constantly" profited. "Any bold undertaking risks the fortune of the man who embarks on it and of those who trust him. The Americans, who have turned rash speculation into a sort of virtue, can in no case stigmatize those who are thus rash."

Perhaps that was the case in the early nineteenth century, but by the late twentieth century, the risk of failure was only abstractly part of the equation. Consequently, entrepreneurship had a glow that was not entirely deserved, as it was the success stories that drew the eye. All but invisible were those who tried and failed, some of whom rebounded emotionally and professionally, and some of whom did not.

Steve Jurvetson, a young venture capitalist with Draper Fisher Jurvetson in Redwood City, was more aware than most venture guys of the existence of those who did not bounce back; his wife happened to be a psychiatrist, among whose clients were the would-be entrepreneurs who had failed (which in the Valley was pardonable) but who had not maintained their stride (which was not). Therapy has not always been available. Unable to resist investing in the high-tech sector of his day in the late nineteenth century, Mark Twain was financially ruined by his irrationally hopeful investments in the infamous Paige typesetter; heavily in debt, he had to flee to Europe, where it took ten years before he could return with his family, recovered and solvent.

Benchmark invested in companies that fell primarily into one of two categories: seed-stage companies, which consisted of little more than an idea; and early-stage companies, which had begun work developing a product but had not yet launched it. Jurvetson's firm invested in seeds only and saw more proposals than a Benchmark or Kleiner because its door was open to entrepreneurs seeking the smallest amounts of capital. The nation's romance with entrepreneurship could be tracked by the number of proposals that were sent to Draper Fisher Jurvetson: in 1994, 376; in 1995, the year Benchmark was founded, 1,075; in 1997, 2,538; and in 1999, an astounding 12,000.

It is the nature of romance to get far ahead of reality. Even though the number of aspiring entrepreneurs who asked for funding had increased twentyfold in five years, Draper Fisher Jurvetson funded the same number as it had before, averaging fourteen a year. The odds of getting funded would seem to have actually gotten worse, assuming that all proposals were created equal. Perhaps the most discouraging fact of all was this: Even Draper Fisher Jurvetson, which sought to position itself as the most welcoming of any Silicon Valley venture capital firm to the seed-stage entrepreneur who possessed nothing but the wisp of a good idea, screened on the basis of referrals. Over-the-transom submissions from strangers fared no better there than at Benchmark or elsewhere.

Still, some democratization in the background of entrepreneurs could be observed over time. In the 1980s venture funding went to chip deals, computer systems, and biotech; software companies were a barely discernible sliver. Valley companies expected electrical-engineering degrees from everybody, including marketing people. Democratization advanced when software became a valid category in its own right, as in 1989, when venture firm Hummer Winblad announced at its founding that it would invest only in software companies. Liberal-arts graduates began to be hired, not in the bastions of engineering-centric culture like Intel and Cisco, but at software companies like Intuit. Opportunity opened further in the Internet era, when people from literally all backgrounds found their services in demand.

When Bruce Dunlevie met with Benchmark's institutional investors in June 1997, he observed how entrepreneurialism had become culturally accepted in a way that was unthinkable five years earlier. Any lingering stigma that had attached to it had disappeared, a change that had greatly increased the supply of aspirants, roughly matching the increase in available venture capital. "It's a lot less difficult to convince an engineer or the spouse of an engineer to leave Hewlett-Packard and go to a start-up than it was five years ago or ten years ago. These things aren't viewed as risky anymore; they're viewed as 'growth experiences' and a chance for the brass ring. The influx of would-be entrepreneurs and the ability to build teams around those best entrepreneurs—both have improved markedly." This was Dunlevie's answer to conventional wisdom that held that there was too much money now chasing too few good ideas.

■

For an illustrative example of democratization at work in the Valley, consider the case of Eric Greenberg, a voluble East Coast thirty-three-year-old who came West to seek his fortune with little more than a briefcase and a stellar record in sales at the Gartner Group, a company that did research on the information-technology sector. On his own he accomplished what the statistics said was all but impossible: In 1996 he founded a website-services company called Silicon Valley Internet Partners (SVIP); in two months, with a good idea and no contacts, he got $4 million in venture backing; and three years later, SVIP, which had morphed into Viant, went public and quickly traded at a $500 million market cap.

For Greenberg this was a bittersweet experience, as he was no longer at Viant. He had been pushed out a year after the company's founding. The experience left him bitter, with a particularly strong animus against venture capitalists.

"Think about this: It's your idea, you write the business plan, you don't sleep for months, you talk all these people into joining you. There was nobody with me when I got funded, I arranged all the funding myself, sold the initial deals, got the initial employees—it was my idea, my tenacity—and all of a sudden, you get fired and they take your fucking stock away." He paused only briefly to snatch a breath. "It was like losing your kid."

He was eager to save other entrepreneurs from the pain he had endured.

First lesson: Never send a business plan to venture capitalists without first getting a meeting set up. And at the meeting, leave no paperwork behind. He'd left a business plan with a firm that backed a direct competitor that appeared two weeks after his visit. Venture capitalists never sign nondisclosure agreements, so you have no legal recourse in such a situation.

Also, be warned that after you've made your pitch, venture capitalists are craftily evasive and will not give you an outright no. They'll instead say, "Well, we want you to do some homework," or "We want you to think about this, this, this, and that, and come back to us with an answer." If you hear this, it's over, Greenberg would tell you; they're never going to fund you. If a deal is going to be funded, it's funded within ten days. "They don't want to say no, 'cause they don't want to burn the bridge—you might not come back to them with the next deal. If you get lucky and something good happens, yeah, then they'll fund you. But if they want a deal, they're going to jump on it like flies on shit."

He had advice about negotiating terms, employment agreements (protection that most entrepreneurs do not have but should), and vesting rights (vest quickly, he urged). Don't expect that the lawyers you hire will be looking out for your interests—they're in cahoots with the venture guys. "You have to have another set of lawyers that review your own lawyer's work, because if you don't, you'll get screwed." And venture guys can undermine the entrepreneur's interests in other ways, such as liquidating companies quickly in order to turn their own money around. The bill of particulars was a long one.

Greenberg's downfall at Viant was not wholly unexpected. He had never operated under the illusion that he could serve as the CEO, and he and the CEO he had helped hire did not get along. One or the other had to go, and the venture guys formed the decisive swing vote in the matter. "The VCs had no choice 'cause he"—the new CEO—"is the golden goose," Greenberg said afterward. He recognized that his nemesis was "the guy that Wall Street wants; they don't want a thirty-two-year-old kid. They want this guy in his mid- to late forties, who's been there, done it before. That's what Wall Street buys. So they had no choice. I would have made the same choice if I were the VCs." Financially he had done well enough (when Viant went public in 1999, Greenberg's 5 percent share of the company was soon worth $60 million on paper). His beef, it turned out, concerned how coldly he was treated.

To restore his spirits after exile from Viant, Greenberg had gone to Asia for six weeks, become bored, and returned to town without a plan. He had sought out Dave Beirne when he left Gartner, and now Beirne had come out to California himself. Greenberg called him up to see whether he liked his new life at Benchmark. Beirne said yes, and you've got to meet my partners. Before he knew it, Greenberg was invited to become an entrepreneur in residence at Benchmark. EIRs, as they were known, were funded by many of the leading venture firms in the Valley as a source of "deal flow"; by having EIRs tinker with a new business plan while under the same roof, the firm gets the first peek; if it likes what it sees, it also is in the best position to be the earliest investor. At any given time, Benchmark hosted one or two EIRs, who usually stayed four to six months.

One of Greenberg's dearly learned tenets drawn from his earlier experience was that it was best to have many venture firms bidding against one another. As an EIR at Benchmark receiving a stipend of $10,000 a month while he was to figure out the next fundable idea for a new business, he would be legally free to shop the resulting idea around, and the EIR sponsor, on its part, was not obligated to fund his plan. He anticipated that he'd feel uncomfortable not giving Benchmark the right of first refusal and for that reason was reluctant to accept the offer. But he acquiesced.

Greenberg's harsh view of venture guys in general was not all that different from Dave Beirne's own. (At a partners' meeting, when Dunlevie had mentioned how distrustful of venture capitalists an entrepreneur whom he had just met with had been, Beirne had asked Dunlevie, "Well, how many venture guys *could* you trust with your idea?") Greenberg was a talker, and Beirne was as patient as a therapist. The first idea Greenberg proposed was to open a talent agency for engineers, which would be called Digital Talent. As CAA had done for actors, so Digital Talent would change the balance of power between employee and employer and ensure that bright engineers "don't get screwed." Beirne and the other Benchmark partners, more dispassionate than the recently embittered Greenberg, urged him to consider putting this one aside and coming up with another idea.

The second one, which became a company called Scient, got the partners' interest. Greenberg, looking back upon his pitch, said proudly that he got paid "a six-million-dollar pre-money valuation for twenty PowerPoint slides and no team." The slides were packed with a jumble of ideas. A "market inflection point" had opened an opportunity for "any-to-any computing." There were trends toward massive outsourcing of corporate information-technology services; toward

Windows NT; toward home area networks. Scient would address the opportunities created by these trends, offering IT consulting, systems integration, and outsourcing to clients who sought cutting-edge technology. Even if a number of Greenberg's "trends," all accorded equal weight by him, seemed less than noteworthy, information-technology services seemed a promising business to be in.

Beirne promised Greenberg that he would deliver the right CEO, and with that promise, Sequoia Capital joined Benchmark as investors. Performing another feat of convincing a big-company guy to take a flier on a barely conceived, mote-sized start-up, Beirne hopped to London to bring in as CEO Bob Howe, a senior IBM executive running its $14 billion-a-year financial-services business. Howe was fifty-three, a veteran of Booz Allen as well as IBM, and a person of strong convictions, which he was accustomed to expressing with much physical emphasis. Howe and Greenberg seemed like a father-son pairing. At times Howe was furious with his wayward charge, and Greenberg openly chafed under the authority wielded by the paterfamilias. But most of the time Greenberg was content with his decision to choose fortune over fame, and while holding the formal position as company chairman, he concentrated on his assigned role: recruiting engineering talent to the company.

■

When Eric Greenberg, a workaholic, pushed himself to exhaustion, he looked to Dave Beirne, who had wrestled with his own workaholic tendencies, like a mentor in AA. Beirne knew how to buck Greenberg up. Regular exercise, for example, was one step he suggested for restoring some measure of balance to Greenberg's life. Every daily call, Beirne would say, "Hey, how was your run this morning?"

"Didn't go."

"Eric, you've got to go, man."

Beirne worked well with Bob Howe, too, who was a scratch golfer; he and Beirne played together, and Howe had an opportunity to vent. When Greenberg and Howe weren't getting along, Beirne figured out what needed to be fixed.

Scient was a company that needed to earn credibility in order to persuade corporations to entrust their digital futures to its care, so Beirne flipped through his mental Rolodex and invited two heavy hitters to the board: Fred Gluck, McKinsey's former managing partner and most recently the vice chairman of Bechtel; and Mort Myerson, Ross Perot's right-hand man at EDS and Perot Systems. Gluck accepted, and Myerson seemed inclined to, also. After flying in, he said, "I did EDS. Did Perot. But this is the biggest vision I've ever seen. If you pull this thing off, it's huge."

Unlike Webvan, whose launch was too far away still for it to be actively looking for lots of executive talent, Scient was going for a big bang. It was at just the right stage for Beirne to help with recruiting, and he did so with the possessed determination of a weight lifter in harness determined to show everyone that a bus *can* be towed. As in the Ramsey Beirne days, he went maniacal, personally interviewing each of Scient's first thirty hires.

■

Scient had set up its office in San Francisco, and in late March 1998 Howe came down to Menlo Park, with Eric Greenberg, to introduce himself to Beirne's partners and talk about plans. He was expected to have extracted from Greenberg's original mishmash of ideas a crisp, succinct message that Scient would carry to its prospective clients.

The message on the PowerPoint slides he brought was still rather vague, however. "Scient is a savvy results provider with a point of view. Our experts help clients cultivate electronic business solutions through harnessing emerging technologies." The trend toward adoption of Windows NT had disappeared, but there were many opaque slides about the New Bottom Line, the New Business Fabric, Building and Cultivating the Business Layer, and dozens of others that would induce sleep if Howe were to run through them. But he didn't. Relying on a born showman's instincts, he abandoned his script, shrugged off his jacket, loosened his tie, and extemporaneously entertained on the fly.

Instead of pulling out the upcoming year's budget in Excel, he reached into his satchel and pulled out an oversized, lined green sheet—a real, pre-1-2-3, pre-Excel spreadsheet. The partners laughed at the sight of a seasoned IBM veteran, about to lecture them on emerging-technologies services, pulling out an antique like that.

"My parents have one of those," Dunlevie said.

"I know computers are great, but"—Howe lifted the sheet—"I know how this thing works." He looked at it a moment and said the plan called for having 130 people hired by the end of the year and $12 million in revenue. He rattled off his desired revenues for succeeding years: "Twelve million, thirty, sixty, one-twenty, two-fifty, five hundred—then I go play golf."

As long as he ignored the slides, he was clear: Scient's business would be the services that converted businesses into e-businesses. He didn't mention that it was Greenberg who had figured it out, even if he couldn't articulate it well. No other company had yet successfully staked out this specialty as its sole business. Perot Systems had some e-commerce experts, as did EDS, Andersen, and IBM. But in each case, they were scattered across a large organization.

These same organizations were distracted by Y2K-related consulting. "All my old friends are busy now," Howe said. "EDS, IBM, Andersen. You want to be a programmer till January second, 2000, then you want to be a lawyer. You've got all the big people in the world who could possibly take a position here fundamentally diverted. They're making a lot of money, but they're also in agony. At IBM, they will probably put everybody who speaks anything like Chinese on the planes because the banks in China will not function in the year 2000. The fourth- or fifth-largest economy in the world will come to a halt in the year 2000. So they're diverted. So you pick the sweet spot in the market. You've got your competitors diverted.

"The real trick for us is in two or three years to get a significant position. We want to be two hundred fifty million as fast as we can. We want seven hundred to a thousand of the most talented people in this business that Eric can recruit. And that in and of itself will be a competitive weapon. When Andersen and all those guys wake up midway through the year 2000, decide they want to play here, hopefully we'll be ahead of them, we'll have a market position, we'll have a strong-enough place that we can keep moving the business."

Scient's first clients were so desperate for help that they were willing to pay to have Scient guarantee the availability of its consultants. Beirne noted that there were currently 575,000 openings for technical people in information technology.

Why could Scient assume it would be able to get the scarce technical talent that no one else could? Howe explained, "Number one, we have the monster recruiter here. We've got this recruiting machine going." He wrapped an arm around Eric Greenberg's neck. The second reason was that Scient's sole focus on electronic commerce would be attractive to the programmers with expertise in that nascent field, who felt they were invisible within a leviathan like IBM or EDS. "They go from being on the extremities of these giant organizations where they worry they're going to be extincted at any point of time, to the heart of the business. What happens is, the more focused we are, the more of those people we get, the more people we attract—it's the same thing we did at the IBM Consulting Group."

At that point Kevin Harvey, who had founded two successful software companies himself, expressed skepticism about Howe's contention that Scient would be able to reuse software code on multiple projects.

Howe didn't back off an inch. By this point, he had taken off his tie with a dramatic whipping motion and unbuttoned his shirt. "This isn't hard to execute. You want to know why? At the heart of this is a client who desperately needs to be able to compete here. They're going to be very price-insensitive, because I have a service, guys, that is at the gut of their ability to compete and win in the future! To me that says, I can execute that, even if I build every one of them from scratch, and make a fortune. What is reusable is the knowledge we're going to develop in building every one of these"—and he slammed the table repeatedly with his fist as an accompaniment to each word: *"The guts, core competency, capital that we'll win on is knowledge, boys!"*

The partners laughed.

Howe had his audience in his palm. "Make no mistake, we're going to fuckin' kill 'em."

"I actually want a job," Beirne said.

"When we get this leadership position, and we get ahead of these guys, and we build more sexy things, and critical things, than anybody else can, the *fuckin'* world will come to my doorstep." When Howe was excited, he forgot to honor polite convention and convert *my* to *our*.

A few minutes later in his spiel, he remembered to nod to Greenberg. "And as long as we've got that cougar here to recruit 'em—"

Beirne explained to the others: "Mort Myerson calls me and goes, 'Bob Howe—that guy's reputation is awesome; Greenberg, he's a cougar.' "

"What we need help on," Howe asked, fishing for client prospects, "is if you've got good contacts—"

"Absolutely," Rachleff said.

Howe was silent, signaling the end of the performance, but everyone's ears still rang from the profane sermon he had just delivered. Bruce Dunlevie paid homage by jumping to his feet and giving him a standing ovation. Rachleff asked Howe if he would be kind enough to return every Monday.

Standing in the doorway on his way out, Greenberg told a couple of the Benchmark partners the plans for the next round of financing. Scient's valuation in the December seed round had been $6 million; now it was March and Scient was looking for investors at a current valuation, in the new math of the New Economy, of $180 million, which, it turned out, it had no difficulty finding. Greenberg exulted, "I think we're the greatest play in the Valley right now. It came farther than I thought it was going to go in three months, let me tell you. I'm glad you guys didn't fund Digital Talent." They laughed together.

"That's our value-add," Rachleff joked.

"We always do the second one," Dunlevie said.

■

How was Scient's new vice president of marketing working out?, one of the partners asked Beirne at a meeting a few weeks later.

"Great," Beirne said. "He was a little too excitable at first. He'd go out on a sales call, telling companies, 'When you put this e-business strategy in place, you'll be able to rip your competitors' heads off and shit down their neck.' Howe thought that was going a little too far." The partners laughed.

"Howe thought that was going too far?" Dunlevie asked.

"He said, 'We can say that to ourselves in the car, but we don't say that to the client.' "

"I actually thought that was printed on their business cards," Dunlevie said.

■

To anyone who had known Eric Greenberg before he came to Benchmark, back when he could talk of nothing but the mendacity of venture capitalists, their lack of scruples, their callousness, the new Eric Greenberg, the 1998 model, would not have been recognizable. At an industry conference Andy Rachleff saw Greenberg praise Benchmark in the most glowing terms.

Rachleff told the others, "Eric's done a hell of a sales job on our behalf. That's the value of a happy EIR. They spread the word like no one else."

"He's going on the board of *Red Herring*," said Dave Beirne. The magazine focused on the business of high technology and venture capital.

"Eric is?" Kevin Harvey's voice became high-pitched in his excitement. "That's *huge!*" High fives.

■

If Eric Greenberg thought it, he said it, without editing. Not just exuberance and business ambition were visible, but also the deepest of cravings, the seat of the existential *I was here, damn it!* yell into the void. Here's a shortened e-mail message that he sent to everyone at Scient at the end of 1998:

> To the Greatest Group of People I Have Ever Worked With,
>
> We will accomplish things that would surprise the greatest optimist! The world is our oyster.
>
> As my great friend and mentor, Bob Howe, says: "We have it all to play for."
>
> Dreams come true. Our company is living proof. We are off to the greatest start in the history of our industry, but so what. It is about the journey and the end game: to build the greatest services firm on earth that is the preeminent influencer in the next stage of our economy. Big dreams?
>
> Yes.
>
> Look what Edison and Bell achieved through their innovations: GE and AT&T.
>
> Let's shape the next 50 years of our economy together. We can. Bob cannot. I cannot. The Silicon Valley VCs cannot. We together can. It is a collective effort of the best people doing their best work.

That is the only way we become legendary over time and build an enduring legacy. I know that I personally do not want to be forgotten by the world when I eventually pass on, and I hope you do not either. Scient is a means by which we can all make contributions and live forever—through our work-product and company longevity and quality.

This is the company we are building. Believe it. It is real. Recognize when momentum is going your way, and ride it!

6. Room at the Top

"**G**od is not on the side of the big arsenals, but on the side of those who shoot best."

Voltaire's words had been used by the Benchmark partners to solicit capital for their first fund. Would institutional investors welcome another first-time fund such as theirs? Their prospectus optimistically quoted Daniel Webster: "There is always room at the top."

They had sought $85 million at a time others were raising $250 million, reasoning that small is beautiful. Whatever the size, Benchmark's backers expected the capital to be invested in a reasonably short period. With a smaller fund, the Benchmark partners would not feel pressure to invest in deals of only borderline quality, merely to put money to work. A smaller fund should be attractive to entrepreneurs, too, they reasoned. Each investment the partners would make would mean one more board seat that a partner would have to take, so with a smaller fund, they would avoid the danger of shortchanging an individual entrepreneur by having to serve on too many boards.

They successfully raised the fund, but one should look back and note the fragile position of the shooters without a large arsenal, of Benchmark itself, and of its tiny portfolio companies. Successes in a portfolio naturally draw attention, but the stories of companies that do not take off in a dramatic fashion, the ones that falter, are invaluable for reminding all bystanders that the start-up business is actually hard, even in golden times. The brave talk at Benchmark's inception—that young sharpshooting David will win over Goliath—was not borne out immediately.

Of Benchmark's first ten investments, two—Compact Devices and C. W. Gourmet—went out of business without glory. Xantel, which makes PC-based office-telephony hardware, almost did. A small stake in PointCast, the online news-delivery network that was the toast of the Valley in 1995, had brought with it endless headaches as the company groped for a business model while bleeding red ink. Jamba Juice and Broadbase, a software company that developed tools for analyzing large databases like customer lists, did moderately well. PictureVision, which developed a system for digitizing snapshots, could have sunk out of sight were it not rescued by Kodak. Benchmark's very first investment, Silicon Gaming, was done with Kleiner Perkins and initially did the best of the first ten. It was the first to go public—but then the stock sank. It appeared that the brightest star of the early batch would be the eleventh investment, in Genesys Telecommunications Labs, one of Bruce Dunlevie's companies, which made software for routing telephone calls from customers in large corporate call centers.

The collective value of a typical venture capital portfolio will go down before it goes up—the pattern is called the J curve—because the companies that are not going to survive die before the best performers begin to shine and pull the value of the portfolio up with them. That, at least, had been the pattern in the past. In Benchmark's case, even though the partners would later talk about their first year of investments as a time of gaining their sea legs and learning how to refine their group approach to investment decisions, and even though the poorest investments were clustered in the very first group, Benchmark never passed through the dip of the J. By the end of its second year, boosted by sixfold gains from Genesys and Silicon Gaming, Benchmark reported to its investors that to date the fund was returning at a rate exceeding 100 percent annually. That's the beauty of a portfolio effect.

■

Entrepreneurs do not have the luxury of holding a basket of eggs, however; their egg, usually their only egg, must not break. Often the biggest threat to the embryo is not adult birds of prey, the entrenched competition from the Fortune 500, but rather carnivorous fledglings, fellow start-ups, some of which will have first-mover advantages and perhaps better capitalization. In eBay's case, at the time it was still sitting in the nest and Benchmark had invested in it, *The Economist* estimated that there were more than 150 online auction sites on the Web. One of those was far ahead of the rest, backed by Kleiner Perkins, and was already a public company with a market capitalization of about $175 million.

Onsale's founder, Jerry Kaplan, was at forty-three a well-seasoned entrepreneur with a Ph.D. in computer science. But he could as well have been a showman. He launched Onsale's website in 1995 just as his memoir, *Startup*, hit bookstores. The book spun an engrossing story of how Kaplan had, in essence, flushed $75 million of Kleiner Perkins's money down the toilet in a vain attempt to make a go of Go Corporation, which produced an operating system for pen computers. He had dusted himself off and launched Onsale, creating a bidding experience that he described as "part Las Vegas, part P. T. Barnum, and part Price Club."

He had to start out with just his and his partner's money because Kleiner Perkins and every other venture firm he shopped the business plan to had turned him down. When he launched the company, John Doerr publicly derided Kaplan as being far out of his element, noting that he "doesn't have any merchandising or mass-marketing success." Amazingly, Kleiner Perkins later decided to let bygones be bygones and signed up to back Kaplan once again. Kaplan likened his ongoing ability to raise capital to the workings of Hollywood: "Just because you make *Waterworld*"—referring to the soggy 1995 flop whose reported budget of $175 million was the most expensive to date— "doesn't mean you're not ever going to make *Titanic*."

Kaplan's original business vision was to provide merchants with an online auction site for baseball memorabilia, and initially its offerings were eclectic, including Mickey Mantle autographed baseballs, manufacturer's discontinued computer equipment, fine wines, and the last caboose in use by the Duluth, Winnipeg & Pacific Railroad. He relied on professional merchants or closeout houses, but by structuring Onsale as a commission-based business, he anticipated Auction Web/eBay's model.

Kaplan quickly shed all lines other than closeout computer equipment; he also shifted away from commissions and instead purchased the closeout merchandise, gambling that Onsale could make a higher margin by taking ownership of the goods than if it remained content with small commissions. The inventory and price risks were tricky, especially so in the computer hardware business, where prices declined daily.

The problem seemed to Kaplan and his backers to be merely theoretical. The company could boast that it was already modestly profitable before it went public, and it appeared to hold special appeal to male buyers in search of computer gear. Ron Rappaport, a Zone Research analyst, described the appeal of Onsale to those buyers: "They go out, they find a good bargain, they hunt it, they kill it, they take it home. And then they're proud of it. They hold that carcass up in front of other Web users and say, 'I got this same computer for twenty bucks less!' "

Even if it wasn't twenty bucks less, the hunters returned happy. Kaplan, the showman, could not resist telling the world that Onsale bidders enjoyed the hunt so much that they ended up paying online at his site more than they would have for the same goods in a physical store. A new television set that would normally cost $245 was sold at auction for $340; an $800 notebook computer was won with a bid for $909. "We're shocked at what prices these things go for," he said; he offered by way of explanation the site's tapping into "competition, winning, beating other people."

Onsale's trumpeting of the opportunity for "beating other people" is about as antithetical to Pierre Omidyar's eBaysian culture as it is possible to imagine. At eBay, every completed auction with more than one bidder did of course involve someone beating out someone else. But where Onsale fed blood lust, eBay averted its eyes and pretended the bidding process was entirely bloodless, and instead devoted its efforts to promoting amity. Omidyar would have been content to remain the disengaged pacifist, letting auction buyers choose between it and the warrior philosophy of Onsale, but in September 1997 the barbarians came right to eBay's door.

First, Onsale attacked with what eBay feared was a multimillion-dollar spending blitz on exclusive portal deals. Second, rumors were launched that Onsale was going to add a new auction site that would depart from the closeout computer-equipment business and instead be modeled after eBay's, involving individual sellers offering a wide variety of items to individual buyers.

Until this point, eBay had not spent anything on marketing. It only had eighty-five thousand listings on the site, but its computer systems were too fragile to sustain any more traffic, so questions about a marketing budget had been moot. In fact, before the installation of a new system, eBay had to limit to ten the number of items any given seller could list. But when Onsale began to lock up portal positions, public investors seemed to feel that Onsale was securing an impregnable position; as September progressed, the trading price of Onsale's shares jumped and now, in just five months, were trading five times above their offering price of $6. Onsale's market cap had reached half a billion dollars.

Let's remain calm, Bob Kagle urged Omidyar and Jeff Skoll (Meg Whitman had yet to be hired). He said that the portals would not deliver the "competitive preemption" they were selling to Onsale. They would segment their sites, simultaneously meeting the strictly legal terms of the contract with Onsale yet selling advertising space to Onsale's competitors. Let Onsale spend its money there; Kagle favored low-cost guerrilla marketing. Throwing big bucks at portals, whose touted benefits had not been independently confirmed by research, would burn up cash without establishing the eBay brand. Experimental, inexpensive trials with Yahoo and AOL were inaugurated instead.

■

In mid-1997 Jeff Skoll received a call from Onsale: Would eBay like to sell its customer list? No, it would not, he replied. After this conversation, eBay's engineering staff noticed that bots—software agents—were crawling all over the eBay site, vacuuming up the e-mail addresses of buyers and sellers. Their source was traced back to Onsale. EBay had an attorney send a letter demanding that the crawling stop. Sorry, Onsale replied. Didn't realize it was going on.

The night before Onsale launched its new site, Onsale Exchange, several hundred thousand eBay users received e-mail from Onsale, offering free listings to sellers as an introductory enticement. EBay denounced the e-mail as spam and issued a furious press release, "Internet Community Outraged by E-Mail Assault," in a vain attempt to stir up media attention. Onsale shrugged, saying that it wasn't spam, it was "value-added e-mail." Michelle Kaplan, Jerry's wife, dropped in on the eBay chat room and invited everyone to "come on over to Onsale."

On the same day that Onsale Exchange launched, another competitor, Auction Universe, was relaunched, under the aegis of its new owner, Times Mirror. At the eBay offices, a conference room was dubbed the War Room and decorated with sheets of camouflage and dog tags. The executive staff met daily to plan responses and revive one another's spirits; eBay was feeling encircled by much better capitalized competitors. And when, in December, eBay's listings remained flat for the first time ever, it looked as if eBay's remarkable ride was over.

■

That was the low point. In January listings picked up; Meg Whitman agreed to come on board as soon as she could extricate herself from responsibilities at Hasbro; and Onsale apparently was not doing so well, because it extended its free-listings offer. Bob Kagle had some news for his Benchmark partners: Jerry Kaplan had approached Pierre Omidyar about merging Onsale and eBay, suggesting that John Doerr and Bob Kagle join the two of them and figure out a deal. Kagle reported to his partners, "Pierre talked with Meg, and they decided they were going to use the excuse, 'Geez, we're just hiring a CEO, and want to get that all integrated and everything.' I told them I thought that was *not* a good idea." Kagle predicted that agreeing to even talk about the merger would lead to Kaplan and Doerr urging Omidyar to abort Whitman's being hired. Kagle coached Omidyar to say instead: "This deal makes all the sense in the world, and it's bound to happen, there's no doubt about that at some point, but we just have to get public first and have a relatively fair valuation for comparison to make the decision on it."

"In other words," said Kevin Harvey, who relished cutting through politesse, "We like this deal—when *we're* buying *you!*"

"The 'fuck you, die' thing," said Dave Beirne.

"No," Kagle corrected, "a friendlier version than that. So Pierre is going to call Jerry and let him know that."

■

EBay had an enormous advantage over the competition that it only then, under challenge, was coming to appreciate: a nicely balanced critical mass of sellers and buyers in each of hundreds of categories. This delicate balance had been achieved through the natural evolution of the eBay ecosystem, without the intervention of any guiding hand. If in any given category there were too many sellers compared with buyers, the sellers would have been discouraged and quick to jump to eBay's rivals to try their luck there. If there were too many buyers, and in order to win an auction one had to offer up a ludicrously high price, this too would have led to mass defections. Fortunately for eBay, the number of sellers and buyers, while growing exponentially, had remained well apportioned.

EBay's users remained loyal for another reason: feedback ratings. Buyers, after a transaction, could send in a report about their experience with the seller, which future prospective buyers could consult; sellers had an identical opportunity to evaluate their experience with the buyer. Over time, both sellers and buyers accumulated a number of positive-feedback ratings at eBay, a neatly quantifiable reputation, that they were loath to abandon. The eBay "community" stayed put.

■

In May 1998 Jerry Kaplan probed again, this time approaching Bob Kagle instead of Pierre Omidyar. There's only one winner in each category, so the two companies should join forces, he told Kagle, who recounted the conversation to his partners. If eBay and Onsale remained competitors, at best they would always have to explain why the one was different from the other.

Bruce Dunlevie laughed, mimicking Kaplan speaking to Kagle: "You're profitable!"

"That's right," Kagle said, continuing in the same spirit. "Our margins are ninety, yours are ten; let's start with that, then we'll go from there."

"Ours is a good business, yours is a shitty business," added Harvey.

Kagle granted that Onsale was doing some things well. Kaplan had been at his gracious best when he said that he just wanted to be part of the winning team and did not himself need to be TheGuy. We'll get a banker to figure out which company would get what percentage of the merged entity, he told Kagle. Whitman could run it. He suggested that the new company be called E-Sale—the place to come to buy and sell anything.

Bruce Dunlevie asked Kagle if Kaplan had shut down his person-to-person auction. No, Kagle said, it was still in operation. It presently had 7,000 listings, placing it fourth in size among person-to-person auction sites. Collectors Universe, which was second only to eBay, had 22,000. And eBay had 450,000.

"I was thinking," Kagle said, "why would you want to dilute what eBay has with all that crap? I still feel that way, ninety-nine percent to one percent. But there was one thing that did impress me, and the systems side is very, very well run. The guy who is running operations for them is out of Schwab. I think their downtime is measured in some tiny infinitesimal fraction of what ours is. You know how you get that 'server's busy' all the time at eBay? Part of it is they've got a fraction of our traffic. But still.

"So Meg's going to meet with them, just to chew the fat a little bit. I still think it's stupid to diffuse the pure play. But it might make sense after going public. Stay tuned."

That Kagle would not categorically rule out a merger did not sit well with the others. Bruce Dunlevie would not let the conversation end there. It was time to administer the same medicine that Kagle administered to other partners whom he thought needed to take a firm stand—what Kagle called the "spine stiffenola."

Dunlevie lifted his chin high and looked across to Kagle with a face of incredulity: "What I heard you just say is the real reason to buy Onsale is they have a good MIS guy."

No, Kagle demurred, he was not proposing an acquisition. EBay's systems could be improved, that's all.

How much customer overlap between eBay and Onsale, Kevin Harvey asked.

"That's the key question," Kagle said. "I said, 'Jerry, I just don't see it.' He was giving me this thing about the mall. I said, 'Look, the people who hang out at the mall are not the people who go to the flea market.' He said he has data. So I said we're open to data, and we'll take a third-party look at the data and see what we can learn. If there's a huge amount of customer overlap, then there's something to think about, right? But if there's relatively little, which is what I suspect—if there were more, his Exchange would be doing better."

"Right. By definition."

"So I just don't believe it," Kagle said. "I think he's blowing smoke."

"He's good at that," Andy Rachleff said.

"Here's my view of the cultures," Kagle said. "EBay is the fair, open, honest marketplace that treats people the way people want to be treated and all that. And Onsale, I can tell you from being there an hour, is make-a-buck. It makes sense. Discount merchants. Toward that end, they've done some things pretty well there. For example, I spent ten minutes or so with one of the merchants who's monitoring all these auctions in real time, figuring out how many do we offer tomorrow, and where do we start the bidding, and how many weeks of inventory do we have of each one. They're turning their inventory on average in three weeks' time, which is amazing, at that level of business. That's not a terrible business. It's just no eBay. Whether you would *ever* want to take the execution risk of merging them together is a real question."

What are the numbers, Dunlevie wanted to know. How much do they lose on how much revenue? What's the break-even point in their business?

"Well, they have broken even in the past, at one point."

"Before they went public," Rachleff pointed out.

"Right, before they had to start buying traffic," said Dunlevie.

"Exactly," Kagle said. "All he told me is, 'We're six to twelve months away from breaking even again.' I was reading tough quarter on his face. We'll see. He seemed a little too anxious."

Harvey, like Dunlevie, remained extremely skeptical of Onsale's business model. "Only on the Internet do you see this kind of revenue multiple on ten percent gross-margin businesses. That's going to go away. Unless you have a brand that's bigger than life."

"Unless your business is *huge*," Dunlevie said.

Kagle now seemed less ambivalent. "There's a lot of reasons to keep eBay pure-play. The story. The community. The culture. Everything."

Rachleff laughed. "Bob, I don't think you're getting any push-back!"

7. Privileged

ithin the Benchmark office, investments and valuations were most often referred to with extreme brevity. "Two at six" neatly encapsulated an entire deal, referring to a $2 million investment at a $6 million premoney valuation; there was no need to spell out that the investment would buy a 25 percent share of the company's equity ($2 million into $8 million, the postinvestment total).

Sometimes nouns would be used: A "hundee" was a convenient way of referring to $100 million ("What will it trade at? A couple of hundee?"). A "buck" equaled $1 million; a "nickel" was worth not $50,000, but $5 million. So in this monetary universe an entrepreneur was better off if the venture guys put in a nickel rather than a buck. What you never heard was what Hollywood scripts put in their mouths: "mil" for million. Bob Kagle would jokingly use "bilski" for a billion dollars, with a *b* he exaggeratedly aspirated in a self-mocking, Dr. Evil way, but neither he nor his colleagues spoke of "mil" for million.

The other notable linguistic taboo concerned the convenient two-syllable substitute, "VC," for the six-syllable original that referred to themselves. No matter how many times entrepreneurs blithely talked about VCs, the VCs referred to themselves as "venture guys" or even venture capitalists, cumbersome though it was. But never as VCs. Was it because of the unsavory associations attached to their own profession? After all, it was the phrase used by others when the venture guys were the objects of vilification, so the taboo was a tacit acknowledgment of the less-than-high regard in which they were held in those quarters that were even aware of their existence.

The compensation practices in the venture business originated in traditions whose original functional justification no one today can recall. Venture capitalists, theoretically, could draw compensation like other categories of knowledge workers, charging entrepreneurs on an hourly basis for access to their expertise. And the suppliers of the capital, their limited partners, theoretically could hire the venture guys as staff members to do the investing in-house, on a straightforward salary. Many corporations over the past four decades have dabbled in venture investing attempting to do just that, and all have foundered, not necessarily because a salary per se is inherently flawed but because it is comparatively unattractive. Compensation based on a percentage of the investment gains was five to one hundred times as great (or even more) for counterparts doing exactly similar investing in independent venture firms. Good corporate venture guys always defected to the much better paid alternatives in the free market. If the corporation sought to make the compensation of its in-house venture guys competitive, then it soon discovered that the people in the venture department were making more than the CEO, and that produced another set of problems.

When talking about their work with the public, venture guys did not go out of their way to correct a misunderstanding that theirs was a job involving personal financial risk of the most extreme sort. In fact, they had the best of all worlds: a claim on a percentage of future investment gains, as well as a steady, guaranteed income that the limited partners paid as an annual management fee, usually 2 percent of all capital under management.

The fee income, however, was pocket change. The real money came in the form of "the carried interest," a quaint, confusing term that was shortened colloquially to "the carry," which was 20 to 25 percent of the profits to be made investing Other People's Money. If a starting kitty of $500 million became a portfolio of investments worth $5 billion, then a 20 percent carry would mean the venture guys would get, after repaying the original $500 million, a fifth of the $4.5 billion in profits, or $900 million, to divide among themselves, and their limited partners would get the remainder.

In the 1980s it often would take seven years, even the full ten-year life of a limited partnership, to know the likely outcome of a basket of high-tech investments, but in the late 1990s, Internet time and a bull market combined to greatly accelerate the process. By year two of a fund, all of the capital would be invested, and the firm would raise a second fund, and two years later, a third.

The officers of foundations and university endowments did not like paying the carry, that 20 percent vigorish, but they preferred to pay up in order to gain entrance to a venture firm with a demonstrably successful track record that put it in the top tier of fund performance, rather than pay less to a firm whose performance was weaker. The difference in returns between the top quintile and the bottom was large, especially when the market sank. In the eyes of the limited-partner investors, it was also better to park one's money with a nonstellar performer that was a known entity rather than one without any track record; they were extremely wary of unproven first-time funds.

When Benchmark formed in 1995 the prevailing carry was 20 percent; Kleiner Perkins alone had created an aura that permitted it to charge 30 percent. Plotting their entry, the Benchmark boys contemplated the same problem of differentiation in an already crowded marketplace that the companies in their future portfolio would face. Instead of setting themselves apart by offering to charge a carry lower than the prevailing industry standard, they instead decided to charge 30 percent, like Kleiner, and right out of the gate. As a marketing ploy, it worked well—it got attention, even if it scandalized and angered some investor prospects.

One of the first places the Benchmark boys visited was the office that managed the endowment of Stanford University, which had been an investor in both TVI and Merrill Pickard, the firms from which Kagle, Dunlevie, and Rachleff came. The university was the partners' alma mater, so it would be all the more fitting if Stanford invested in their fund. But when they sat down and explained the unusual nature of their terms, the color drained from the face of the Stanford manager, who had waited twenty years for a first-time fund to approach him so that finally he could have the chance to reduce the customary carry. Here was a delegation that had the audacity to ask for 30 percent. He showed the visitors the door, and then called his counterparts around the country to try to marshal a united front of opposition.

The Benchmark partners had added a twist to the usual terms, calling their carry "performance-based": It would be 20 percent until the original capital was repaid and "the risk is gone"; then it would go to 30. Rather than raising as much capital as possible and charging a flat management fee like everyone else—"wallowing in fees," the Benchmark guys called it with contempt—they instead would raise smaller funds and also charge a declining management fee as the returns from the investments came in and the carry grew. With this structure, they could not sit on their butts and rake in the fees, regardless of the performance of the individual investments. They also pledged to put in 3 percent of the fund's capital from their own pockets, instead of the industry standard of 1 percent.

The gamble paid off. Despite Stanford's success in persuading two institutions to withdraw their oral commitments to Benchmark's fund, other investors stepped forward and the partners secured the $85 million in institutional capital that they had announced they would raise. At Bob Kagle's urging, the partners started business by giving their secretarial staff meaningful pieces of the carry, which would make them millionaires in short order.

The partners knew they were extremely well paid. What they could not understand was why their colleagues on Sand Hill Road trolled for more tax breaks than they enjoyed already, lobbying Washington through their trade group, the National Venture Capital Association, and state capitols. Dunlevie brought in a letter that Tom Perkins had sent, inviting him to join in an upcoming meeting Perkins had set up with the chief of California's state tax board to protest "unfair taxes for small businesses on the Internet." Dunlevie read the letter aloud and muttered, "The people who live in Livermore and Tracy and commute five hours a day—*this* would be at the top of their list of concerns, I bet."

Kevin Harvey had some sarcastic annotations, too: "It's so hard to be a start-up now. Most have to stay in business a year before they make a hundred million—it's so unfair."

The Benchmark boys were not interested in pretending that they and their portfolio companies were oppressed by the greedy hand of government. They were not interested in John Doerr's lobbying group, TechNet; nor were they interested in the libertarianism of Cypress Semiconductor's CEO, T. J. Rodgers. All but Kagle were uninterested in the NVCA. Kagle, however, had not lost that student-council improve-it-or-stop-complaining impulse of his high school and college days. He was elected to the NVCA board and volunteered to serve as program chair for the 1998 meeting, which would commemorate the organization's twenty-fifth anniversary at the Ritz-Carlton Hotel in San Francisco.

■

"It is a *privilege* to serve entrepreneurs!" Kagle delivered his opening speech at the NVCA anniversary meeting like a preacher addressing a sullen congregation of sinners. He sounded the scolding theme every chance he got and had Ted Turner fly in to talk at the gala dinner about "Social Responsibility and Giving Back." Turner's speech would be a stream-of-consciousness ramble that audiences allow only the extremely rich to indulge in. But his you-can't-take-it-with-you homily made no more visible impact than Bob Kagle's plea for a renewed emphasis within the profession on serving the entrepreneur.

Everyone in attendance was in a dark suit, and euphoria was in the air. In a buffet line, one gentleman with silver hair told another, "I haven't felt this smart since 1968." He added, "If we start thinking it's our brains, we're in trouble."

That sort of self-admonishment was the voice of the minority, however. Self-congratulation was the theme that recurred in panel after panel. Kagle did his best to curb it from his perch at the podium. At one point he bared one of the profession's most sensitive secrets. "I'm often asked—too often—by an entrepreneur, 'Why is the venture capital industry so financially rewarding?'" Looking out across a room filled with several hundred people who composed what must be the highest percentage of multimillionaires that room had ever seen, he continued, with polite sarcasm: "I cast about for the name of that one fund that lost money, sometime in the 1980s."

The standard answer that the industry always reverted to when asked to defend itself was that "the rewards are commensurate with the risks." But how can an entrepreneur swallow that when the venture capitalist is the one who gets to distribute risk across a portfolio, Kagle asked. And the more informed entrepreneurs would also point out that whatever risk the venture guys assumed, it was risk that did not extend to much of their own property—"it's *other* people's money," the limited partners', that is at risk, Kagle noted.

This less-than-heroic depiction of venture capitalists was not winning friends and influencing people in that ballroom. How more pleasing it would have been to hear the John Doerr stump speech, the "we are part of the largest legal creation of wealth in the history of the planet" bromides. Doerr's perspective assumed that a trade-friendly global economy, free of superpower conflict, was no more deserving of acknowledgment than oxygen in the air.

Kagle offered to his audience of venture capitalists only one path to redemption: continual acknowledgment that it was the entrepreneur who deserved the credit for wealth creation.

The applause was muted. Audience members had come not to hear a sermon but to mark their own collective ascendancy within the world of finance. As the meeting proceeded, it became clear that what had drawn many to this meeting, which was closed to the public, was the opportunity to boast.

Benchmark Capital's "fundamentally better architecture"—equal partnership, equal decision-making power, equal compensation—was a heretical arrangement, judging by the testimony of panelists. Pat Cloherty, of New York–based Patricof & Company (whose Mephistophelean partners were dished up in Michael Wolff's 1998 book, *Burn Rate*), spoke of her firm's highly evolved hierarchy: analysts, associates, senior associates, principals, and at the apex, partners. Sonja Hoel, a young venture capitalist at California-based Menlo Ventures, described how her firm's year-end bonuses were based on a point system that would do a Pentagon-sized bureaucracy proud, carefully documenting "deals out the door," replete with negative points, too, assigned for undesirable "performance metrics." As a profession, venture firms were most comfortable with wide skews of compensation; in one case, the most senior general partner arrogated two thirds of the entire firm's carry just for himself. (In 1995, when Benchmark announced its structure of equal compensation for all partners, a partner at Boston-based TA Associates sniffed in the *Venture Capital Journal* that that was "communism"; Bruce Dunlevie, upon being told by the reporter of the comment, guessed that "the guy who said that must have been a senior partner.")

One topic that did not come up was the homogeneity of the profession. Notwithstanding the appearance of Cloherty and Hoel on panels, this was an overwhelmingly male assemblage. The venture capital guild remained conspicuously more white and more male than any other profession one could think of—except, perhaps, the world of high-tech executives in Silicon Valley. Unlike law, medicine, or university teaching, where the profession was entered via an academic route, and thus its composition amenable to change in step with the changing composition of graduate enrollment, venture capitalists came primarily from the executive ranks of the high-tech world in which new ventures were started; the still lagging underrepresentation of women and minorities in the wider high-tech economy would undoubtedly mean the venture capital world would lag in acquiring a more heterogeneous look. In the meantime the entire industry would appear to be a restrictive club.

The one panel least likely to be seen again was "Living Legends," which put on the stage the venture industry's preeminent names from the past. They had been venture capitalists for decades, an experience that gave them some perspective on the giddy times of the present. Was Tom Perkins exaggerating—he did not appear to be—when he said that when Kleiner Perkins opened its office in 1972 the telephone never rang; he and Gene Kleiner only made outbound calls; and the pace was so slow that they had only a single secretary, who worked half days? Peter Crisp, of Venrock Associates, a firm decades older than even Kleiner Perkins, reminded the audience that investments used to be made with the expectation that it would take eight or ten years before an exit could be made, and "now you sell companies before they have revenues!" IVP's Reid Dennis used his time to take up where Bob Kagle had left off and scold: "There are very few of us who have a concept of philanthropy, and it does the country a great disservice."

The champion curmudgeon was Don Valentine, who founded Sequoia Capital in 1972, the entertainingly irascible figure from the old days when high-tech revolved around the chip industry (Valentine had been one of the fair-children at Fairchild Semiconductor and a founder at National Semiconductor). Valentine was a bulky person, with a gravelly voice and a disinclination to smile. Politesse was not in his repertoire; once when an interviewer asked him about mistakes he had committed in his venture capital career, Valentine attributed most of the blame to "horrible" CEOs, a couple of whom he volunteered "to put into a cell with Charlie Manson for a couple of years." Valentine was a scold, but of a different sort; service and philanthropy were not what he was there to talk about—rather it was the venture capital business itself, which was run, he maintained, by incompetents; 20 percent of the partners did 80 percent of the work; valuations had lost all pretense of being based on anything real. "I'm not sure what business I'm in, nor what you're in, but we're not in the venture capital business.

"We have billions when we used to have millions. We have limited partners ripping the hinges off the door to get into the next fund, which confuses us." Don't think for a moment that that means we know what we're doing—we don't, he said with finality. "The stock market in the 1990s has covered up our ineptitude." At the moment, the industry had more money to invest than it knew what to do with, and exits were better than ever before. "I think we'll look back on the 1990s, like the periods of Greece, as the Golden Age." And after the rise would come the fall. These remarks struck an outside observer as perfectly reasonable. But the audience appeared to receive them instead as entertainment, grinning like the masochists who sit at the front tables in a comedy club.

Aside from Kagle's head being visible above a sea of suits, Benchmark as an entity had a low profile during the two-day meeting. In the program itself, Kagle had pulled strings in such a way that participants had fewer, not more, ties with Benchmark—he relished the idea of eschewing the program chair's traditional prerogative of packing the program to promote his own firm's profile. Dave Beirne was the only one of the partners he had dragooned to be on a panel; Beirne had refused to go on "Young Turks Speak Out" and had grudgingly consented instead to go on "Managing a Career in Venture Capital."

It was an assignment that he did not look forward to. He had not even been in the business a full year; how could he presume to speak on "managing a career"? He arrived at the meeting room just before the panel was to begin, and all heads swiveled to watch his entrance. For most, it was the first opportunity they had to glimpse this person they had heard a great deal about.

His copanelists lectured about ideal educational and professional backgrounds for venture capital, the salaries and share of the carry that associates and junior partners can expect at a typical firm, and the strategies for speedy promotion to full partner. The entry-level position of associate, and the next rung up, senior associate, typically earned $82,000 and $118,000 in salary and bonuses, respectively, but were excluded from receiving a slice of carry, the gains that produced the bulk of compensation. A compensation specialist explained how once a senior associate was promoted to junior partner, the lowest rung of the ladder to receive a portion of the carry, the compensation jumped upward; even a tiny, 2 percent slice would give the junior partner an additional $3.4 million over the course of four years of investing, assuming a slow rate of investment and modest return of 20 percent annualized.

The lecture on compensation was intended to depict the state of affairs at a typical venture capital firm; it incidentally highlighted the contrast between the typical firm and Benchmark, where there were no associates, senior associates, or junior partners, and where the annualized return would soon pass 200 percent. When it was Dave Beirne's turn to rise and speak, he paused a dramatic moment before beginning (what the audience did not know was that he had thought the format was going to be only question-and-answer; he had no remarks prepared). He could not speak for others, he began cautiously. A firm's culture is what is most important, and to him Benchmark's founding principle of an equal partnership had been essential: "Same salaries, same carry, one person, one vote, no managing director."

Regardless of where younger venture capitalists worked, there was one universal way for them to promote their own careers: Serve entrepreneurs, the Benchmark refrain. "This isn't the old days—there's no longer an old boys' network," he noted, so when capital was a commodity, service was the only way to differentiate oneself. "Managing a Career" was simple: "You will succeed," he advised, "by helping others succeed." In his own case, he had discovered so far that it was his prior experience as an entrepreneur, not in high-tech executive search, that had proven to be most useful to the entrepreneurs he was working with. "It's hard to help entrepreneurs if you haven't had the two A.M. sweats, haven't made a payroll." Beirne stayed politely for a few minutes to talk with the well-wishers and curiosity-seekers who gathered around him, then he excused himself and disappeared. None of the other partners appeared during the two days.

■

The following Monday, toward the end of the partners' meeting, Andy Rachleff turned to Bob Kagle and suggested that Bruce Dunlevie should have been placed as the chair of the "Living Legends" panel at the meeting, instead of Geoff Yang of IVP.

"Didn't want to cross over into self-promotion," Kagle said, without his usual animation.

"By the way, you know I'm not finding fault," Rachleff said.

No, Kagle said, looking down at the table. But before the event, his Benchmark partners had been "dissing the whole thing as a waste of time. I got more support out of my distant related friends" at other venture capital firms.

"Then we're at fault," Rachleff said, chagrined.

"No, no." Kagle looked uncomfortable. "I'm just saying, Hey, I got a big message of lack of interest."

Kevin Harvey agreed with Kagle. Anything Kagle had tried to suggest about their participating had been met with resistance. Harvey included himself among the guilty parties.

"I think we *are* at fault," Dunlevie said. He was regretful for having let Kagle down personally, but he detested the NVCA. "I think it is a bogus association, as you know. I think it's self-congratulatory and back-patting, and I think all that stuff they do in Washington is disingenuous to get lower capital-gains taxes. Not for everybody else in the world—just for venture capitalists. I think it's highly politicized, distasteful to me.

"But if you're the head guy on it, the question is operative: Is there something we should be doing? We should all have been there, I see with the benefit of reflecting on it, if only to support you."

Kagle addressed the others: "You don't want to be perceived as thinking you are too cool for all that stuff, or thinking it's beneath you or something. If it's worth John Doerr's time, it's worth our time almost by definition." He laughed at flattering Doerr and went on to talk about Dave Beirne, who was out of town at that moment. Kagle said Beirne, as the newest guy to venture capital, would have learned a great deal if he had gone to listen to the "Living Legends" panel.

The panel members had "built the industry, right? But somehow it wasn't worth his time to do that. It just seems like we've taken our macho thing to the limit and we need to come back from that a little bit. That's how I feel. 'Cause there's a lot to learn from a lot of people in the world."

"I hear you," Rachleff said. "We should have been there. In the future, let's make sure when another one of us is in this situation that we be supportive about that. The Kleiner Perkins guys do what Doerr did on this one all the time—they always stock their panels. I'm a cynic, I look at it that way. Whenever he's on Louis Rukeyser, all he mentions are Kleiner Perkins companies. It's a total promote."

Harvey had just as strong a visceral distaste for the National Venture Capital Association as did Dunlevie, but he was willing to see Kagle's point. "My thesis, which is probably wrong, has been that marketing myself to venture capitalists is not the best use of my time. You're taking the view that we can really learn something, and that's a good thing."

■

On Sand Hill Road, the venture capital world brought together for-profit and nonprofit constituencies in an abstract sense (nonprofits were the principal limited partners) and a concrete sense (the Benchmark offices were owned by a nonprofit). But the two worlds intersected in the most literal fashion, in a venture called Charitableway.

This was Andy Rachleff's deal, one that stood apart from the rest of his portfolio of network-equipment and telecom-related investments. His investment decisions demanded mastery of arcane technology that the others jokingly distilled down to "moving bits faster"; they relied upon Rachleff to keep abreast of these fields. However, Benchmark's organizational culture deliberately bound the partners tightly together, regardless of investment specialization, and that, in turn, gave each partner the freedom to make investments—like Charitableway—that did not necessarily fit a neatly labeled cubbyhole.

The concept originated in conversations that Rachleff had with Pete Mountanos, a rapid-talking fifty-year-old entrepreneur with the energy of a twenty-year-old. Rachleff was forty years old, and wore his hair on the long side, falling over the tops of his ears; his manner of speaking was the opposite of Mountanos's, measured, free of excited extremes. Rachleff's speech, like his partners', was also free of regional accent. He had grown up in New Jersey, and gone to the University of Pennsylvania and Stanford business school.

Rachleff had been impressed with Mountanos when Mountanos was working at Microsoft, which had recently acquired his start-up, VXtreme. After Mountanos completed his employment contract and left Microsoft, the two had lunch. When Rachleff invited Mountanos to list his ideas for new businesses—Mountanos said he could reel off ten good ideas off the top of his head—Rachleff heard the idea for Charitableway and said, Stop right there. Do that one.

At Microsoft, Mountanos had chafed when the company put pressure on all employees to give to the United Way because he could not easily direct to whom his donation would go. Wouldn't it be great, he proposed, if there were a website where you go to look for information on charities, choose the charity you wished to donate to, and then have your company match the contribution. It was an adaptation of the same principle of self-direction that had made 401(k) plans such a popular alternative to traditional pension plans. Give people choice, Mountanos said.

Rachleff was immediately excited by the idea. The Web offered an opportunity to solicit donors at electronic brokerages, at online auctions like eBay, and at media-related websites, making a painless way to donate, say, stock that was just sold or to put an item up for a charity auction. And a largely automated system could slash the 18 percent in overhead charges that the United Way took off the top in administrative fees, and still leave room to make a profit—if the world was ready for a for-profit solicitor of charities.

Popular acceptance might have seemed unlikely, were it not for the extremely negative publicity that the United Way had drawn to itself in recent years. Just when Benchmark, along with Softbank, invested in Mountanos's new company—Charitableway received $8.3 million, at $8.9 million pre-, a generous valuation for a mere idea—the local United Way brought the spotlight upon itself when it discovered halfway through the year that it had lost track of its own expenses and was short $11 million in funds promised to one hundred recipient charities. In the wake of the revelations, the executive director was fired, the majority of the board of directors resigned, and an emergency fund-raising campaign was launched to make up for the shortfall. "If you make it not-for-profit," Rachleff argued, "what do you expect? You need a profit incentive to drive efficiency."

Mountanos first set up operations in Benchmark's office. For Rachleff, this was a company for which it was especially fun to recruit employees. "You can do well while doing good. Everyone gets it. That's how we filter on the people." Within six weeks of moving into its own office in Palo Alto, the company had twenty people and had already outgrown its space.

With glee, Rachleff told his partners, "Our dream came true: United Way tried to stop charities from doing business with us." Mountanos had been worried that this would come to pass, but Rachleff welcomed it. "Unbelievably boneheaded move!" He changed his voice to sound like a United Way official, speaking to an agency that was a beneficiary: "If you work with those guys [at Charitableway], we won't give you money." Rachleff laughed at the thought of the United Way wanting to prevent agencies from receiving donations that did not come through its own hands. "Hello? It's like a large company suing a small company. All it does is give it credibility."

At a company board meeting, Mountanos reported that a professional consultant to charities had recently called him, inquiring about a position.

"How much do you make now?" Mountanos had asked him.

"Four hundred fifty thousand a year."

"How can you make four hundred fifty thousand dollars as a fundraiser? How do charities rationalize it?"

"I only focus on large, individual donors. And it's important that I live in their neighborhood."

Mountanos added that the man had said that in dead seriousness, and the charity paid him enough so he could live in Atherton. "I was stunned: 'I have to live with my donors.' " Mountanos shook his head, incredulous.

The company's board turned its attention to the question of whether to change Charitableway's name, to distance it from the United Way. Adopting a made-up name was a possibility, but Mountanos, thinking of Yahoo, was leery of a name that appeared to be too *cool*.

"Any other names being considered?" asked Andy Rachleff.

"No. All the URLs have been taken. Charity.com—the guys there said they wanted to see our business plan before they'd talk to us, signaling they'll want something astronomical."

"What's astronomical?"

"A hundred thousand dollars."

"That's not astronomical."

Mike Homer, a board member who had been the vice president for marketing at Netscape, nominated "humanrace.com," a candidate that Mountanos had mentioned that he owned. "Human Race is a great name."

"I got that for fifteen hundred dollars. I was on the board of that company, it was dissolving, so I said I'd buy it." Mountanos was reluctant to discard the company's current name. "I've got to say, a lot of people just love the name Charitableway. It's self-explanatory." Even if he could be persuaded to look again at other alternatives, "the names we might go try and buy, we've never fallen in love with any more than with this one."

The name remained. But his phrase "fallen in love" lingered, a reminder of the unusual conjunction here of business and romance, of hoping to do well and hoping to do good.

8. Name Your Price

In Dave Beirne's rookie year, he fell in love, for the right reasons, with the right deal, and his more experienced partners, for reasons that were almost as good but not quite, held back. Ex-romantics who had been burned in the past, they couldn't help but emphasize the shortcomings of Priceline, the you-name-your-price airline-tickets service that had just been launched. To them it smelled like a promote, an unproven concept play with no clear prospect of making money. They fought with Beirne over the issues with a sharpness that was not commonly seen in the conference room, and yet love was love, and Beirne would not let go of it.

That Benchmark even had the opportunity to consider an investment was due to Beirne's mastery of the art of voice mail. So testified Jay Walker, the founder of Priceline, based in Connecticut; when he received Beirne's "You don't know me, but we're going to be friends" message from out of the ether in May 1998, he was sufficiently intrigued that he returned the call, even though he neither sought nor needed capital from Benchmark. Walker, forty-two, was a marketing-oriented entrepreneur who "makes a living," as he put it, inserting advertisements in envelopes with billing statements. It was a decent living at that—his net worth was in the hundred-million-dollar range—and it had permitted him to set up his own private research outfit, Walker Digital, whose Ph.D.s were given a charter to do applied marketing research that would lead to new, patent-protectable business ideas. It was one of those hothouse-bred ideas that had turned into Priceline, which was funded by Walker and a host of well-connected backers on the East Coast, including principals of General Atlantic Partners. GA, a $4 billion outfit, boasted that it was the "world's largest private equity investment firm focused on information technologies." Still, largest or not, it couldn't boast of the experience in building "world-class teams" that Beirne could, so Beirne managed to talk his way through Jay Walker's door. After flying out to Stamford and spending seven hours with him, Beirne had secured Walker's interest.

When he first told his partners about Priceline, Beirne did not minimize the risk; there was a ton, and he needed to do more due diligence. But he pointed to the heavy hitters that Walker had attracted to his board. Rick Braddock, who used to run Citicorp, was, in Dave Beirne shorthand, "a total stud," and Nick Nicholas, former co-head of Time Warner, was "another total stud." If this thing works, he said, it's the kind of thing you'd be proud of when it goes public—"Yes, we were in Priceline." He mused quietly, "I think it could be everything as big as what Amazon was to books."

He had won the opportunity for Benchmark to invest, but this was not a raw start-up, so it was pricey. He was hoping to work out terms that would give Benchmark half of a $15 million financing at a $60 million premoney valuation. The $7.5 million investment—a partnership record—would secure a 10 percent stake.

"Only a ten percent stake?" Kevin Harvey asked.

"If we had the ability to own ten percent of Amazon.com when it was at a hundred fifty million bucks, we'd have done it, right?" Beirne countered.

"What about the fifty other deals at that price that we didn't do?" Harvey asked. "I could be persuaded if there's real revenue mo. I wouldn't do this on the come."

What was the financial history of the company, Kagle asked. It had been intended as a neutral question, but it touched upon a vulnerable spot. Jay Walker had put $15 million in himself, and $10 million had been raised already from directors like Braddock and from GA. "So there's twenty-five in it already?" Kagle asked incredulously. This was equivalent to five typical Benchmark investments combined.

Beirne nodded quietly.

"Little fire going on?" Harvey needled, alluding to a cash bonfire.

They're spending a ton of money on traditional advertising to establish the brand, that's all.

Dunlevie couldn't resist: "Little fire going on?" He flapped his arms up and down: "They need a big guy with the bellows!"

Turning his ire on Harvey, Beirne said, "I think you have every right to be as much of a prick as you want to be after you meet it. But meet the company."

Later in the meeting, Harvey returned to the issue of the disappointingly small slice of equity available for Benchmark. "You've already called me a prick," he reasoned aloud, "so I've got nothing to lose at this point."

"No," Dunlevie corrected, "you have the right to be a prick after you meet it. It's far gentler!"

"The thing could be a couple billion dollars," Beirne reminded everyone.

■

Initially, Beirne suggested that a couple of the partners hop on a plane and go visit Priceline as soon as possible, but Jay Walker offered to come out to California to meet with everyone there instead. The next week, Walker and Priceline's chief financial officer, Paul Francis, appeared at Benchmark's office, attired in the ties and sport jacket and suit that visitors from the East Coast stubbornly wore, knowing that they would be greeted with West Coast informal. In this and his medium stature and unlined round face, Walker was unremarkable. To an inattentive listener, his manner of speaking sounded chirpy, like that of a sales guy just a mite too eager to please.

The partners were uniformly resistant to the pitches of sales guys, but as soon as Walker dispensed with the polite, we're-glad-to-be-here chitchat, it was instantly clear that this visitor was unusual.

His opening lines were proud declarations: I am an entrepreneur! Have been so for about twenty-five years. I build businesses for a living!

Headed for hubris, he then expertly turned course and in the same, matter-of-fact declarative mode, said that most of the businesses he had built over the years had failed, so he knew a lot of ways how *not* to do something. His most recent venture, NewSub Services, was his biggest success to date, doing $250 million a year, but even this he was careful to politely deprecate, referring to its advertising inserts as "all that garbage in your credit card statement that irritates you."

This was preamble to a presentation that would run almost three hours, an extended lecture in applied marketing theory that would set a local record for length yet leave the Benchmark partners entertained and awed. With an academic's attachment to conceptual labeling, Jay Walker walked the Benchmark audience through demand collection systems, conditional purchase offers, primary and secondary demand fill, plug-in demand, bounce-off demand, and numberless other concepts. A prospective Priceline customer seeking an airline ticket might not know what to bid, Harvey wondered aloud. "We've got names for all this stuff," Walker replied without a moment's hesitation. "What you're talking about is performance anxiety." What about customers that would try to submit multiple bids, beginning with ridiculously low ones? Walker had a name for that, too: "the pinging problem," named for the "ping" command used to test a network connection.

A banquet of concepts, each dish a minifeast, presented in methodical order. Each potential problem identified had a matching solution in place.

On Priceline, prospective customers named the price they were willing to pay and the dates they wanted to travel, and gave a credit card number ("proxy transfer"), which was used by Priceline within one hour if a fare at or below the price bid was found. The fine print included the following: agreeing to fly on any flight, other than a red-eye; agreeing to the possibility of making one stop en route; the tickets were nonchangeable and nonrefundable; and no frequent-flyer miles were earned. This set of restrictions, Walker argued, made the tickets a flat-out inferior product—so inferior the airlines thought Priceline would not find anyone interested in it. But they were wrong; they didn't realize what Walker and his marketers knew, which was that the business was all about price, price, price, and when you were done, it still was about price. And yet the airlines didn't have to worry that Priceline tickets would hurt their existing fare structure because Walker's system implanted "deeply embedded uncertainty" that rendered the tickets complementary to, not competitive with, conventional tickets. (Bruce Dunlevie took an immediate liking to Walker's phrase; for months afterward, he would mischievously slip "deeply embedded uncertainty" into group discussions.)

Our biggest competition, Walker explained, was cars and couches; Priceline's system "collected demand" from people who would not otherwise be flying. And by promising to get back with an answer within one hour—why one hour? Glasses in an hour, photos in an hour; consumers already understand the unit—Walker was deliberately creating in the consumers' mind the idea that Priceline was a virtual gladiator fighting on their behalf: "It's going to take us an hour to knock on everybody's door, punch him in the jaw, give him your offer, and get back to you with an answer, but be assured we're out there working for you!"

Walker's colorful metaphor got a laugh out of Andy Rachleff. Encouraged, Walker pretended to be an imaginary customer: "The bastards are out there working for me! Yeah!"

In fact, the bastards were working for the airlines, too, simultaneously, consulting with their revenue-management departments and tailoring arrangements to provide what Walker described to the Benchmark partners as a "dream come true" for airlines: These new customers could be plugged in to a reservations system wherever an airline wished. As an industry, the airlines annually had $38 billion worth of empty seats that they could not fill without weakening their existing revenue-maximization models. Now Priceline said to them— and here Walker picked up and waved a thick pile of computer printouts, bids that Priceline had collected from its website the previous week—here's $5 million of credit card–guaranteed demand, from every city, to every city. It's yours if you want! The average marginal cost of putting an additional passenger on a flight was only $20, so any fare that the airlines charged above $20 was gravy, profit that dropped right to the bottom line of the airline. "Which is why this is so powerfully attractive to the airline," Walker said, grinning.

But was it actually so "powerfully attractive"? Kevin Harvey mock-innocently asked how many of the major airlines had Priceline lined up, and the answer was only two, and relatively small ones at that: America West and TWA. Harvey's follow-up questions exposed an additional problem: Priceline was unable to secure tickets at a deep discount, so it was selling tickets for below its own average cost in order to secure some customers. An inconsistency appeared: The airlines, which a moment before Walker had described as enamored with Priceline's "plug-in" demand, were also saying to him: "I'm not giving you the best prices. I'll just give you some of my worst prices. Sell that shit for a while." And even subsidized, Priceline was only able to fulfill one out of every twenty offers.

"I'm the resident pain-in-the-ass," Harvey said to Walker, apologetically. "I'm just trying to think this through." If your filter works as promised, providing nonbusiness travelers exclusively, what's to keep a United Airlines from selling similar tickets off its own website?

"Okay, let's be Sears," Walker proposed, back on the safe terrain of marketing theory. Imagine you walk into Sears and, ignoring the price tags on all the merchandise, you heed a big sign that hangs over the cash register that says, NAME YOUR PRICE! TELL US WHAT YOU WANT TO PAY! He moved his hand from left to right, as if he were reading a sign that was right in front of them. "Are you ever going to pay attention to retail prices at Sears again?" Walker demanded. "Ever?

"We can talk the theory all day long," he said—indeed he could, as the clock showed—but now he took up the question of the possibility of a deal. "What got us on a plane was what Dave said, which is, 'Look, we have what you guys really need. The missing piece of your puzzle is the world-class operating team. You're going to succeed, but you'll succeed more quickly if we help you recruit a CEO and the team who will take this from a couple-hundred-million-dollar business that it's going to be next year to the couple-billion-dollar business it ought to be.' " What Beirne had had no way of knowing in advance was that Walker was that rarity—like eBay's Pierre Omidyar—an entrepreneur with no wish to operate the business he created. So the prospect that Beirne had dangled before him, of getting the perfect CEO who could accelerate Priceline's growth, had piqued Walker's interest. "We can't do better than you, Dave, is our belief," Walker said, turning to him. "Everywhere we go, that's what we're told."

At the same time he paid the compliment, Walker was also careful not to overstate his readiness to discount the current valuation of Priceline in order to cut Benchmark in. He had no set number in mind, but the range of possible values began at $60 million and extended up to $250 million, depending on which assumptions and comparable valuations were used; with impressive detachment, Walker coolly analyzed the rationale for both low-end and high-end valuations. He then anticipated how negotiations between the two sides would proceed:

"David, you're going to argue that we ought to take the bottom end of that number for the world-class team, and we're going to argue, Okay, how do we know we're going to get the world-class team? And how do we know what they're going to be worth when they show up here, since there's always a discount risk for people just coming and not working out?"

Since we're not actively shopping for capital, Walker summed up, this isn't about the money per se. It's really about two teams—your team, our team. We've got a multibillion-dollar asset here if played right. We're not greedy; we're not pigs. We're players. Game theorists that we are, we understand the game trade. And we're not afraid to make a trade for the right set of circumstances.

He said he'd be flexible, but he did not say Name your price.

While Beirne walked the guests to the elevator, Harvey and Rachleff exchanged looks of amused fright.

"The economics I call terrifying," Harvey began.

"I was really surprised to see the negative gross margin," Rachleff said. He shook his head and laughed. "They sell the thing under cost."

"But they're going to make it up on volume," Dunlevie added drily.

When Beirne returned to the room, the partners piled many compliments upon Jay Walker; Kagle called him "a totally compelling dude, just *totally* compelling—one of the smartest economic thinkers I think I've ever hung with." Dunlevie agreed. Even Harvey, usually the stingiest with praise, allowed that Walker was a "charismatic guy." Everyone but Beirne had experienced cognitive dissonance, however: Walker was so impressive, and seemingly had thought through every contingency, yet at the same time the facts were anything but positive.

"I'll paint a negative picture," Harvey offered. "He's paying a shit-load of money for traffic. The customer experience right now, the hit rate, is bad. I don't believe that you have positive testimonials when only five percent of your customers are successful. To have any leverage with the airlines, he needs to keep feeding that customer-acquisition fire. That's a boatload of money. There's a chance he just never gets there."

Beirne had a counterexample at the ready from their own portfolio: PointCast. It lost a million subscribers each quarter, yet at the same time a million new ones signed up.

Yes, but PointCast managed to acquire more than a million customers without spending what Jay Walker had already spent in four weeks marketing Priceline, blanketing the country with radio commercials and print advertisements featuring William Shatner, the former *Star Trek* actor. His professional identity had no apparent connection to the Priceline message, but Shatner's was a familiar voice and face, and renting his seal of approval conferred instant familiarity upon his sponsor. From familiarity, it was a short—if illogical—hop to instant credibility, but such is the magic of celebrity testimonials. Jay Walker had a good ear; the Shatner message was savvy. The only aspect that was second-guessed was Priceline's expensive choice of *The Wall Street Journal* for full-page advertisements, where the demographic characteristics of the readers did not seem well-matched to Priceline's target audience.

Mother-in-law research, which encompassed relatives who lived well apart from *The Wall Street Journal* readership, augured well for Priceline. "I didn't come from money," said Beirne, who predicted that relatives from his family and his wife's all would travel on Priceline. In fact, "every person I know, outside of the people that I hang with right here—they'd all travel this way."

And judging by the mesmerizing performance of Jay Walker that morning, you had to figure that when it came time to raise additional capital, Priceline could spin a spellbinding story, even more compelling than Webvan's. And Walker's personal commitment to his vision—the partners had learned that Walker had invested not $15 million but $20 million from his own pocket—was something few entrepreneurs were in a position to demonstrate with such force. Beirne liked the idea that Walker could sit across from any banker and say,

"I'm in." Still, Priceline had not proven that it could get one of the top six airlines. If it did not succeed in doing so, then the air-ticket business might fail to break even. Walker had grandiose plans for expanding name-your-own-price into many other services, but as Kagle said, the airlines were "do or die" for Priceline.

"The wheels are shaking on this thing right now," Beirne conceded, but then again, if Walker had already signed one of the major carriers, Benchmark would not now have the opportunity to invest.

"This is Webvan," Harvey said, meaning here was another company that would require far more capital than the others in the portfolio, and the risk of failure would not diminish as it soaked up capital.

"It's kind of weird to be very excited and scared to death at the same time," said Kagle.

Webvan was the right touchstone. So was this as scary as Webvan or less so? The capital-intensive nature of Webvan was daunting, but on paper, at least, Louis Borders could show that the economics should work out nicely. In the case of Priceline, all the partners knew with certainty was that Jay Walker could sell plane tickets for $200 that cost him $225.

"And he's not getting a lot of supply!" Kagle noted.

Harvey was laughing so hard he barely got the words out: "We're selling at a ten percent loss, and supply is the issue!"

"Two negatives make a positive, right?" Beirne said, maintaining a straight face. He let the jokes die down, then moved to drafting a proposal: How about offering to invest at $60 million pre- to get 10 percent ownership immediately, and another 5 percent that would be tied to successful hiring of a CEO and the rest of the company's senior management team? Added up, it would mean writing checks for more than $10 million.

Harvey: "Terrifying."

Dunlevie: "Exciting."

Kagle: "Exactly!"

"Is that a nervous laugh?" Beirne asked Kagle.

"They're *all* nervous laughs," Harvey explained.

■

"I'm just getting limber," Bruce Dunlevie joked, swinging a bat in pantomime as if it were he, and not Beirne, who followed Priceline immediately with another mighty swing, TriStrata. This was a tiny Silicon Valley company that developed encryption software; no one had heard of it, even though it had been founded four years previously, because it had yet to release its first product. Yet it asked for an outsized pre-money valuation of $85 million, higher than even Priceline, and sought a $15 million investment from Benchmark, double that being considered for Priceline. In one breath, Beirne was asking the partners to approve not one but two investments that were an order of magnitude richer in valuation than the typical early-stage start-up. When recruiting Beirne to the firm the year before, his partners had encouraged him in his desire to pursue the biggest deals, the biggest swings. But now, confronted with his requests to loosen the spigot and let the capital flow, the partners collectively gulped.

"I'm an eight on this deal," Beirne declared, 8 being an uncommonly high vote on the scale of 1 to 10, even for a deal's advocate. TriStrata was a prototypical Dave Beirne deal. It carved out a large business opportunity—its software, if it delivered on what the company promised, would safely protect from unauthorized eyes all data and messages that traveled within a corporation's computer network. Conceivably, the software would one day be installed on every personal computer in every office. It was a deal well-matched to Beirne's strengths because the company's prospects could be measured indirectly by the association of brand-name people of accomplishment, who in this case included the founder, John Atalla, the father of PINs, which had made bank ATM networks secure two decades earlier, and Tom Perkins, of Kleiner Perkins fame (and one of the "Living Legends" at the NVCA conference), who had already invested his own money in TriStrata. And it seemed to be a good match also because the company was "a make"—it needed a CEO and a senior management team.

Two other elements made TriStrata attractive to Beirne, though he may not have been conscious of their pull. Like Priceline, TriStrata was not actively pursuing capital from venture firms—no company looks better than the one that professes it does not need your money. And only Dave Beirne would find the last element appealing: the

challenge of winning over an entrepreneur who had an unusual background. John Atalla was not a typical Silicon Valley wunderkind; he
was Mitteleuropa, in his seventies, a technologist, and someone who
did not like John Doerr or venture capitalists in general. Beirne's specialty was finding ways to connect with literally anyone, and when he
met Atalla, he could distance himself from the other venture guys—
Beirne presented himself as an experienced entrepreneur, like Atalla,
and of course he was a recruiter, the person who could bring in the
people who would ensure that the old man could leave a legacy.

When John Atalla had come to the Benchmark office to meet a
few of the partners, it was Beirne who knew what he wanted: listeners—extremely patient listeners—who would show interest in a me-
andering discourse on Europe and his background and his
philosophy of life. Beirne composed himself into a sculpture titled
"Rapt": leaning toward Atalla, both elbows on the table, fists support-
ing his head, eyes unwaveringly focused on the speaker. Bruce Dunlevie, too, wore an attentive mien. Kevin Harvey, however, repeatedly
hopped out of the meeting to take phone calls. To Beirne's distress,
Harvey was oblivious to the psychology underlying the encounter.
Didn't he understand? Atalla wanted to build a relationship with the
firm—in the phrasing of one of the partners, Atalla "wanted to date
before he fucked." (Harvey's view of the same scene was quite different: The old man evaded all specific questions about the business and
the technology, clear evidence that he was "full of shit.") Like Jay
Walker's, Atalla's presentation went on for almost three hours, but it
left the other partners drained, not excited.

Dave Beirne's courtship of Herr Dr. Atalla—what venture guys
would call a "sell situation"—succeeded. Beirne called him at the end
of the week following the visit, thanking him for the opportunity to
look, but explained that there was no prospect of an agreement on a
deal because the valuation and investment sought were way beyond
anything that Benchmark had done before. Atalla wouldn't hear of it.
Talk to the other board members, he pleaded with Beirne. "You *have*
to be an investor in my company. You have to be on my board." He
was willing to accept a lower valuation so the investment would be
more attractive. "Make the fucking numbers work!"

"Clever, very clever" was Kagle's reaction when he heard of the conversation. "I don't mean Atalla's being dishonest," he hastened to assure Beirne, "but I'm just saying he's very clever." He and the others were leery because even though Perkins was on the board, along with John Young, a retired president and CEO of Hewlett-Packard, and Bill Zuendt, the former president and COO of Wells Fargo—hitters all—the company lacked a business plan. Atalla promised profits of $10 million in the first year of sales but had no idea what revenue was expected; four years after its founding, and with its pilot product ready for launch, it had yet to hire a single marketeer or salesperson.

Dunlevie mimicked Atalla: " 'All we're focused on around here is profits.' " More realistically, Dunlevie thought TriStrata would do at best $10 million in revenue, but certainly not in profits.

"No way," Harvey said. "There's never been an application in the enterprise that was this global and extensive and involved and everything that's going on, ramping [that fast]."

Rachleff was in the skeptics' camp, too. He couldn't see in this what Beirne apparently saw. "I'm missing something unbelievable," he confessed.

"You spent a half hour with this guy," Beirne said testily, pointing an accusing finger at one partner. The finger swung to another: "You left early." And a third was charged with being present "for maybe a third of the meeting." Beirne's prescription was for the others to use the Dave Beirne method: Spend more time with the entrepreneur to understand the opportunity by relationship-building.

The testiness, however, was an indication of pressure. The Tri-Strata board was meeting in one week and wanted to know whether Benchmark was in or out. Why there would be such a rush to get an answer when the company was ostensibly not seeking an investment was a mystery that no one in the room pursued. Beirne found himself in a delicate situation. He had won an invitation to join a club of swells—Perkins, Young, and Zuendt. Dunlevie himself had offered a roundabout testimonial that a friend of his, whom he revered, regarded Zuendt as "the smartest guy he's ever met." This was august company, so anything but an immediate yes on Benchmark's part would be read as skittishness. Or worse, the TriStrata board might regard ordinary due diligence as an affront to their own reputations. Relationships could be damaged by a misstep here.

It was tempting to trust in the professional judgment of the others because TriStrata's core security technology was, by its nature, impenetrable to all but an elite among cryptographic experts. The Tri-Strata Secure Information Management System, involving installation of its own computers and proprietary software in a corporate network, encrypted and decrypted all data with code that was purportedly "unbreakable." Atalla claimed that he had figured out how to implement an arcane algorithm called "a one-time pad," a desideratum that was based on a long-known cryptographic theory but whose practical realization had eluded everyone else. While other cryptographers had had to settle for a *pseudo* one-time pad implementation," Atalla said he had implemented the real thing. Was there independent corroboration that he had achieved the cryptographic equivalent of converting lead into gold? Only if one accepted indirect evidence. Price Waterhouse had put its best people on the task of trying to break it. "It could not be broken," TriStrata said they had reported. And there were other encouraging signs: Price Waterhouse had already installed the pilot system at a few of its offices and appeared close to signing clients like General Motors, Cigna, and Shell.

"Close to signing," however, was not signed. If ever there was a deal that screamed for due diligence, investigating claims and consulting disinterested third parties, this was the one—and all the more so given it would be Benchmark's all-time largest investment and at the all-time highest valuation. The Benchmark tradition was to do the due diligence before a commitment to invest was made, but here the TriStrata board was pressing for an immediate answer. Responding to the palpable doubts in the Benchmark conference room, Beirne proposed to his partners that Benchmark commit to invest, subject to thirty days of due diligence.

"It's chickenshit," Rachleff spit out, upset at the proposed break with Benchmark tradition. A commitment that was "subject to due diligence" was not a real commitment; it was nothing but poor service to an entrepreneur. It was the sort of clause that leasing companies and buyout firms resorted to, he noted with distaste. If a commitment is to be meaningful, you must do your homework before, not after.

The others were also unenthusiastic about a conditional commitment. Maintaining a good relationship with Atalla was important, so which would Atalla respect more, Harvey asked Beirne. If you say,

"Look, I want to shake on the deal, and we're going to do a month of due diligence"? Or if you say instead, "I want to do one week's worth of due diligence, so when I give you my word, we're done"?

"I think it's a really good question," Beirne replied. "I think my fear on it is if you bring someone in to help do some due diligence on this—say this guy at Netscape who's supposed to be some hot-shit security guy and that person's not, the person shows poorly and that reflects on us. I think I could lose the whole deal."

Kagle gently cautioned Beirne: "We all have our blind spots, right? Our greatest strength is our greatest weakness. And I think in this case, Dave, we're all conscious of the fact that there's a lot of marquee players around this thing. You're all about marquee players. So we need to make sure that you're not getting too colored by that relative to all the other stuff."

"Salesmen are more likely to be sold," Rachleff added.

"I think I can get one of the best CEO's ever to go run this company and build one of the best senior management teams in the business," Beirne said. "I've watched what that does to companies. Now, I've marketed a lot of things that people said were 'fucking stupid'— Netscape was one of them. All I want to do is have an open mind from all you guys to do the due diligence. I don't think people like Zuendt and Young are stupid. They don't put their money in and spend their time on things that they think aren't real."

"No," Kagle allowed, but "the tension here is these kinds of deals are testing some of the fundamental tenets of at least the way we used to think we approached the business. I, for one, am open to learning new things here about all this." He laughed. "But I'm seeing some crazy things that I *never* would have predicted six months ago. And I think there's a lot to be learned from going through this exercise. I'm excited about it."

"Really?" Rachleff asked.

"Yeah." Kagle continued. "I'm where you are on judgment on the deal. But I've got to be open to learning and changing my mind."

"There's way too much interest to leave it—no one's advocating that," Harvey said.

"If I don't play this the way I want to play it," Beirne said, with an implied sigh, "I will have basically left it."

"So how can we help you?"

"You did. Thank you."

Harvey pretended Beirne was a schoolchild receiving swats and mimicked: " 'Thank you, sir. May I have another?' "

Shaking his head at the prospect of an investment at a record-setting price with fundamental questions about its business still unanswered, Rachleff, who had just turned forty, could only shake his head and mutter aloud, "I'm a relic. I must be a relic."

It was true, TriStrata was asking a high price, Beirne acknowledged. As "the cheapest fuck on the planet" he knew it was a high price. So was Priceline. But these two projects could be—and here his low voice went still lower for emphasis—"*franchise* businesses that could take Benchmark over the top."

He was silent. "And if I fail, we've lost some money, but I'm done. So I understand what these mean. If Webvan screws up, Benchmark's going to raise another fund and do just fine. But if I fuck up on this one and Priceline and—"

"Remember pen computing, Dave?" Rachleff said, with a reassuring smile. "You'll do just fine." Everyone but Beirne laughed at the memory of what at the time had seemed like an utter disaster for Kleiner Perkins, and yet hadn't John Doerr marched out of the smoking crater unscathed and funded Netscape?

"I take this very seriously," Beirne said, without relaxing.

"I hear you," Rachleff continued. "I'm sensitive to this issue because this is what we talked about at breakfast before you joined, could you be happy doing these things. I understand where you're coming from and what kind of projects you're involved in. The challenge is, Can you do that still within our price constraints? It's a challenge."

■

The due-diligence issue prevented a partnership decision that day on TriStrata, but Beirne asked for a vote on Priceline. First, though, the group had one more question for Beirne: Which of these two high-priced deals did he favor?

"That's like *Sophie's Choice,* you just choose one," Beirne said.

"If you did?" Rachleff persisted.

"I don't."

"Rank 'em, in your mind."

"They're both terrifying."

"If you could only do one, which would you do?"

"I'm not playing that game, Andrew."

"What do you mean you're not playing that game? Answering helps me understand what you're thinking."

"I'd do them both."

"I heard that, Dave. Just answer the question."

"It's like saying which of your kids you want to survive, Andrew."

"No, it isn't."

"I've worked both of these big-time, and I like both of them for different reasons. They both, I think, have unbelievable upside."

Dunlevie joined Rachleff in trying to extract an answer, but Beirne would not, could not, favor one of his babies over another. Harvey tried another angle and asked whether Beirne would do Webvan again. At that point, the Webvan investment was almost a year old and another year remained before it would launch. Yes, he would, Beirne said, but Harvey confessed he was uncertain whether he himself would vote in its favor again.

"I think it's important to permit different styles of venture capital," Dunlevie said tolerantly. "Dave's got a style. It's not to say we do every deal"—here his voice climbed high and hoarse—"that's wacky and high-priced!" He returned again and again to the evident fact that "Jay Walker is one of the smartest fuckers we've ever met." So which aspect of the picture was most salient: that Priceline was spending scary quantities of marketing dollars in order to sell airline tickets below cost, or that it was the creation of a great guy, and one should always back a great guy?

The deal that Beirne proposed for Priceline was $7.5 million at $60 million pre-, with warrants for another $7.5 million that, if exercised, would give Benchmark a 15 percent stake, the minimum acceptable to the partners.

Beirne ripped off a blank sheet from a legal pad and tore it into strips for the vote. Each partner was to select a number—by custom, an integer only—from 1 to 10: 6 or higher expressed approval; 4 or less, disapproval; a vote of 5, the neutral refuge of cowards, was not permitted. After the ballots were returned, the votes were read off but no cumulative or average number was calculated. The partnership formally bestowed its approval to any deal in which three of the five partners voted above 5, but in fact the votes on investment decisions were merely advisory, information for the advocate—the ultimate decision maker—to digest.

Kagle could not move. "This is the weirdest feeling I've ever had, sitting here voting. I'm trying to get in touch with what that really means. To have voted on so many things and never have had this feeling before is a weird thing for me."

Harvey looked up at the ceiling for a long while. "I have to think about this."

Rachleff asked Beirne, "If you had a whole portfolio of these, would you be comfortable?"

"He already has!" Dunlevie answered for him, setting off laughter.

Comfortable? "Only if they're successful," Beirne answered helpfully.

Kagle finally wrote a number down, folded the paper over, and tossed it in Beirne's direction. "I couldn't decide whether I was a 3 or a 7, and I couldn't get anywhere in between."

Beirne read off the notes: "Kev is a 6 with the deal" that was on the table at 60 pre- "and 4 without."

"It won't be this deal," Harvey predicted, accurately as it turned out. "There's no chance."

"Andy's a 7, Bob's a 7, and Bruce is 7.25."

Dunlevie explained, "Once I've been introduced to decimals, I'm going creative." The others laughed. "Bob, you've unlocked a whole new world for me. The integer thing was really cramping my style."

■

In May 1998, at the same time that circumstances led to the speedy completion of the TriStrata deal, the negotiations with Priceline faltered. When the partners asked Beirne for an update the week following the vote, his expression was pained. The Benchmark offer of a $60 million valuation had been rejected—Priceline's other investors had argued that Benchmark should pay up at the current price of the internal shares for the employee pool, which would come out to $80 million.

"So do you feel like it's too high-priced for you to want to do it? Or do you feel like it's too high-priced for *us* wanting to do it?" Harvey asked Beirne.

"Too high-priced for us to want to do it."

" 'Us' including you?"

"No."

No one spoke. Beirne's anger was manifest in the way he now spoke at a barely audible level: "I see sphincter squeeze. It does me no good to call for a vote, get four 4s, and not be able to go from here."

"Also does you no good to assume you know the answer," replied Harvey.

"I think I know the answer," Beirne said. "Braddock's got his own money in this. GA's got personal money in this. I mean, we're playing with guys that are worth billions of dollars or hundreds of millions of dollars. They think they're playing in the big leagues and we're in Little League. That's fine."

More silence.

Kagle tried to offer a compromise that both Beirne and the partners could live with. What about relaxing the partnership's 15 percent ownership minimum? Why not have Benchmark take a smaller piece as a passive investment, that is, one in which Beirne would not serve as a director on the board?

Beirne kept his voice low, but the thought of missing the opportunity was too much to bear. "I think if this is what we think it is, if they nail one of the top six carriers, this will be such a massive company. The fact that we've sold ourselves into a position of owning 15 percent of it, I think, will be unbelievable. And I do think there is a shitload of work to do." It would also mean a return to "living in the tube," traveling to and from Connecticut. He was game, but to settle for only 7 or 8 percent? He didn't finish the thought out loud.

"You think we're chickenshit today," Rachleff said, "you should have seen us when we first got started."

"I didn't say we're chickenshit. I—"

"But we are," Rachleff insisted. "We are, to some degree."

One argument in Priceline's favor, Harvey suggested, was that even at an astronomical price, "we're in an environment where the company doesn't have to be successful for us to make money."

Kagle recoiled at the thought of backing a company that could exist only atop a stock-market bubble. "I'm never going to sign up for that program. You're betting too much on things that are out of your control."

Dunlevie had another proposal for Beirne. Benchmark would put $10 million in at the asking price, and Beirne would take on hiring the CEO but not go on the board. It would be a way of playing a more active role in the company's growth without having to use up a board slot on an investment in which the equity stake was small. This proposal, Dunlevie conceded, did undermine Beirne's original rationale for leaving the executive search business for the venture capital business.

Beirne shook his head no.

"Why not?"

"That was the business I was in. I would actually make more money personally, a shitload more money, if I was just building the senior management team of Priceline."

"That's not clear to me, either," Dunlevie said.

Oh, no? Beirne said that at Ramsey Beirne he and his colleagues made over $3 million recruiting the senior management team in four searches just for @Home. "That's a pretty good return on your time," Beirne argued. But he insisted the money wasn't the issue; it wasn't why he was doing what he was doing.

"But you do seem to have an emotional barrier—" Harvey ventured.

"I came over to do this to stay involved with the companies that I work with." The thought of being the one who would recruit the CEO for Priceline and then have to step to the sidelines, when a GA partner would be the one who got to hold a seat on the board, was too frustrating to contemplate. "I did that for ten years, that's what ripped my guts out. I didn't come to do this for money." If that had been the case, he said, "I'd just have retired."

The discussion turned to other matters, but Dunlevie came back to the suggestion that Benchmark buy a small piece and Beirne would help Priceline get its CEO. Don't let your ego get in the way, Beirne was told. "You'll get all the credit you need if you get a great CEO and the thing's worth two billion dollars and we own eight or nine or ten percent of it. You'll close the CEO, get off the airplane, get back to work here, and let that guy build the company." If what Dunlevie called the "non-board-seat option" was unacceptable to Beirne, well, then so be it. They could then walk from it with equanimity.

It wasn't as simple as that, though. Writing a $10 million check—even larger than that for TriStrata—and "not watching 'em—I can't get there," Kagle said.

"I'm syncing up with that," Harvey said.

"I didn't say 'not watching them,'" said Dunlevie.

"You know what I meant."

Rachleff had a compromise: "Writing five and not going on the board—that intrigues me."

Beirne would not budge. There was a lot of hiring that Priceline would need to do; a small stake would not justify the work entailed. Harvey and Dunlevie took a break and did riffs on the fact that the Priceline staff was "on loan" from Walker Digital. How committed could they be to seeing Priceline through hard times when they could shrug, abandon ship, and land softly on firm ground at their old jobs?

"That breeds some very scary behaviors, generally," Kagle said in a serious voice. "The fallback. Entrepreneurship is not a place to fall back."

The discussion made clear that none of the other four partners supported the idea of buying a 15 percent stake at the new asking price; that would mean writing a check for close to $15 million. When Beirne asked everyone how they felt about walking away from Priceline, Rachleff spoke for the others: "There has to be a point at which one walks on every deal."

Beirne had spent the past week preparing emotionally for this outcome. He had set for himself the task of reducing this to a purely emotionless business decision, and by the previous Friday, he said, he had "got there." Now the outcome he had dreaded was upon him. He could sense before it happened formally that he was about to lose Priceline. He remained outwardly composed, but he had deceived himself when he said he had purged all emotion from his system.

"If you do the portfolio approach, Andy—I've thought about that a lot since the meeting you called me stupid in—I've got to think that if I did both these deals [Priceline as well as TriStrata], and they're both eighty—just say eighty pre- or whatever the fuck they are, absurd—one of them is going to hit, one of them has to hit, and I bet it's really big. The likelihood that both fail and we lose all our money in both of them, I think, is near impossible."

"Well, you sort of had me until you said that!" said Kagle, setting off laughter among the others.

Was Beirne looking clear-sightedly at the first half of the risk/reward equation? Rachleff pressed. It seemed to him that Beirne was reducing risk to a question of the height of expected payoff, as if an outcome short of a couple billion dollars would then be a "bad risk." Instead, Rachleff suggested, the risk lay in whether the Priceline economics ever worked. Rachleff paraphrased Beirne's apparent position: "If the reward potential is huge, then it doesn't matter as much what the risk is."

On that issue, whether huge upside should render conventional risk less important, Harvey sided with Beirne, and over time would become the leading advocate among the partners of paying up at any price to buy into the deals with the highest upside potential. Here he was concerned not so much with the financial risks entailed by taking on two high-priced, high-risk deals simultaneously; rather it was with what might be called the "psychological risks" for Beirne. After spending a harrowing year working to keep PointCast, yesterday's big bet, alive—a task so consuming that he did not make a single new investment in all of 1997—Harvey knew better than anyone in the partnership what the psychic toll could be when a high-profile company hit turbulence. And if Harvey, the Zen master of emotional detachment, had experienced the woes of one of his portfolio companies as one long, sleepless nightmare, what would happen to Beirne, who despite his declarations to the contrary was constitutionally unable to "take the emotion out of it"?

Yes, one of the two plays might work, Harvey allowed. "But the one that doesn't will kill you. Especially you. I know you. You'll die."

His partners were willing to invest $5 million in Priceline but not $15 million.

Rachleff tried one more time to persuade Beirne to accept a smaller equity position and not go on the board. Using Beirne's own optimistic assessment of Priceline's prospects to make the case, he began, "It all gets back to if you think it's going to be worth a billion dollars, it's better to own—"

"Andy." Beirne cut in sharply, impatiently, the emotionless façade gone. "I think it's going to be worth *more* than a billion dollars. How's that?"

Then why not put $5 million in, Rachleff persisted in his usual calm voice.

Beirne remained adamant. Why not instead put $15 million in?

Kagle jumped in. "Here's why, Dave. It's real easy. We take three times the amount of risk to do that. Three times the amount of risk is *huge*, in whatever risk/reward ratio you're calculating."

Impasse. Seeing no hope for progress, Beirne ended the discussion without comment. "What else do we have to talk about?"

■

That the rookie could smoke out and haul in the biggest deals out there was a stellar feat, one that is retrospectively obscured by the tactical mistake Beirne committed when he gambled that he could persuade his partners to pay up for both TriStrata and Priceline simultaneously. In hindsight, it was arguably the biggest mistake he made in his first year. The gamble prevented him from declaring a favorite between the two; he was so busy winning and protecting the opportunities to invest, on the one hand, and trying to pull his reluctant partners along with him, on the other, that he never had time to step back, look hard at both deals, and compare the relative risks and likely rewards. Consequently it was happenstance that determined which of the two was funded first, in effect determining which of the two Beirne got to do. The other partners' appetite for high-priced deals, never strong in the first place, was more than sated once the offer to TriStrata was immediately accepted and the initial offer to Priceline was not. How many stuffed thirty-pound turkeys could one eat in one sitting?

The Priceline opportunity was not definitively closed in May 1998 when Beirne failed to win partner support for buying in at $80 million. He kept in touch with Jay Walker, talking regularly throughout the summer, and Walker remained open to a Benchmark investment. He was still interested, amazingly, even after he solved Priceline's CEO problem by persuading board member Rick Braddock to take on the role. The conversations with Beirne also continued after Price-line landed Delta Airlines, the breakthrough with a major carrier. But as the weeks passed, and Priceline's business grew, its valuation naturally went up correspondingly. Like a hot-air balloon, Priceline at the beginning had lifted off slowly, uncertainly, as if it would never be able to ascend above a treetop—you looked away for a moment, then back, and it was rising out of sight and soon gone. The chance to grab a trailing tether line when it was still "only" $80 million had vanished.

Six months later, in November, Beirne was still talking to Walker and Braddock about a Benchmark investment, and even after Price-line completed another round of financing involving others (at $535 million post-), Benchmark was offered another chance to buy in, if Beirne was willing to help the company recruit a chief operating officer. The partners and Beirne rehashed the issues, but if they had troubles reaching consensus when the price was $80 million, there was no reason to expect them to do so at $535 million.

And then the story unfolded far away. Priceline's IPO was at the end of March 1999. The shares were priced at $16 and ended the day at $69; its market capitalization of $9.8 billion was the highest first-day valuation ever achieved by an Internet company. From there it swung up and down with a vengeance, but mostly up. Not even a month later the stock reached $120, giving it a $17 billion valuation. Jay Walker's net worth had jumped to $7.5 billion.

■

Dave Beirne had gotten to Priceline when the balloon was within reach, but his partners, moving more cautiously by dint of experience, were two steps behind him. What no one foresaw at the time was that this would turn out to be the last moment when Beirne would be frustrated by their wariness. During that summer in 1998—and due undoubtedly to some extent to the consciousness-raising experience of the Priceline debates—the others came around to Beirne's position that for some must-do franchise deals, the potential upside did render risks irrelevant, and in those cases price should be no object. By the early fall, Dunlevie was nonchalantly advocating, and getting unanimously supportive votes for, an investment in a seed deal, Handspring, which planned to design and build a new handheld computer for the mass market but which had no employees other than the two people behind the Palm, Jeff Hawkins and Donna Dubinsky, and was at a $60 million post- valuation. It was deemed a we've-got-to-do-it deal, a category that had never existed before.

Afterward, every time Beirne heard another one of those ubiquitous Priceline commercials on the radio, he would have to grip the wheel hard so as not to run off the road. How close they had gotten to participating in that one, if only the collective threshold for high-priced investments—for the wildest, close-your-eyes-and-hold-nothing-back, spin-into-a-human-corkscrew kind of swing that Priceline was—had been raised in time.

9. World Class

The TriStrata deal progressed swiftly to completion, closing in July 1998. The primary corroboration of Atalla's cryptographic claims had come from the former chief technology officer of Price Waterhouse, who Beirne said was a glass-is-half-empty sort of person, and this expert had positively raved about TriStrata's technology. And Beirne had accompanied Andersen Consulting's best cryptographic expert on his first visit to the company, and his report had been positive, too. The better the technology looked, the easier it was to explain the company's undeveloped business plans and financial models. Here was a company run by Dr. John Atalla, a technologist, focused solely on the technology—and Atalla looked to the Price Waterhouses and Andersen Consultings to take care of selling it to their web of corporate clients, which absolved him of the need to worry about such details.

In the end, Benchmark invested $6.5 million in TriStrata, whose valuation was pegged at $97.4 million, a partnership record and an even higher valuation than initially proposed. The partners gave Beirne their support for a clean deal, without a due-diligence clause; TriStrata accepted without delay; and the deal was done. It marked a milestone: a $100 million price for a company that had yet to collect a penny of revenue.

In Dave Beirne's view, the primary risk in the deal was in finding the world-class CEO ("world-class" was the adjective that always preceded "CEO"). He knew just the person for the position, too: Paul Wahl, an executive board member of SAP, the giant software firm based in Germany. Since 1995, Wahl had served as CEO of SAP America, a subsidiary whose revenues had grown from $650 million in 1995 to $2.2 billion in 1998. He knew how to build large organizations, sell to large organizations, and oversee complex software technology. He was the perfect candidate for TriStrata (and, incidentally, as a German national with senior-executive experience on two continents, was literally world-class).

Eight months previously, TriStrata had retained Dave Beirne's old search firm to find a new CEO, but the search had still not been completed. When Beirne called back to New York to suggest Wahl's name, he learned that Ramsey Beirne had already designated Wahl as their number-one choice but Wahl had said he was not interested. (It was an intelligence test: One job oversaw $2.2 billion in revenues; the other, zero. Choose.)

His former Ramsey Beirne colleague did not have the prior relationship with Wahl that Dave Beirne had, however. It had begun three years previously, when Beirne, having heard a lot about this up-and-coming SAP executive, had called him with one of his I-have-nothing-to-sell-just-want-to-develop-the-relationship calls. Wahl granted him a half-hour meeting at a New York hotel—at 6:30 A.M. They had a chat, and Beirne's face and personality were registered in Wahl's mind; that's all that was needed. Beirne didn't need to keep the tie alive with periodic hellos—in fact, sparing Wahl such calls was part of the Dave Beirne method. When Beirne called next, which was twelve months later, it would be because he had an open position that he thought would be of interest. Beirne was then searching for the CEO position of Healtheon, a Kleiner Perkins–funded company. When Beirne brought Wahl and John Doerr together, Doerr did not sell Wahl hard, and Wahl passed. But the experience gave him an opportunity to get to know Beirne better.

It mattered not a bit that Ramsey Beirne couldn't get Paul Wahl to take a look at TriStrata. Let me talk to him, Beirne said.

"Paul, I've invested in a project. I want you to trust me. I just want you to come out and meet the founder of this company. Hear what we have to say. Worst-case scenario: investment of time on your end with another great person in the world, and no strings attached." He did not tell him the name of the company.

When Wahl flew in, Beirne met him for breakfast to brief him on the company, then took him over to TriStrata's office to introduce him to John Atalla. It was a Saturday, and Beirne later had to leave to catch a flight to New York. But when he got to the East Coast, he called Wahl and extracted from him a commitment to make a second visit to Silicon Valley in three weeks and spend another day with Tri-Strata. "Paul, put it on your calendar right now."

This was the visit that Beirne called "the selling situation." He, John Atalla, and board members John Young and Bill Zuendt all spent time with Wahl individually, selling. Beirne knew that everyone possesses something he called "the driver," the basic seat of motivation, and Wahl, the reserved German, had come around when alone with Beirne to revealing his own interior hopes. An offer was presented and the candidate was hooked. He flew home that Friday to Philadelphia to discuss the offer with his wife. He promised to give Beirne an answer by Sunday.

When he called, though, it was to turn down the offer with regrets.

"I have to let you know that the relationship with SAP is too important to me. I'm going to stay. The terms of the offer that we outlined? I didn't talk to my wife about them."

"Oh, my God!" Recovering, Beirne asked, "What do you mean? What you're telling me right now—is it equity-related? Is it cash-related? What are the issues?"

"I've learned more about what my needs are. What we talked about—I don't want to embarrass anyone, I don't want to negotiate, I don't want to get in a bad situation."

"Okay, let's assume we're not negotiating. 'Cause we're not. What we talked about originally is what we thought your needs were. So we framed an offer that met those needs. Now what we're saying is, What we outlined was inaccurate. So let's outline what it is we think you need. And then let me see if I can go get that done before we even get into negotiations."

Wahl thought for a moment. "Okay. What I've learned is, I have a tax issue." A foreign-national CEO facing a large visa-related income-tax liability and a move to an expensive area needed reassurance that he would have the means to live well. Beirne listened, then went back to the TriStrata board and obtained better terms.

He called Wahl. "I'd like to formally extend the following offer to you." Beirne proffered 10 percent of the company (up from 7 percent) and $300,000 in cash compensation—half in salary, half in bonus—and a million-dollar loan so Wahl could pay off the tax liability he'd incur by leaving his current German employer for an American one. The loan was for five years and secured by Wahl's TriStrata stock. It was to be repaid if the company went public, which would make repayment easy; if the company did not go public, the loan would be forgiven. It was a sign-on bonus in everything but name.

"Great! I'm going to go talk to my wife. We're basically done. Let me get past this part." The next day he called Beirne back.

"Dave, I regret to say I've got to stay at SAP. I talked to my wife. I cannot believe the negative reaction I got from her. She almost cried. She's so upset that we're going to have a massive life change again. She spends a ton of her time in Germany now, 'cause I travel eighty percent of the time anyway. Going to California versus Philadelphia—it's even farther away. I've been married for too long, my family is too important. I just have to walk away."

"I thought your wife wasn't going to be an issue."

"David, I didn't think it was going to be an issue."

"You know, Paul. I hear that. But I can't accept it. 'Cause I think you're saying no for the wrong reasons. You're saying no because she's afraid 'cause she doesn't have the data. I'd really like to invite her to meet us, to learn about this, so she'll understand why you were so excited about it."

"I'll ask her if she wants to do that. But I don't think that's the issue."

"You've got to balance some things here. The question I have for you is, Are you going to change your work habits at all if you stay at SAP?"

"No. I do what I do—it makes me happy. My wife has married me, knows what makes me happy, and I'll continue to do what I do."

"I'm not asking you to work a minute longer than you do right now. Not to do anything different than you do. But just to do it in a situation where you can actually get the psychic reward that you deserve for building a great company. *Plus* the financial reward that will give you the ability to set yourselves for life. You can retire whenever you want to spend your time with your wife."

Wahl's resistance weakened. "Okay. Let me talk to her." At that moment Wahl's wife was in Germany.

"Don't do this over the phone," Beirne said. "Fly to Germany. If SAP won't pay for it, send me the bill. Go see her face-to-face. Tell her you love her. Tell her this is what you need to do to be happy. And that it won't be worse than what you're doing now. But only better for you and your family down the road."

Wahl did as Beirne suggested. Flew to Germany and got his wife to agree to the move to California. On a Saturday Beirne faxed to Germany the offer letter. Wahl called him and agreed verbally, then resigned from SAP on Monday. He had to fly back to the United States immediately for a visit to a large SAP account in Memphis, and he set off without having signed the offer letter. This was in deference to the SAP board's request that he give them forty-eight hours to draft a counteroffer.

Wahl zipped from Germany to Memphis, then back to Germany, where a counteroffer was waiting for him at his hotel. He conferred with Beirne, who convinced him not only to reject SAP's offer but to do so face-to-face. Beirne thought that it was the only way Wahl could convincingly convey to SAP that his mind was made up, that he was not ambivalent and vulnerable to being turned around. But Beirne's tactic was a calculated risk: Wahl *was* ambivalent.

"Before you leave," Beirne said, "I'd like you to sign the offer letter I sent you and fax it back."

"I don't have a copy with me."

"Well, I just happen to have one with me." This was a gambit: Beirne was at home and did not have a copy of the letter there. "I'm going to send it right now. I'd like you to authorize it and send it right back to me."

"I'm leaving for the airport in ten minutes."

"Give me fifteen minutes."

Beirne drove quickly the half mile to the Benchmark office, faxed the letter, and got it back signed. First the oral commitment, now the written. That's when he knew he had his man.

Before hanging up, Beirne had said to Wahl, "The other thing is, the board would like to invite you to the board meeting next week. We have so many strategy discussions. I'd like you there. It's important for you to be a part of it, and I'd also like you to bring your wife."

If Wahl was in California, he, ipso facto, would not be in Germany, prey to SAP's unceasing blandishments. Wahl's resignation was effective immediately, but SAP was begging him to work for four weeks to provide transition. Four weeks, Beirne thought. In Germany. Totally exposed. I'm fucked. I've got to get him out of there.

Beirne had already begun preparations for the invitation days before. He told the other TriStrata board members that he wanted to send Wahl and his wife first-class air tickets to come spend the weekend in San Francisco. "Let's have a board dinner and welcome him to the family."

To make the right impression, all members of the board needed to be present to show collective appreciation that Wahl was joining this tiny company. The problem was that Tom Perkins was bobbing on a yacht somewhere in the Mediterranean, the pastime that after his retirement from Kleiner Perkins seemed to occupy most of his time and attention. He lived the life one would expect of a very wealthy character in a Danielle Steel novel—but his story was nonfiction: He was married to Steel. Beirne insisted that Perkins show up for the board dinner. He told Atalla, "Call Perkins and tell him he has no choice. He wasn't part of this interview process, he wasn't part of the sell process. He's got to attend the board meeting, he's got to attend dinner. We've got to show that we are committed to this human being."

Thinking about the arrangements he'd made with the hotel, his real estate agent, the spouses of the other board members who would come to the dinner, too, Beirne was excited about the Wahls' arrival. In his office, he said, "His wife will love meeting everybody. We'll show 'em we're real people." And tactically, it would get Wahl engaged with his new company immediately—and out of Germany.

■

When Beirne had decided to do the TriStrata deal, he'd believed the biggest risk in the deal was in finding the right CEO, and now that risk had been eliminated. But his focus on the CEO search was his past speaking. Out of view were two other basic risks in this deal: technology risk, that is, would the encryption technology work as promised; and market risk, the question of whether large corporate customers would pay for TriStrata's yet-to-be-released software.

When Paul Wahl headed for his new home, TriStrata may have looked no different from any other venture-backed start-up in the Valley that occupied leased offices in the land of cubicles. But up close, it sat apart from the others, at the bottom of the "trough."

The term comes from the shape of a graph that venture guys draw. Think of the life-cycle stages of a company: raw start-up; developing the product; revenue-producing; almost public. Theoretically, if markets operated efficiently, the risk/reward ratio for an investment made at any one of those stages should be about the same. Investing in a raw start-up would entail high risks with potentially high rewards to match. At the other end, companies that are about to go public are low risk because they have customers and revenues; the rewards for investments at that stage are commensurately low, too. An investor pays an expensive price to enter a deal with a company that is about to go public, so it is not possible to get a huge payoff in the difference between that price and the post-IPO price. But even if the reward is small in an absolute sense, the relative reward theoretically is always matched to relative risk in the same ratio as it is in start-ups.

In practice, this is not the case for companies at the intermediate stage of still developing a product. Here an investor has to pay up, usually at a valuation for the company that is at least three times that of the raw start-up stage, but the risks have not been reduced proportionately. Think of a U-shaped graph showing the rewards divided by risks. The left top of the U is represented by the high reward/risk ratio of a seed-stage company, and the right top is where one finds the high reward/risk ratio of an about-to-go-public company. And in the middle, the trough, are the companies in the development stage where history shows a pattern of comparatively low prospective reward married to high risk. When Benchmark raised its first fund in 1995, it explained to its institutional investors that it was going to specialize in first-round funding of the early-stage companies, one of the two places where the high reward/risk ratio was found. It would avoid, the partners said, "feeding in the trough."

TriStrata was at the very bottom of the trough.

Wahl would also soon discover another aspect of John Atalla's business sensibility that harkened back to a pre-modern Europe and made the company distinctly unlike its neighbors in Silicon Valley: nepotism. Owning 90 percent of the company before Benchmark's investment, Atalla regarded TriStrata as the family business and had installed his son in a director-level position. Secure in his father's protection, Bill Atalla acted as if he were a minister with an all-company portfolio and ranged widely. No one at the company dared to voice a critical peep. It was unlikely that Wahl would regard this as helpful, or even innocuous.

■

Beirne got a call from the public relations person at TriStrata about the imminent announcement of Paul Wahl's appointment. She had a message to pass on. "The Atallas"—the plural suggested that the son felt co-equal with the father—"want to know why we're making a big deal of this announcement. Why don't we just wait a few weeks and not rush it?"

"That's not John Atalla," Beirne said. "That's Bill Atalla. Have Bill call me."

"Why?"

"Because he doesn't understand the magnitude of what we've just done. We just recruited the CEO of SAP America! This is the most important event in the history of this company!" TriStrata had remained out of public view for four years; here was its chance to make a public splash. Beirne continued, "If we don't leverage this opportunity, we're clinically insane! Have him call me immediately."

When Beirne told John Young, the chairman of the board, Young too was aghast at the Atallas' reaction. "Holy shit! How do they not realize—I mean, this guy is almost nuts to be joining this company. It's got no revenue. It's got no customers. It's nothing. It's a total gamble. He's got a two-billion-dollar revenue company with a fifty-billion market cap. And he just joined a company with twenty-five engineers, no marketing, no sales, no finance, no customers, no revenue!"

Beirne drove over to TriStrata's office to meet with the company's public relations staff and the outside PR firm that had just been hired. Getting out in the TriStrata parking lot, he took long, furious steps as if rushing to a street rumble with a bat in hand. But before he reached the conference room, he had stowed his anger out of sight. As Beirne had expected, Bill Atalla was present and his father was not; it was in such meetings that Atalla Junior was at his insufferable worst, running the meeting and doing most of the talking. (In college, what had set Beirne off more than anything? "If it was handed to you . . .") For an hour Beirne remained quiet, waiting for an opportunity to offer two minutes of suggestions without appearing to step on toes.

The question, he finally got to ask everyone, was, Do we make a big deal rolling out the company publicly, saying it has found the Holy Grail for security? Or should we instead try to generate buzz by focusing for now on a story that was easy for the press to get excited about: World-class CEO joins hot-shit start-up, and save the company's story for later? The latter course offered the media two separate news pegs, and was the course that Beirne pressed for. It was the view that ultimately prevailed.

When Wahl resigned, SAP should have come to the conclusion that it would have to take better care to inoculate its next SAP America CEO with a vaccine to protect him from the entrepreneurial fevers that infected everyone they sent. Wahl's predecessor, Klaus Besier, had left SAP in 1996 to head One Wave, an e-commerce services company based in Watertown, Massachusetts. (Only a year later, amid One Wave's financial difficulties, Besier had left.) In 1998 SAP's chief financial officer, who was appointed as Wahl's successor, was gracious in commenting publicly that he could see that Wahl, in accepting TriStrata's offer, "couldn't pass up the opportunity of a lifetime."

■

Into this sunny picture, featuring a new chief executive officer, came a squall seven weeks later generated by the resignation of TriStrata's chief technology officer. At a partners' meeting, Beirne explained that the departing CTO was "basically the guy with all the knowledge in his head. I spent my whole weekend trying to turn him around."

Why had the guy resigned? Kevin Harvey asked.

"Just finished his Ph.D. at Stanford. Working for Dr. A. has been a bitch."

"Does he like Paul?"

"He likes Paul. We have maybe about a twenty-five-percent chance of keeping the guy. He thinks the technology is terrific. He thinks that John has hyped too much." Atalla's claim of having succeeded in developing a system that was a "one-time pad implementation" was not supportable; the CTO said TriStrata's system was merely *based* on the "one-time pad" concept. "It's just words, but in the crypto community, we're going to get crushed because we don't have exactly what Atalla says we have. I think part of this guy's issue is he's wondering, Do I want to be part of this?" Allegations that Bill Atalla had sexually harassed a fellow employee had surfaced in a lawsuit.

"That's the son?" Dunlevie asked.

"The son."

"Ah, so he's got all kinds of features," Harvey said.

"Right. So, Bill Atalla should have been terminated immediately. John stuck by his son. And I think John lost a lot of the love of the people. So I said to Paul Wahl, when I met him this week, 'So, you're going to find out if we're going to hit the curve.' "

"What's the background of the CTO?" Dunlevie asked.

"He was at Sun Microsystems doing encryption stuff and getting his Ph.D. in cryptography over at Stanford. Smart guy. He's not someone I would fight for, except he's got all the engineers—they're there because of this guy, and he's got all the knowledge in his fuckin' head. Atalla's the vision, but John couldn't read code now to save his life."

"Seems like this would hinge on how much he likes Paul. If he really likes him a whole lot, he wouldn't have resigned."

"Well," Beirne said, "if it's not too little too late. Paul went out to dinner with the guy and his wife Saturday night. Spent time with him again yesterday. Wahl is all over it. Atalla has not paid the people—no increase in compensation for anybody, shares are really limited. They don't communicate, so the guys up in the back don't even know. Paul's learning all this, what's really going on in the business."

Things were not as they had seemed. For Beirne these discoveries were at first disquieting, then exasperating, and eventually, infuriating.

10. All e-, All the Time

During 1997 e-commerce had become an increasing preoccupation for Benchmark. EBay's organic growth was a source of encouragement, of course, but it also made its example anomalous; what other e-commerce business was likely to grow 40 percent a month without a marketing budget? Benchmark's other early e-commerce bets had given the partners pause. E-Loan, an online mortgage service, had been growing slowly; and Louis Borders's Webvan was a long way from setting its vans in motion.

By the spring of 1998, however, the combination of the expanding popularization of the Web and the pioneering evangelical work done by Amazon, eBay, and others for the greater cause of e-commerce produced the feeling that now, finally, was the time for venture capital to make significant bets on virtual stores.

At a partner meeting in March, the partners kicked around the idea of calling up the limited partners to raise another $100 million for a new fund that would be devoted exclusively to e-commerce, what Bob Kagle called "all e-, all the time." It would serve as a marketing tool as well as a statement about sector bets. Benchmark would be the first firm to establish such a fund.

Without looking up, Bruce Dunlevie flipped through the pages of a new issue of *Forbes* he had brought along that was devoted entirely to e-commerce. The companies featured comprised a list of prospects: Auctions Online; Fashionmall.com; your-kitchen.com;

Reel.com; eToys. Each was briefly discussed, and Benchmark connections to some of the entrepreneurs from previous endeavors were uncovered.

Reading from the list, Dunlevie came across one that seemed the most fun imaginable: "Sporting goods and equipment: Sports Site." Even better, no travel required; it was based in San Jose.

"Don't even look at it. Fund it!" Dave Beirne shouted facetiously.

"Exactly," Dunlevie said, still flipping through the magazine pages. "That is pretty cool." He resumed his methodical recitation of categories and prospects.

Bob Kagle had Dunlevie stop when he touched on the category of selling art. This was a subject dear to his heart. "Art is huge," Kagle said. It was also a category of goods that would lend itself well to the online medium. Conceivably, one could have in a single place listings of every work of original art available for sale in the world and could search by artist, medium, subject, or any other characteristic.

What the partners were looking for were categories that were ripe for "disintermediation"—removing a middle layer in the distribution chain. In this case, that layer was the twelve thousand or so art galleries in the country.

"Huge market," Kagle insisted again. "All kinds of bad selling tactics there. Ugliness." It was ripe for the introduction of a more efficient form of matching buyers with the art they sought.

■

The discussions led to a surge of redoubled efforts to identify and investigate dozens of e-commerce companies that were aiming for a broad consumer market. That spring Benchmark backed PlanetRx, an online pharmacy that would compete head-to-head with Kleiner Perkins–backed Drugstore.com; Dave Beirne went on the company's board. One that came close to getting funded but ultimately did not was GreenTree, which offered vitamins and nutritional supplements on the Web, but not prescription drugs. Another deal that passed preliminary muster was Sparks, which was preparing to sell greeting cards online.

Kagle was Sparks's advocate, and his pitch to the partners emphasized the unique ability of the Web to offer what no physical card store was able to: a definitive selection of cards, easily searched, that could provide what entrepreneur Felicia Lindau called the "Aha!" discovery—the perfect card for an occasion. The largest card stores carried about one thousand cards; Sparks would start with five thousand and move quickly to thirty thousand. The greeting-card industry in the United States was one of those businesses whose size one was likely to underguess: $7.5 billion annually.

The entrepreneur, who was thirty years old, possessed what Kagle thought were terrific marketing instincts.

"This is not a rocketship," Kevin Harvey said, interjecting a characteristically cooler tone. "This isn't something that's going to move a boatload of sales in its first year."

"Here's my question," said Kagle. "This is central to the beast here. Bruce said it earlier—as a result of the advent of Amazon, he's increased his book gift-giving by a factor of—?"

"Twenty."

"So the question is, how much primary demand for cards is unlocked by removing the friction from the process? Not so much as a substitution for the cards you do send today, but for cards you otherwise may not send. That could be a really big number. I don't know. It's just a hunch. But I know I personally would send a lot more cards this way. A *lot* more. 'Cause I like the idea of cards." Cards were a way of establishing connections. Dunlevie had a soft spot for deals that combined the business world with the literary one; Kagle's soft spot was for a deal like this that could be described as being in the business of emotional connection, making the world more *a*ffective as well as effective.

"What I'm concerned about," Dave Beirne said, "is the ability for eToys or Amazon just to take a small fraction of the best cards, make them available there, and all these major sites just lock you out."

"Skimmin' the cream," Kagle said.

"Skimmin' the cream," Beirne affirmed. "It's good enough. We've all settled for good enough."

Sparks did not yet have an operational website—it was little more than an entrepreneur with an idea—but the risks were deemed run-of-the-mill. Benchmark went ahead and invested $2.3 million in a deal that appraised the value of the company as $6.2 million prior to the financing.

■

A friend of a friend brought another e-commerce deal to the firm: a plan to dispense eyeglasses on the Web. Bob Kagle and Bruce Dunlevie took the initial meeting with the entrepreneur. Later, they reported back to the group.

"I've actually been doing a fair amount of mother-in-law research," Kagle said, "including, this weekend, I bought my mom some new glasses back in Michigan. I think there's zero chance that Web dispensing works. Zero. With today's solutions. I don't see any way you get around trying on frames." He and Dunlevie had urged the entrepreneur to do some basic consumer research to see what consumers thought.

Yes, there was a problem, the entrepreneur conceded, in getting the physical prescription for the glasses from the optometrist. And he could not offer prospective customers a way of trying on glasses, which was indeed another obstacle. His fallback position was almost sad: His system would work for customers who wanted to purchase second pairs of glasses. This did not have a galvanizing effect upon the Benchmark partners.

Dunlevie reported that the previous week he had coincidentally met with another eyeglasses-on-the-Web company called Optical Planet. They had solved the problem of getting hold of customers' prescriptions by avoiding the problem altogether: They sold nonprescription sunglasses only. As for the problem of fitting glasses, they showed Dunlevie their website, where a visitor could click on a model of Arnold Schwarzenegger, have the selected glasses pop on Arnold, and rotate the model in 3-D.

After the demonstration, Dunlevie, thinking he was missing something, had asked the entrepreneur, "Is that all?"

"Yeah!"

"You don't do prescription glasses?"

"No, that's too hard."

You had to give the entrepreneur credit for his straightforward answers.

Dunlevie returned to consideration of the first deal and mocked his own aversion to spending time shopping. He said, "I am such an

I-don't-really-care-if-it-fits-or-looks-good-just-give-it-to-me-so-I-can-get-out-of-here shopper." He sheepishly confessed that if he tried to buy eyeglasses online, he'd buy three pairs in three different sizes, hope one fit, and throw the others away. He and his partners all laughed at the absurdity of this.

How would a marketeer define a one-of-a-kind customer like Dunlevie, Kagle wondered aloud. He rocked his chair back and smiled at him: "That's a segment of 'Are you completely price-insensitive?' "

Benchmark declined to invest.

■

As the e-commerce initiative gathered steam, Bob Kagle placed art online at the top of his list of categories that he'd like to work on. The usual stringent screening out of strangers did not apply in such cases; on the contrary, strangers were the very people the venture capitalists sought. Having no way to advertise an interest in a particular business to prospective entrepreneurs, the venture guys got on the phone and figuratively knocked on doors. In August Kagle identified the top three prospects in the online art business that had websites up and running: artuframe, based in Chicago; Barewalls.com, in Cambridge, Massachusetts; and ArtSelect, in Iowa. In Silicon Valley, several newly formed companies were also talking about entering the business, but the three Kagle had identified already had businesses in place, and some had purchased art-related keywords at Web portals like Yahoo. Artuframe seemed the furthest along of the bunch, so Kagle "beat the doors down," as he put it, to get in to discuss an investment. He and Dunlevie flew to Chicago.

Artuframe was owned by Bill Lederer, who was thirty-seven years old but not a member of the youthful digerati. Offering fine-art posters online was a business that he had grafted upon a traditional art-supplies and framing business that had been in the family for many years. In appearance and manner, he looked more like a middle-aged insurance broker than anything else. But he impressed the visiting Benchmark partners with his expertise in the framing business and with his passion to make artuframe successful. Kagle and Dunlevie invited him out to California to meet the other partners.

■

In preparing the others for the visit, Dunlevie explained that he most liked the fact that artuframe had assets in the analog world, not just the digital one. He said, "They actually have to do things. To the extent that the winners in e-commerce are actually going to have more complexity and vertical integration, this is more along those lines. I think this whole thing hinges on this guy, and the more time we spent with him, the more we thought he was a pretty cool guy."

When Lederer arrived on Sand Hill Road to talk about his business, he came in a dark suit, which might as well have been a shiny black tuxedo for the way it stood out. He also was not a figure of commanding self-assurance. He had brought along with him a much older man, a friend whom he had asked to serve as an advisor as he visited this unfamiliar corner of the business world about which he clearly had heard some unsavory stories.

As Lederer talked about his hopes for artuframe, it became clear that his background set him apart from Silicon Valley entrepreneurs in another way. His deceased father was a dominating, openly acknowledged influence, who had instilled in his son the lessons of the Depression: Never go into debt; never relinquish majority control of the company. Bob Kagle was the perfect Benchmark partner to serve as Lederer's advocate.

Lederer's presentation went on much longer than planned—he was as garrulous as a life-insurance salesman sitting beside an uninsured prospect on a transcontinental plane flight. His advisor tried to hurry him along from across the table with hand signals, but Lederer was determined to talk through every detail of his grand plans for art online. The emphasis was on the future, not the present, because the artuframe website had only been up a short time.

In the discussion among the partners afterward, Lederer was appraised as being a smart, thoughtful person, but his "tell-'em-and-sell-'em, tell-'em-and-sell-'em" manner of salesmanship was not well-matched to this audience.

"I think he's still shackled by the specter of his small-thinking father," Dunlevie said. "The guy just has no frame of reference on what he's doing. Like coming out of the analog marketplace and stumbling into the digital world." But there were positive aspects to artuframe's story too, and it was not too late to act. Dunlevie continued, "*Nobody* has first-mover advantage in this category yet. Whoever raises capital, with some good advice and recruiting, is going to win, I believe. How big the sector is, I don't know." However, the art business looked better than that of Sparks, Kagle's greeting-cards-online company. "The average selling prices are twenty-X higher."

"Yup," Kagle agreed. Rachleff and Dunlevie discussed whether Lederer would be able to perform well as the CEO as the company grew—in other words, would he "scale," and if not, would he be able to accept that judgment? Dunlevie thought he would. "I think he wants to be rich, not famous."

The Chicago location would make it hard to help Lederer build the executive team, Beirne said, speaking from his experiences as a search guy. Recruiting high-tech talent to Chicago was tough to do: Players wanted to be with other players. Chicago's weather didn't increase its allure, either.

"What scares me about this market," Beirne said, "is kind of the same thing on PlanetRx. When you don't have a major distributor, you don't have a major player, you have this real big fragmented industry. You think, Okay, it's a great opportunity to go in and disintermediate all this bullshit."

Kagle was a one-voice chorus. "Right!"

"Then again," Beirne continued, "there's a bunch of quirks around traditional, small little nichey businesses like this. They operate that way for a reason." So maybe what seemed to be a large opportunity was illusory.

Undeterred, Kagle returned to Lederer. "That's kind of why you like the domain experience of this guy relative to other people in the segment. 'Cause he would be able to navigate that."

One partner's vote fell short of a 5, but Kagle had the majority of approving votes that he needed, and after a few days of noodling on it and discussing the issues with Dunlevie, he decided to invest.

■

If Bill Lederer did not look the part of a Fast Company–bred entrepreneur, neither did Stu Weisman, M.D., a forty-three-year-old gastroenterologist who had established a thriving endoscopy center in Redwood City, California, but in early 1998 was experiencing some midcareer restlessness. Among the options he considered for himself was launching a business that would market to physicians PalmPilots that would simplify writing prescriptions.

When asked why he contemplated abandoning his successful medical practice, in addition to the reasons one would expect to hear—making doctors' lives easier, removing errors from misfilled prescriptions, making the world a better place—he included an unexpected one: envy. It seemed to him that his social world was filled with guys who had their own start-ups or were venture capitalists who did nothing but service start-ups. At parties, everyone else talked about business; he wanted to participate, too, but his professional world stood apart and he did not have the right vocabulary. Entrepreneurial fever in Silicon Valley had spread even to community physicians.

Weisman got an opportunity to advance his still-unformed ideas about his own business through the father of his son's best friend. The two eight-year-old boys were on the same soccer and basketball teams and often slept over at each other's houses. Their families became friendly and planned a vacation together in Maui. The first day on the beach, when the two fathers began talking for the first time about their professional interests, Weisman discovered that they shared more than he could have guessed. The other guy was a venture capitalist who a year previously had spoken with his partners about his wish to do an e-prescriptions play almost identical to what Weisman wanted to pursue, but none had come along. Weisman had ten days to talk almost nonstop with the guy—who was Dave Beirne. At the end of the trip, Beirne asked Weisman to come in and pitch the guys when they returned to California.

That Beirne would get excited about Weisman's idea for a company yet to be born was in itself of interest because the deal was a different kind of proposition from, say, Webvan, where the potential market was enormous and the entrepreneur, Louis Borders, was a marquee name, or Scient, with an experienced entrepreneur and a marquee senior manager from IBM. Instead, this was a deal that pivoted on Beirne's confidence in reading an individual, a yet-untested entrepreneur.

After Stu Weisman's visit to meet the other partners, Beirne explained why he was enthusiastic about doing a deal. The company that would eventually assume the name ePhysician had no office and no employees; Weisman himself had not yet resigned from his practice. This was a classic "seed-stage" company: a guy, a business plan, and nothing more.

"I think this guy is incredibly entrepreneurial," Beirne said. "I think he is a total winner. I think he has looked failure in the face multiple times and kicked its ass. He's an out-of-the-box thinker."

Anticipating the question of whether this could grow into a sufficiently large business, Beirne maintained that it could. Pharmacies already pay 25¢ a transaction to prescription-management arms of insurance companies, so there already was a transaction-based revenue model in the business.

He returned to his estimation of Weisman. "I think the guy will work his ass off. He's smart. And he's a winner—he's proven it."

Weisman had impressed Bruce Dunlevie, too, who bestowed upon him a superlative comment in Valley jargon: Weisman was a "good guy." Dunlevie wondered, however, "How many doctors are really going to change their behavior?"

"Exactly," said Kagle.

Technology was adopted slowly, Dunlevie continued. Just that morning he'd called a guy at Lucent, the telecommunications and networking-equipment giant that, among other things, was the world's largest manufacturer of voice-mail systems. "I said, 'Is he there, please?' They said, 'No, he's traveling.' I said, 'Can I leave him a voice mail or e-mail?' They said, 'He doesn't use either one.'" This didn't augur well for ePhysician, he thought. "Doctors are pretty fiercely independent."

Dunlevie viewed ePhysician as a plausible start-up but not likely to become a billion-dollar-valuation, world-class big company. None of the adjectives that Beirne usually applied to deals he advocated seemed to apply here.

"I agree with that," Beirne said. But that didn't change his stance. "I think the guy's a winner. This is a good soul. He will bust his hump for this company."

"Well, but he might be a winner in an eight-million-dollar business. Which doesn't leverage your skill set." Dunlevie hastened to add, "I'm not shittin' on the deal at all; I think it's got a lot to recommend it." But he pointed out the absence of natural scale effects. "I think you've got to have somebody call on every fuckin' doctor. This product is sold, not bought. So it's got field sales-force economics. You've got a lot of constituencies you've got to corral at the same time. It's business-model complexity, which, again, I'm not scared of. It just takes longer, takes more money, it's slower. And I don't see this thing having any upside tornado effect, like a TriStrata or Priceline or something, where there's word-of-mouth, potentially. So I think this is just a good hard slog."

"This will take a huge amount of the time out of the doctor's life, which they hate—this constant communication back and forth between the pharmacy—it takes that away."

"See," said Dunlevie, "I'm not buying that that takes a huge amount of time out of the doctor's life, or that they're constantly dealing with this problem. I just don't buy it. I think that's bullshit."

"Stu says it is."

"Well, Stu's got a little bit of a vested interest here. He's one guy—he's got seat-of-the-pants research."

Maybe, Bob Kagle suggested, the way to begin would be to fund the development of a prototype, test it with a critical mass of doctors, see what the adoption rate felt like, and then decide whether to throw money in.

Dave had already suggested to Weisman that he keep his practice for two days a week, work on the business the other days, and see what the market research told them. "He thought about that, and he came back and he said, 'No, that's chickenshit. I've got to go all the way, or this won't happen. But I appreciate the thought.'"

Despite his reservations about market and technical risks, Dunlevie spoke out against the proposal to offer only a small amount of capital for experimentation.

"You're saying there is no partial pregnancy, no matter what?" Kevin Harvey asked.

"Not for a guy who's built a practice, is chairman of all these committees at Sequoia Hospital," said Dunlevie. "I don't think it's fair to a guy of that standing. If this guy were twenty-three years old and had this idea, and his dad was a doctor, then I'm all for the two-hundred-fifty-K investment." But for Stu Weisman, Dunlevie knew it was all or nothing.

Beirne added more details about Weisman's past accomplishments. "He got a wife, from an Italian family that all lived in the same town, to pick up six months into their marriage and move across the country to start a practice where he had no relationships, didn't know *any*body when he got out here. He can sell, too."

"Is he Italian?" Kevin Harvey asked in apparent seriousness.

Beirne couldn't believe the question. "Weisman"?

Rachleff, the only Jewish partner, laughed, shaking his head. "You're good," he said, marveling at Harvey's obtuseness.

A million-dollar investment in ePhysician at a $2 million pre-money valuation would buy a third of the company, but a million was insufficient, Harvey said, and Kagle, muttering in a low voice, agreed.

"I think you need to make sure the company has got plenty of financing to get itself in great shape to do a second round," Harvey reasoned. Putting in more money now would mean Beirne would not have to spend time raising more money soon. "The scarce commodity here is not money, it's Dave's time."

"And I do think time-to-market is an issue," Beirne said. "I think there's a possibility that someone's going to walk through his door one day and go, 'I've got a new thing I want to show you.' People were doing this on the PC. Someone's going to figure out how to do it with the PalmPilot."

"So why two million?" Rachleff challenged. "Why not do it as a three- to four-million-dollar start-up?"

Maybe they should go with a higher number, Harvey said. "Dave is 'Go big or go home.' You can't go big or go home with a little bitty bat."

"You just have to hit 'em a lot," Beirne said.

Would Weisman abandon the game if he discovered that adoption turned out to be slow, Rachleff wondered.

"He's *selling* his practice," Dunlevie pointed out.

"I hear ya."

"He's not buntin'."

Harvey would be glad to invest $2 million, $3 million, $4 million—whatever Beirne desired. But he asked Beirne if he would like to first spend a couple of weeks gauging the degree of market risk, learning a bit more about the likelihood of doctors adopting the Pilots.

"So what do you have to do to get there?" Beirne asked. "Do you have to go around and talk to fifty doctors with one of these and say—"

No, you don't have to call on fifty people, Rachleff said.

"I'm not worried about calling fifty people. I called twenty-five dealers on Autoweb"—a deal that he had ultimately decided to turn down.

"I think ten [face-to-face] interviews would tell you a lot more than calling fifty people," Kagle said.

Dunlevie cut in. Go to four guys at local clinics, show them a Pilot, and ask them to imagine using it to scribble prescriptions and then sending them to the pharmacy by putting it in a cradle and pressing a single button. "If two of the four say, 'Yeah, that's cool,' that's pretty informational. If all four say, 'No fuckin' way' . . ." He didn't have to finish the thought.

"They're going to say the same thing we said around this table," Beirne predicted, "which is, 'Yeah, sounds good. Yes. It makes sense.' "

"I'd like to hear that," Rachleff said.

"Maybe," Dunlevie said. "I'd like to talk to two doctors that aren't Stu, that's all."

The discussion returned to the terms of an offer. Even Rachleff, the most wary of the group, was now comfortable with putting in more money, rather than less, paying a higher valuation but obtaining a large percentage of equity. The offer would be $2 million for a 40 percent stake.

Beirne ripped four slips of paper off a loose sheet and passed them to his partners.

"Okay. Can I have your votes?"

"Can we have *your* vote?" Dunlevie asked, reminding Beirne that tradition dictated that the advocate express his own vote first.

"I'm a 7. I think, you look at an Autoweb, or something like that, that I could have done—we'd have had to put so much more money to work." And in the case of ePhysician, he would not have a "loose-cannon entrepreneur," someone who pursued whatever whim came to his mind. Beirne collected the slips and read off the numbers. "A 6. An 8. A 5.5 from Bob—you're not allowed to do 5s. A 6 from Kevin."

Kevin Harvey scolded Kagle: "You were the first one to ever say 'You can't do 5s.' "

"He was the first one to say it was *not* true, too," Dunlevie pointed out.

"Such is the nature of Bob," Harvey said.

"I think this will be a good deal for you to do," Dunlevie said to Beirne. If the data collected from the doctor visits came back positive, this would make Beirne's fifth company, and by the following summer, after two years in the saddle, he expected he'd be a director for eight companies. This would be what his Benchmark partners considered the maximum number of directorships he could hold without diluting the quality of service to the entrepreneurs, and fewer than the twelve or fourteen directorships that the competition up the street assumed per partner.

"I'm at a 6 on the deal, and an 8 in a portfolio sense for you"— Dunlevie meant that this one helped to balance other deals in Beirne's portfolio, the ones that did not begin with a small, reasonable valuation like ePhysican; ePhysician also had the virtue of being unlikely to burn a barnful of cash. "I think you *will* make it successful. I just don't think it will be Healtheon."

"I think it's a good deal for me to do, too. I need one like this."

With a $2.5 million check from Benchmark and an offer to set up shop at their office for as long as he needed until he could find his own space, Dr. Stu Weisman committed that most quintessential American act: the reinvention of self.

11. Buds

One day after the Benchmark partners had finished a meeting with entrepreneurs who were pitching a home-improvement-services deal, Bob Kagle gave in to the temptation to show off a little. He was certain that no one else in the room knew power tools like he did. "Let me see a show of hands," he directed. "Number of guys who own a 'saws-all.'" Only one other hand went up beside his: Kevin Harvey's.

"Yes!" Kagle exclaimed triumphantly with a laugh. The men had been separated from the boys.

"Okay," Harvey continued. "Number of guys who use it for cutting deer in half." Now all the others laughed hard: Harvey was the only hunter in the group.

Harvey's hobbies and family background were difficult to pigeonhole. His father was a professor of math at Rice University; his mother, an attorney. His family was what he would describe as "middle-middle class," but he had grown up in a Houston neighborhood that was mostly working-class and low-income.

In high school he became best friends with Rob Shaw, one of six kids in a single-parent family that was food-stamp poor. They spent more time together than most buddies because both worked every possible moment they could at Weingarten's, a Houston grocery-store chain where Shaw had landed a job first, then gotten one for Harvey. Harvey didn't do homework—a math whiz's prerogative—nor did he participate much in extracurricular activities. Instead he worked at Weingarten's.

Harvey and Shaw were also early business partners. When they were fifteen, they decided to buy a car together. They consulted the classifieds and headed for the seller of a promising Opel. Harvey didn't know how to drive, but he had insisted as the two walked up to the house, "Let me do all the talking, okay?" The asking price was $1,500. Harvey walked in and quickly initiated negotiations: "How about thirteen-fifty?" The seller shouted gleefully in a language that sounded like Arabic, added a whoop of happiness that required no translation, hugged his wife, and danced around the room. Shaw drily said to Harvey, "Good negotiating."

Since both Harvey and Shaw were underage, unlicensed, and uninsured, they parked the car midway between their two houses, with the understanding that if either's parents found out, the accused would claim it was the other's car. Unfortunately, the Opel was not destined to provide years of faithful service; it blew up six weeks later.

With a parent on the faculty, Harvey was able to go to Rice tuition-free, and since he was a National Merit Scholar, room and board were covered. But he loved to work, to the exclusion of attending classes. A friend got him a job doing programming for the Houston school district, and it wasn't long before he, along with Shaw and another friend, formed their own company, Styleware, which produced word-processing software for the Apple II. Harvey was the CEO, and in its first year the company pulled in $1 million in revenue; in its second it earned $3 million. A year after Harvey graduated (barely) from college, Apple's software subsidiary, Claris, bought the company for more than $5 million. At the age of twenty-three, Harvey had $3 million in his pocket.

The terms of the sale required that Harvey work for Apple for two years. He tried to persuade Shaw to move with him to California, but Shaw decided to stay in Houston and see what he could make of himself on his own, without the help of a brilliant best friend at his side. He founded Synergy, a reseller of accounting-software packages that evolved into a systems-integration business that would do well, $10 million in revenue annually.

When Harvey's employment contract with Apple expired, he set off to start another company, Approach, which would bring out an easy-to-use database program for Windows. Unlike the days when mail-order sales of Styleware's software would simply take off with only minimal spending on advertising, this time he would have to get shelf space in retail stores, and for a marketing blitz that would cost $2 million he knew he needed the backing of a venture capitalist.

His first encounter with venture capital left a sour taste. He approached Sequoia and Hummer Winblad, both of which committed to doing a deal. But when Ann Winblad heard that Microsoft had its own easy-to-use database in the works, she withdrew, and Sequoia said, If HumWin's out, so are we. Two months gone, and nothing to show for it.

His salvation was a young venture capitalist at Merrill Pickard, Bruce Dunlevie, who made bets on entrepreneurs, not on the prevailing winds in the industry, a contrarian bent that had enabled him to sail through the pen-computing era profitably. Dunlevie liked Harvey's "We're going to outexecute everybody" bravura.

Approach got its product out before Microsoft, and selling at $250 a copy, it did $5 million in revenue in 1992, a terrific start. But when Microsoft shipped Access for an introductory price of $99, a mind-bogglingly low price at that time, Approach was in trouble. One of Harvey's sales managers told him that he'd just been called by his own grandmother who had bought Access because she'd heard it was such a good deal—and she didn't even own a computer. It was time to look for a much larger partner, and Lotus stepped in, paying $23 million for the company.

Once again, Harvey submitted to golden handcuffs for two years, but at the end of the contract, Bruce Dunlevie and Bob Kagle invited him to join them in the new venture capital firm that they were just about to set up. He did not leap. Venture capitalists had a negative reputation; his own experience prior to meeting Dunlevie had shown him why that reputation was deserved. It would mean "going over to the dark side," as he joked with friends.

■

Several years later, after Harvey had joined the firm, and after Dave Beirne had followed him, Beirne good-naturedly gave Kevin Harvey and Bruce Dunlevie a hard time about not mingling with others at an industry conference the three had just attended. Beirne reported to the other partners in a voice that hid all trace of sarcasm that Harvey and Dunlevie "just blew the place away, schmoozing like I've never seen. It was awesome." Then Dunlevie reported the truth with the voice that turned hoarse whenever he spoke about his own foibles: He had ducked out of the conference in the middle of the afternoon and gone back to his room to check e-mail and make all the phone calls he could think of. When he had run out of things to do, he still couldn't face returning to the conference: "I thought, 'I don't want to go down and eat Ben & Jerry's at the ice cream social.'" So he had stayed in his room and watched a movie—Harrison Ford in *Six Days Seven Nights*. "It was terrible."

Beirne smiled at Dunlevie's social cowardice: "You fuckin' prick." Beirne laughed.

Unperturbed, Dunlevie continued. "I had a cranberry juice and a sudsy water, together. Watched this movie, read a book." He asked Beirne for credit for making it down for dinner.

Kevin Harvey fell equally short of Dave Beirne's expectations. "You know what it is, Dave?" Harvey said. "You're a better networker. Bruce and I are both terrible at it. We sit and talk to each other." He laughed. "I thought I never wanted to be a venture guy because I thought venture guys just had to schmooze all the time, which I hated. Then I went to some conference with Bruce, and he just stood around and talked to me. I said, 'Shit, I could do that.'"

In the first year as a venture guy, what he called the "belle of the ball" phase, things went so well that the job verged on being boring. Benchmark's first investment had gone public, and PointCast appeared to be the Next Big Thing. Then PointCast imploded. The founder built a bunker and dug in, refusing to admit the need for help, and the struggle to keep the company from becoming a large, smoking crater became unofficially Harvey's full-time job. At some point that year he was no longer the belle of the ball.

Having come through that, however, in 1998 he made six promising investments and now had a more realistic view of the work entailed in venture capitalism, which served to make him more, not less, engaged. And with eBay leading the way, the partnership's e-commerce companies were opening up possibilities that were unimaginable when Benchmark had formed.

There was a huge business to be made merely supplying consulting services to e-commerce companies. Look at Scient's start; it was hiring talent as fast as it could, and it still had more clients than it could accommodate. When he spoke with his old buddy Rob Shaw, still in Houston, Harvey tried to get him excited about these possibilities. Get into e-commerce consulting, Harvey advised. There's a problem with that suggestion, Shaw told him: I have no clients down here who are asking for that kind of help. Silicon Valley was not just ahead of Houston; it was too far ahead for Harvey's insights to be of help to Shaw's business.

Until Houston joined the New Economy, Shaw had time to dabble and learn something about e-commerce for future consulting gigs. For a proof-of-concept site that could be shown to prospective clients, he thought to himself, why not try selling watches on the Web? He had recently discovered that no store in Houston offered a discount on a Cartier he had wanted to buy his wife, yet it was possible to get a discount by other means. He had just run into a college buddy, Sean McNamara, who was a watch guy. McNamara had assured him he could get any watch he wanted at 50 percent off retail.

Shaw took his idea to his number-two person, James Whitcomb, who had also been a friend of Kevin Harvey's. Whitcomb shot Shaw's idea down: "Stupidest thing I've ever heard. Another one of your failed ideas"—a reference to some expensive experiments the two had already engaged in at Shaw's initiative. Shaw also ran the idea by Harvey, who was lukewarm about watches but thought that even if the project failed as a stand-alone business, Shaw would learn about the most advanced technology for building an e-commerce site. This was the argument that brought Whitcomb around, too.

As they looked more closely at the existing Web watch vendors, Shaw and Whitcomb saw that the incumbents did not carry inventory. A customer would "buy" a watch, then the company would scramble to find a supplier who had the watch in stock. Newwatch, as they would call their own experiment, would try to beat the others by carrying inventory, which entailed buying two existing terrestrial jewelry businesses. This would be a bet of half a million dollars, an entire year of Synergy's profits and double the amount they had bet and lost the last time they'd tried something adventurous (writing their own small-business accounting software in the face of Quicken's QuickBooks).

"I want my day," Whitcomb told Shaw. "If we get one off the ground, I want to run it." Shaw said fine. He'd be chairman and continue running Synergy on a day-to-day basis, and Whitcomb would be Newwatch's CEO.

They bought the jewelry businesses and launched their site. They failed to get business the first month. They had no money for buying advertising, but Shaw assigned his best, high-torque programmers to a guerrilla-marketing platoon, whose mission was to find ways to make search engines like Yahoo and Excite come up with links to Newwatch whenever a visitor typed in *watch* or any related variation in a search. The search engines had software that would eliminate the simpler forms of deception, such as packing a Web page with hidden keywords. To trick a search engine required ingenuity, and the programmers relished the challenge. They succeeded in their mission. Visitors to Yahoo who typed *Rolex* in a search could get two hundred listings—all of which took them to Newwatch. The site now got half a million hits a month, then 750,000 hits.

Visitors were also pulled in by a virtual slot machine—"Win a Free Rolex!"—that was placed on the home page. And they had hired Sean-the-Watch-Guy McNamara, who was available to any customer who called in seeking technical information.

In only its fourth month, Newwatch was doing close to $400,000 in monthly sales. Even more enticing, the average order size was $455, and $90 of that was profit. These latter numbers were figures that Amazon was unlikely to see anytime soon.

They'd bootstrapped it and off it had gone. Almost too fast. They were inventory-constrained and lacked the capital to keep adequate watch inventory in stock. The company needed venture capital to fund its growth. Rob Shaw had back-door access to Benchmark that any other entrepreneur would greatly envy. But it was that very friendship with Kevin Harvey that complicated things, making it not so easy after all. Shaw brought Newwatch to Harvey, saying, I think this business is terrific, but I don't want these discussions to hurt our friendship. Harvey, in turn, said he would not be comfortable having Benchmark invest in a company that sold only watches; it did not seem to him to be a large-enough business to show up on the partnership's e-commerce map. But perhaps he could invest a small amount of his money personally. In any case, he'd be glad to provide feedback and make calls to help Newwatch get in to pitch other venture firms in the Valley.

Shaw and Whitcomb came out to California and met with Kevin Harvey, Bob Kagle, and Bruce Dunlevie. Harvey made arrangements for them to meet with HumWin's young partner, Bill Gurley, whom Harvey did not know well, but Gurley had known expertise in e-commerce, and besides, he was from East Texas and might hit it off with these old friends from Houston. If Gurley wanted to invest, perhaps Benchmark could then do so, too, and leave the delicate matter of negotiations to an impartial party, the other venture firm.

After meeting with Newwatch, Gurley couldn't understand two things: If it was such a great deal, why had Benchmark sent it over to him? And how could Newwatch operate so inexpensively? Where were its expenses? Shaw had explained that he and Whitcomb ran a tight ship; nobody, including them, was paid more than $40,000 a year.

■

When the Benchmark partners gathered at the regular Monday meeting, Harvey sketched the deal for the partners who had not met with the visitors from Houston the previous week. He began by saying, "Rob Shaw, my closest friend," and dispassionately reviewed the strengths and weaknesses of the business. He was most concerned about Newwatch's lack of authorization from the major watch companies. Harvey concluded, "I think he who goes biggest and first is going to be one of the few authorized dealers. Then there's going to be some barrier to entry."

His Houston buddies had half convinced him the distribution rights could be secured. If a sufficiently enticing amount of money were put on the table, the watch manufacturers would be willing to risk the wrath of their existing dealers and sanction a new distribution channel that offered online customers discounts. He told the partners, "They think if they write a big-enough check to purchase some inventory, like half a million bucks, that they can get Rolex."

Without the complications of Kevin Harvey's friendship with the entrepreneurs, Bob Kagle was guardedly positive about the company's prospects. The category seemed to him a good one, were it not for a seemingly intractable problem: infrequent purchases by customers. It seemed similar to the deals they'd looked at involving selling cars on the Web, which they had ultimately declined to invest in.

"What's the friendship risk?" Beirne asked, meaning what was the risk that Harvey's friendship with the entrepreneurs might interfere with his making hard decisions, such as whether to seek a new CEO.

"High," said Harvey.

What about plans to sell used watches?

"No plans."

"That's a *big* business," Beirne said. Newwatch should not pass up the opportunity to sell high-end used watches.

"They think that's an eBay business," Harvey explained. "'Cause you can't get the inventory."

"The high-end watches are not an eBay business. Some of these watches go for twenty grand."

"Trade-ins, Kev," added Kagle. If you could facilitate somebody selling his old watch, he would be much more willing to buy a new one.

"One of the things we haven't talked about," Bruce Dunlevie said, "that I like a lot is they have this guy who is a watch *nut*—one of Kevin's buddies. You go to the jewelry show and everybody knows this guy. The existence of that in the mix, as opposed to two guys slapping together a website, is pretty important."

Harvey toted up the minuses, "the hair on the deal." Number one: The company was in Houston. Number two: The entrepreneurs were friends. Number three: Whitcomb, though "rock solid," tended to think small. Somehow he would have to be persuaded to lift his sights and not be so tightfisted. Prudent spending can be overly prudent: Newwatch had eighteen employees, but their average pay was only $8 an hour.

As Harvey enumerated the issues, he kept returning to the risk of endangering his friendships with the entrepreneurs.

How about having another partner serve on the board, Beirne suggested.

"I could." Harvey spoke slowly. "I don't know which is worse." If the firm were to fund the deal, should he be the Benchmark representative, and jeopardize his friendship if the founders' abilities were to fall short and the two had to be swapped out? Or should he have someone else serve, but in so doing jeopardize his friendship because the two guys were looking forward to working with him, not with a stranger?

"Life's too short," Kagle said. "Do it yourself. Have some fun with your buds."

"How big a business can this be?" Beirne wondered aloud. "If everything executes incredibly well?"

The business plan claimed $700 million in annual revenues in four years, but even Harvey was skeptical. Perhaps $250 or $300 million was possible, however; after all, the U.S. watch market alone was an $8 billion business.

Based on the valuations of retail companies with similar profit margins, Newwatch could easily be worth one times its annual revenue. So if it were able to reach $250 million in sales, it could be a $250 million company.

"This isn't a slam-dunk deal, no way," Harvey said, backing off. "I want you guys to meet it. I think there's a lot of big questions."

■

Kevin Harvey briefed Rob Shaw on what his partners had said. Some of them, he said without mentioning names, had initially been concerned about the fact that Newwatch carried inventory, but Harvey thought they now understood why it was necessary. EBay, the blockbuster e-business that lacked inventory, had set impossible expectations for all e-commerce deals that followed.

Harvey also said—and this was hard—some partners did not think Whitcomb was fully up to the job of CEO. Shaw swallowed. It sounded to Shaw as if his old comrade in arms was saying, "Rob, if this was being brought to me by the president of Rolex North America, we'd love it. But because it's being brought to me by you and James, we're not sure we like it." His friendship with Harvey had always been based on what Shaw called, with pride, "sincere straight shooting," and so, as painful as it was to hear, it was what your best friend needed to say, delivering the hard news straight up.

Harvey also prepared Shaw for the contract negotiations ahead, if the partners voted to approve an investment. The negotiations were going to be the most awkward thing the two of us have ever been through together, Harvey said. We're going to have to negotiate the value of the company, equity, composition of the management team, the terms. We'll have just as plain-vanilla a contract as we can, Harvey said, cutting everything down the middle, disproportionately beneficial neither to Benchmark nor to Newwatch. Harvey would offer the fairest valuation he could determine, and they'd negotiate from there.

When Rob Shaw hung up the phone, he had already decided that there would be no negotiation about the valuation. But he worried that his partner would blow up the future talks with Benchmark. James Whitcomb thought Newwatch's valuation was already $100 million.

"Kevin will offer us a fair value. We're going to take his value regardless of what it is," Shaw told Whitcomb.

"What if it's only a million dollars?"

"If it's a million dollars, we're going to take a million dollars. We're going to take his offer."

"He's going to start low and expect us to negotiate up."

"You don't understand the relationship here. The relationship is not based on playing bullshit games." Shaw believed Kevin Harvey always did the right thing. When Styleware was sold, even though Shaw formally had not owned equity in the company, as soon as the deal was closed, Harvey paid him for the stake Harvey had orally promised him. In discussing the negotiations with Whitcomb, Shaw was unbudgeable: "The relationship is based on what is fair. He's not going to be willing to go up or down." After considerable arguing, Whitcomb gave in; the two agreed to take whatever the offer was.

■

After Dave Beirne met with Shaw and Whitcomb, it was not clear he'd support an offer to Newwatch. At the next partners' meeting, Harvey tried to recall what Beirne had said to him immediately after meeting with Newwatch. Wasn't it "We wouldn't be funding them if they weren't buddies of yours"? If Beirne was correct, Harvey told everyone, then "we shouldn't fund them."

"My exact quote," Beirne protested, "was 'These two guys—*in Houston*—if you did not have a relationship with them, that you trusted them and thought they were great—we would not be funding this deal.' Is my guess. That's different than what you said."

"Do these guys show as well as the other entrepreneurs we fund? That's what I'd like to get everybody's thoughts on," Harvey said.

"I personally would have done this deal," Kagle offered. "Except I hate Houston. *Hate* it! But other than that—natural mo, man, there's nothing like it!" He laughed. "It's workin' already!"

There was momentum in more than revenue. This four-month-old business had just turned profitable, Harvey informed the group.

"That takes me from an 8 to a 9" on the ten-point voting scale, said Bruce Dunlevie. He could see making a reasonable-size company, even without adding product-line extensions. He added, "And I don't mind Houston . . ."—he paused a beat—"for *you*."

"They sure understand their business," Andy Rachleff said admiringly. "And I turned a couple of people on to the site, who just got really excited about it. I know some friends who have already bought watches."

What value should Benchmark place on the company? Bob Kagle thought $4 million would be fair. Harvey did not.

"You'd have to find another four-million-dollar company with three hundred K of revenue before I'd agree with that," Harvey said with undisguised irritation.

"Boy, that just doesn't seem like that's being close to fair, to me," Rachleff said of Kagle's figure, backing Harvey up.

Not only was the valuation too low, Harvey said, it was wrong to err in any direction but a generous one because the entrepreneurs were not going to show the deal to other venture capitalists on Sand Hill Road.

"Treat people the way you want to be treated." Rachleff used the refrain often.

"Have they made a proposal to you?" Kagle asked Harvey.

"No."

"Would you feel more comfortable if they did that?"

"Aw, they won't. I asked them to. And they just said, 'We don't know. Just tell us.' " Newwatch already had a proposal for financing from a Houston-based venture capital firm that gave them a $10 million valuation.

"This guy knows you pretty well, doesn't he?" Kagle said. "Puts you in a very difficult position right now, right? It does."

"Your challenge is," Beirne addressed Harvey, "and it's almost impossible to do—if you didn't know these guys, and they were just entrepreneurs who came through the door, in Houston, with what they have—positive and negative—"

"And assuming they acted the same way, as if they didn't know me," Harvey said.

"Correct."

"And there was a competitive dynamic in the deal, right?"

"I assume the group that offered ten pre- is probably a C player at best," Beirne said. "There's a big difference between Benchmark, in the heart of Silicon Valley, for this company, and a Texas investor."

"Sure." Harvey thought a moment and said the valuation for Newwatch should be either $6 million or $8 million.

"Which side are you negotiating?" Dunlevie wanted to know, provoking laughter.

"I don't know. All sides!"

"Here's where I am on it," Dunlevie said. "It's not a huge category. And there's a lot of inventory and availability-merchandising risk, so it's not a no-brainer. The fairer price for a tier-one investor is eight, and Houston discount gets you to six. That's the logic I go through to get there. Accel would do it at ten or twelve. Benchmark or Kleiner Perkins would do it at eight."

"Well, I'm going to ask for the broad hunting license," Harvey said.

Kagle tore up strips of paper for the vote and passed them out. The only partner who did not vote above a 5 was Beirne, who put in 4.9.

"Have you ever voted for any deal I've backed?" Harvey asked of him, with a tinge of irritation.

Beirne, placed on the defensive, kept his anger in check. He spoke with exaggerated calm, but his lower jaw muscles twitched involuntarily. "I think I've voted for every deal you've done. Abaco. When.com. Red Hat. Remarq. Been positive on every one."

"I'm not criticizing you—I'm not putting pressure on—I was just trying to place it in context."

"I think this is going to be a lot more work than you think. Out-of-town board. You've got friend issues. You've got channel problems—they have to get authorized, so there's business risk on top of all the other stuff. And I don't think you're going to own enough of it, Kevin, for the risk you're going to take."

"A third doesn't do it?" Harvey asked.

"I'm trying to be as honest as I can. It'd be so easy to write down '6.' "

"Interesting spine-stiffening discussion," Dunlevie interjected.

"I love ya, Christ," Beirne said, facing Harvey. "I'm just trying to—"

"I appreciate it. I want to know what everybody thinks."

"I think the friend issue, when it's predicated on noncommercially circumstanced acquaintances, is very real," Dunlevie added. But he pointed out that the entrepreneur-in-residence program deliberately allows the partners to become friends with the entrepreneurs. "It can be a big advantage, not just a complication."

Harvey told the group about a conversation he had had with Newwatch's young CEO, Whitcomb, about his future in that role. "He said, 'So you guys think I can do it?' I said, 'Yeah, at least in the early part. In the long term, this may be big. We may want to go hire the CEO of Macy's or something.' And he said, 'Great.' "

"I think if this company were here, it'd be so much easier for you to manage this," Beirne said.

"If this company were here, there'd be two investors—we'd own fifteen to twenty percent of the company," Kagle said.

"If this company were here," Dunlevie corrected, "we'd pass on it 'cause the price would be too high."

"Okay," Harvey said, bringing the discussion to a close. He had the partners' authorization to offer a deal on terms that sat in the middle, equidistant between the low and high valuations that had come up in the course of discussion. Unbeknownst to his partners, however, Harvey had used his hunting license to change a key term that brought the effective premoney price up to $7.2 million, close to the highest valuation mentioned, rather than the face value of $6 million.

The vote was in late October, and the deal closed in December. In the meantime, Newwatch's Christmas-shopping business took off. "It's screamin'," Harvey would say jubilantly as he walked around the Menlo Park office. "It's screamin'."

■

"You guys hear that Newwatch sold a ninety-thousand-dollar watch?" Harvey announced.

"Yes!" Kagle said.

"That's a good dollar-gross margin," Rachleff said with under-statement.

"Made the quarter!" Kagle said.

Beirne wanted to know one thing: "Free delivery on that?"

12. The Art of the Deal

Ninety-nine times out of a hundred, the partners approved an investment and the formalities were taken care of by the attorneys, Benchmark's and the entrepreneur's. The partners gave no thought to the possibility of an annulment during the six, eight, or ten weeks it took for the attorneys to exchange and sign off on the legal documents. When artuframe, pleading higher-than-anticipated marketing expenses, found itself in a cash pinch even as the docs were being readied, Benchmark immediately wired the company $500,000 as a bridge loan to get it through the interim.

Artuframe turned out to be that one-in-a-hundred case, however, where things were not what they seemed. When Bob Kagle had met with the company's Bill Lederer in July, Lederer had projected $2.2 million in revenue by the close of the fiscal year in October. The projections were part of the disclosures that the investment decision rested upon. Truthfulness in representing the facts of the business was an assumed precondition in any deal.

As the summer passed, Kagle requested several times that Lederer send him data about revenue and website traffic, and Lederer never did. "Well, you know, the accountants are looking at them," Lederer would say. The artuframe site had only opened in June, so being slow to document what was a brand-new online branch of the business did not arouse suspicion. The eBoys went ahead and voted their approval in early September and wired the bridge loan. The next month, Kagle told Lederer that he would be swinging through the Midwest and could get started right away in joining the board, even though the paperwork had not yet been completed.

Two days before Kagle was to leave on his trip, Lederer called him with some unsettling news. "We've got some of the numbers pulled together, and we're going to be way under plan."

"Ah, what's 'way under plan'?" Kagle asked.

"Well, I prefer to share that when you get here."

When he arrived in Chicago, Kagle learned why Lederer had been so reticent. The company was likely to show not $2.2 million in revenue for the fiscal year, but $150,000.

Discovering such a material shortfall in the company's finances was one shock. The second was seeing the poor judgment of Lederer in hiring a couple dozen more people and pumping up the marketing budget. The company was now burning $600,000 a month. Artuframe had built up a huge sluiceway, ready to handle the rushing waters of a $30 million river of annual e-commerce revenue, but what came in was less than $200,000. There were only three thousand online customers to date.

Bill Lederer had shown some good judgment, too, in Kagle's view. Kagle had challenged him to devise a better name and Web address for the business than artuframe, something that would be less limiting and more "aspirational," as Kagle liked to say. In response, Lederer had delivered the goods: He had arranged for the purchase of the "art.com" Web address for $450,000 from its unlikely previous owner in the helicopter consulting business (Advanced Rotorcraft Technology). Every month, 150,000 people typed in "art.com" blindly, hoping to find a site selling art. Kagle reasoned that $450,000 actually was a good deal, compared with the traffic one could expect to get from placing the same money in advertising. Lederer needed Benchmark's capital, however, to consummate the acquisition of "art.com." He also needed money to complete another purchase that Kagle thought made sense, for the definitive database of art prints.

Kagle returned to California to figure out what he should do. Artuframe's shortfall in revenue legally gave him a clear path to abort the deal. But it was complicated by emotional reluctance to separate.

Kevin Harvey joked when Kagle came back that it wouldn't be like leaving at the altar, it would be more like leaving during the honeymoon, and that was an image that Kagle found abhorrent. "I don't like the feel of that; that's not what we're about as a group of guys."

To try to puzzle out a solution, he asked himself the most basic question: Was there going to be an Internet service selling art and framing online? His answer remained unchanged: yes. But it now seemed clear that it might be a much slower haul than Lederer had led them to believe. It might take one or two years before the business achieved the volume that Lederer had predicted would be reached overnight. A long road would mean that it would be a much more capital-intensive business in the interim.

Kagle presented to the partners three options. The first option would be to say, "Look, Bill, this isn't what we thought we were getting into. There's obviously material adverse business conditions from what we had understood and discussed. As a result of that, we just don't have the appetite for the consumer market risk that is being displayed by the business right now." Benchmark would not demand that the bridge loan be repaid; instead, the loan would be converted into whatever small sliver of equity it would be equivalent to at the next financing, when Lederer found another investor. Benchmark would not be involved further, and Kagle would only be able to offer to Lederer, "Good luck."

Kagle paused. "There's a lot of my head that likes that approach. There's a big part of my heart that doesn't like that approach. My gut is sort of somewhere in the middle on it."

The second option was to say, "Okay, the business isn't really in the position that we thought that it was. It's going to take more capital, as well as an adjustment of the company's valuation because of the risk that is now visible." Or a variation of this option would be to break the $4 million investment into two increments. Put $2 million in immediately to see him through the end of January, then reevaluate whether to put the second half in on the basis of seeing whether he could increase his customer base in the meantime.

Everyone in the room, aside from Kagle, kept returning to that astounding shortfall in revenue. Kagle said that he believed that Lederer was caught by surprise as well, but that didn't provide much reassurance to the others. How could he possibly have been so far off? Rachleff wanted to know. It wasn't a rhetorical question. His face and voice expressed genuine puzzlement.

"What was it about the market that led to a hundred fifty K of demand versus two million of demand?" he asked. "What was it that he was assuming would happen that would lead to that kind of revenue that didn't materialize?"

Lederer had thought that more visitors to the site would click their way through to a purchase. He also had acknowledged that it was difficult for new visitors to navigate through the site, and ordering a frame online was still needlessly cumbersome.

The partners also could see that artuframe's growth would be hampered by the relatively small percentage of women who then used the Internet. Sixty-one percent of artuframe's visitors were women, a much higher percentage than the 44 percent that composed the Internet's regular population. Knowing this would be helpful in targeting the advertising budget. But the larger question remained: How big would this business scale, and how soon?

Maybe art online was following the same path taken by books online. The early shoppers at Amazon had begun tentatively, visiting two, three, or four times before they actually made a first purchase. The same pattern was visible among artuframe's customers.

"You could take a lot of different angles about what's the right answer," said Kevin Harvey, returning to the question of what to do about the deal. "The selfish Benchmark thing is to run away. 'Cause I think the use of your time in Chicago for a business that's going to need to be restarted here—that's just big, high cost."

"I haven't met the company," Harvey continued, "but just hearing the data here—the guy showed really bad judgment ramping like this without any revenue. If he was under the impression this was a big-bang category, that's really bad."

Kagle was not willing to be so harsh. He explained that Lederer "comes from the framing business, that's sort of all he knows—all these numbers look gigantic to him, relative to the $400,000 framing-reselling business he had in Chicago before. All he hears about is 'Amazon is *number one!*' And 'You have to be first mover or else you don't win.' I think there are people with the point of view that would say to own art online is huge. And the way you go after it is hyperaggressively, you don't worry about how much money you lose, and you get all the strategic deals. He's got a $1.2 million deal negotiated for an exclusive art-with-Yahoo. That's another thing I didn't mention."

Harvey suggested that one of the options be ruled out immediately—the one that put the original amount in at a renegotiated lower valuation.

"Slow boat to China?" Kagle asked.

Harvey spoke quietly. "Slow boat to China. Could run out of money fast. Already got a huge cash burn."

The company's dire financial situation, with sizable liabilities, meant that Benchmark's capital would be financing an existing balance sheet, rather than financing growth. That was not the case with their other first-round investments.

"Maybe you give it ninety days," Harvey said, "to see if there is any way to acquire any mo."

"Doesn't feel like it's enough to me," Kagle said. "That's no-man's-land, feels like. Sort of know a little but not enough."

"If you put in half of what we're on the hook for," Bruce Dunlevie said, "it goes to do these two acquisitions and Yahoo and he's out of money again. I think it's either walk away or do the big financing at lower cost. I don't think the turn-over-a-few-more-cards-on-the-cheap works."

"What's his morale like?" Andy Rachleff asked.

"What do you think, Andrew?" It was a shame that Lederer had got himself into trouble as soon as he had overcome his natural predisposition to avoid risk. Kagle speculated: "I think he did work hard to exorcise some demons of his father from his own psyche, in order to go for it here. This is my biggest problem walking away right now. I think this guy finally said, 'I'll get out from under the proverbial apron,' and said, 'Goddamn it, there is a big world out there, I'm going to go for it.' And I think that led to some bad judgment."

"And that's motivating to you, 'cause he's getting out from under his father's apron?" Harvey asked, incredulous.

"How do you walk away from him when he . . ." Rachleff asked no one in particular, the question trailing off unfinished. He turned to Kagle. "It's an emotional issue, right?"

"Unh-huh. It's also a what's-right issue."

"I know where you're going from," Rachleff said. "The coldly logical thing to do is walk."

"No doubt about it," said Kagle. "The moral high ground on walking away is to walk away and forgive the loan. It's still not good; it still feels really shitty. But it's the best you can do with walking away, I think."

Feeling shitty? "He represented 2.2 million this year?" Harvey reminded the group. "No quarterly forecast?"

"I'm all into doing the moral high ground, do the right thing and everything else," Dave Beirne said. "But if this is a charity, we're in a lot of trouble. I don't think we should forgive that loan."

"I think it's irrelevant," Harvey said.

"It may be," Beirne pushed on. "But still. I mean, we're worried about reputation on one side. You also don't want to be a pushover on the other side."

"If we make the decision not to go forward," Kagle said, "I don't think we've been a pushover."

"I think this is a personal decision on your part," Harvey said, addressing Kagle. "Because you've got to decide that you feel okay walking away. We can't tell you to do it. I think the logical answer is to walk away. It sounds to me like there's enough evidence of representations being different—"

"I don't think the guy lied to me, I really don't. If I felt the guy lied to me, I would have made this decision within a minute of figuring that out. I don't think he did."

"Let's just back up one second," Bruce Dunlevie said. "The question is, Is there a category here?"

"I don't think that *is* the question," Harvey replied. "'Cause I think the answer is yes. People will buy art online eventually. But is it going to happen from a company that way overramps expenses? Has to get restarted? And you're going to go through a lot of capital. It's going to be slow. I think it's going to be slow no matter what."

Dunlevie still liked the category, however. Artuframe's missteps were merely operational, easily correctable. "They do have the digital rights to this massive number of impressions. And they have a framing factory, that if anybody cares about framing, these guys are the only guys that have that, too." The company had twenty-eight thousand prints in its online catalog and were adding new images at the rate of five thousand each week. Dunlevie continued, "In the electronic commerce world, these guys have some assets that nobody else has. So the highest order bit is: Is there a category?"

"The question is, Does anybody care?" Rachleff asked skeptically.

"If the answer to that is no, then the investment decision's much easier in my mind," Dunlevie said.

Kagle remained hopeful. "See, the answer to me is there *will* be a category, but it needs to be very carefully prosecuted—"

"We *think* there will be a category," Beirne broke in, giving *think* a twist for emphasis. "We don't know that. Just like PlanetRx. We *think* people are going to do prescriptions over the Net. We may find out there is *nobody* that will."

"There're reasons to believe, though," Kagle said, stubbornly. "The current system in the real world is archaic and inefficient enough."

Why not round up another investor, like Softbank, Dunlevie said, suggesting the very opposite of walking away. Say to them, "We'll do four [million], you do four, we get somebody else to do two or three, so we've got a lot of money in the bank now, and we'll go do the category."

The suggestion did not draw anyone's support.

Rachleff changed the subject again, asking Kagle: "Four months ago, if I told you that we were going to meet two companies selling art online and watches online, what would you have said would be the one that would take off?"

"Art. But I wouldn't have thought carefully about the female demographic of it at the time." That's changing, though, he added. Within twelve months, the male/female split on the Internet would be 50/50.

"I tell ya. I think the market's talking," Rachleff said in his measured way. "The beauty of the Internet is you learn very quickly what people are interested in and what they're not. If something works, there's a buzz that goes around, by word of mouth, very, very quickly."

"Right." Kagle nodded.

"We've seen that with software, with RealNetworks, with ICQ— they're based in Israel! Watches? Who would have figured that's a category? I think if something doesn't take off quickly on the Internet, there's a lot of data in that. If it doesn't take off now, you've got to question when it is."

Kagle pondered whether any successful companies had been created on the Internet that had to roll the ball uphill when acquiring customers. "The only one that has even attempted it in a way that's gained credibility, and still doesn't necessarily have a business—that's Priceline. That's the only one where the endemic growth didn't fuel it enough to really be the primary driver. I think. I stand to be corrected—"

"There was demand, though," Rachleff said. "That got traffic."

But set in proper context, artuframe had not done so badly, Dunlevie maintained. He reminded the others, "This thing has been up four months in a category that is not as big as a lot of the other categories that have worked. It's got a more complicated purchasing structure, right? There's the art, and 'Do I want it framed?' But I don't think Amazon ramped all that quickly in its first six months, right? It futzed around. It spent a lot of money on ads."

"You think that's right?" Harvey was surprised.

"Oh, yeah," Dunlevie said. "It's right in their prospectus. They had almost no sales for the first half year."

"But that was, like, 1995."

"I appreciate that," Dunlevie said.

"That there are only three thousand people that have bought anything—it's early days," Kagle said, coming to Dunlevie's and artuframe's defense. "The conclusion that I draw from all that is it's just going to be tougher and slower. I think you'd agree with that, right? It's not that it's not going to happen. It's just going to be tougher and slower."

"Ultimately, everything is going to be on the Internet," Rachleff said, unmoved. The question remained: When?

"I'm not saying do a big bang," Beirne said. "I'm saying, recapitalize the thing and move it out here. It's going to take a ton of work to stay in this game. I'm not up for just forgiving it. I think we are foolish if we do that. That is not the right answer. And I believe in doing the right thing. You don't want to hurt the guy."

But, Beirne said, he was coming to the realization that some online categories simply weren't going to happen. He'd heard that a Webvan rival had filed Chapter 11 the previous week.

Here's the business, Dunlevie explained: "Dried peas and Saran Wrap, delivered FedEx."

"That's the best characterization I've heard of it," Kagle said, laughing hard.

Beirne wasn't laughing. Deals with Web portals had not brought the traffic the rival had needed.

"That's a little wake-up call," Harvey said, now soberly.

"Definitely," Kagle said.

"If you guys listen to that, though . . ." Beirne looked gray and his voice trailed off. "Scares the shit out of me on Webvan. I mean, they only did seven million in revenue? Spending all that money on traffic? Yipes!"

"You've got a regional rollout advantage, though," Dunlevie offered.

"Yeah, they didn't have that three-hundred-fifty-thousand-square-foot automated monster," Beirne said, laughing bitterly.

Returning the discussion back to the artuframe predicament, Kagle mused, "If I could get the burn rate to somewhere between half and two thirds of where it is now and have fifteen months before I had to do the next round of financing, do I think I could create some value here? Yeah. But one of the things that is apparent in that to me is it would be *us* doing a lot of that value creation."

"It's you restarting a company and hiring a new management team in Chicago," Harvey said bluntly.

"Can I go around the room, can I hear?" Kagle addressed everyone. "I appreciate your point, Kevin, that this is a decision I need to make. I'd like to know, given everything you guys know, and everything you can factor in, what each of you thinks you would do in this situation. That would be very helpful to me."

He added a few words appraising Bill Lederer: "Is his heart in the right place? Is he trying to do the right thing? Has he put his ass on the line to make this thing happen? Has he recruited a lot of people and got 'em all fired up about doing it? Is he thinking about the business clearly from a strategic perspective? Yeah."

"I don't know enough about the business," Harvey said, appearing to soften a bit. "I mean, I didn't know they had these digital rights." But when Kagle pressed him for what he'd do in Kagle's position, Harvey lowered his voice and said, "I'd walk away."

Kagle turned to Rachleff.

"I'd pull it and try to find a soft landing or help him with other financing, and feel shitty all the way. I had one of these situations once, where I didn't pull it, and I should have. And it's haunted me ever since."

Kagle swiveled his chair. "Brucester?"

"I'd raise ten or twelve [million] at four pre-, and if I can't get that much money assembled in three weeks, pull it. But I wouldn't raise six or seven. I think you're going to need a lot of runway. And if you could also do the build-it-out-here plan, I think I like that better, though that's pretty problematic. But he has to come back to you about, Okay, you're in a pickle, what are you going to do managing the burn rate, getting more focused, and he's got to come up with the answers, not just hearing from you."

Beirne would take still another position. "I'd cut the burn in half, immediately. And I'd renegotiate the whole deal and bring it out here. I'd keep his framing portion there, that's fine. Just like PlanetRx, we have a distribution facility in Memphis. It's a bitch to manage, but he's there, gives him a purpose."

"Sales and marketing's here, factory's there." Dunlevie summarized Beirne's proposal.

"And you'd still give him the ability to prove something to his dad. And the one thing I agree with in Bruce's suggestion, I'd do it very quickly. Recap or run away."

"And if you can't get it, that's the final piece of data," Harvey added.

The money would be found if Kagle sought it, Beirne predicted—simply on the strength of Benchmark's prior commitment to the deal.

"You'd do that instead of pull it for what reasons?" Harvey asked Beirne.

"'Cause I do believe there's going to be a market there eventually. My big problem with the deal to begin with was the entrepreneur. I don't think he's a great CEO. I told you my concern with Chicago; I don't want a partner traveling. And number two, I didn't think he was TheGuy. With his art experience, you can get some young talent to be the CEO of this company and build around."

"So you deliver the message that he's not a CEO right now?" Rachleff asked.

"That's what I would do."

The final tally: Two partners urged Kagle to walk away immediately; one urged him to raise additional capital immediately; and the last urged him to move the company's headquarters to the Bay Area and find a new CEO.

■

One week later, at the next partners' meeting, Kagle reported that Softbank might put $4 million into artuframe, too. He thanked Dunlevie for the suggestion. It was still uncertain whether a deal could be worked out, but the fact that Kagle was pursuing Dunlevie's suggestion, and eschewing Harvey and Rachleff's advice to walk, was a huge break for Bill Lederer. No one again mentioned the $2 million in revenue that hadn't materialized.

"I'm still working it hard," Kagle reported to the group. "If I can get enough money into it, and the right investor group, I'm probably going to do it. And if I can't, I'm going to shoot it." But Lederer had been doing a terrific job in handling the crisis. "He's cut the company back by fifty percent in the last week."

"Wow." Harvey was impressed.

"So does he know what the plan is?" Rachleff asked.

"Yup."

"And was pretty constructive about it, right?" Dunlevie followed up.

"Yeah, very, actually."

"Those good Midwest values," Dunlevie said.

Kagle noted other encouraging details about Lederer's handling of the crisis. "He went right into full gear. He also said, 'I'm positive I could get traction and first-mover advantage with this thing. And if in twelve months you think there's a better guy to run it, I'll help you find him.' I said, 'What if it's six months, Bill?' He said that would be okay, too."

Kagle had also called Intuit's Scott Cook, whom he knew from eBay board meetings and who also sat on Amazon's board, to get Amazon to take a look and either consider investing or acquiring the company, providing artuframe with a soft landing.

"It's either going to happen quickly or not, either the financing or the acquisition, 'cause Bill is on a very, very short string now."

■

One week later, Bob Kagle had succeeded in bodily pulling Bill Lederer out of the grave. Amazon and Lederer had not been able to agree on terms—even when in desperate straits, Lederer was a stubborn mule—but Kagle had somehow rounded up two other investors, Softbank and Sandler Capital, who put up $8.2 million in addition to the $3.3 million that Benchmark put in. Lederer was under the protective wing of a softie, who happened to also have the connections in the industry to pull off financial miracles. And most amazing of all, Lederer hadn't had to fight his way into Benchmark—Benchmark had found him.

Only six months afterward, Art.com, as it had been renamed, was purchased by Getty Images, the London-based photograph licensor founded by a grandson of oil titan J. Paul Getty. The purchase price was pegged to subsequent performance, but it provided for an approximately fivefold payoff for Art.com's venture investors. It was a respectable outcome, not a home run like eBay but a good base hit, especially considering the company's parlous financial state at the time of the investment just a few months before.

At the time of the sale, Bill Lederer said that the art-framing business was ripe for consolidation because his competitors were not solely interested in making the greatest amount of money, as he was. "I'm a capitalist in a sea of communists," he said with apparent pride. It was an ironic comment from the beneficiary of funding that had been permitted to remain in his hands precisely because his backer had not acted as a flinty capitalist.

13. Getting Out

"Pulling the trigger" is the traditional phrase used in the investment world, conveying the sense that the action has immediate and irretrievable consequences. Meg Whitman arrived at eBay in March 1998. The decision was hers, and she did it, she pulled the trigger, setting in motion the preparations for an initial public offering later that year. These included hiring the auditors. Filling out the management team. Looking over the budget carefully, as the offering would go public off the second quarter's numbers. Setting up the bake-off in which investment banks would compete for the business. Selecting the bankers. Drafting the offering documents. Hiring a speaking coach. Charging off on the road show.

While preparing for the IPO planned for September, Whitman in the meantime had to learn the business, consulting daily not only with Omidyar but also with Kagle by phone for his perspective. She inaugurated new marketing programs—the company was only then beginning to realize that its advertising-free ride had been anomalous. In attending to these things, however, Whitman had to be careful only to touch the dials that needed touching. She did not want to upset the mysterious balance mechanisms already in place in a company that, after the December hiccup, had settled into 30 percent monthly growth.

When she had arrived in San Jose, the one thing she knew she did not have to worry about was the technology side of the business, about which she knew nothing and had no wish to study. But on day two, eBay's servers went down—for seven hours. And when she asked Pierre Omidyar if that had happened before, he told her, sure, all the time. He, Jeff Skoll, and Mike Wilson, the head of engineering, each shrugged and told her, the naïf, that all systems go down, an unfortunate but unavoidable fact of life. They stopped just short of saying to her: Get used to it. Guys, she said, this is a problem. Users *will* go elsewhere as soon as there is someplace for them to go to. The number-one priority needs to be making the system bulletproof. Toward that end, the engineering department's head count jumped from nine to thirty-three. It would not be the last time that the system was overwhelmed, but for the moment the problem appeared to be tamed.

As a marketing person, Whitman was keen to upgrade the company name. How about something exotic, like Cairo? Omidyar, Kagle, and the others defended eBay. The fact that it did not mean anything else was good, it was memorable, and by then it already had a known identity. Whitman was persuaded.

■

Pierre Omidyar had put up his auction site as an experiment in democratizing markets. What originally had burned him, and what he had had no way of doing anything about, was the fundamentally undemocratic nature of IPO's, which allowed the big clients of Wall Street investment banks to profit while excluding individuals of ordinary means. As eBay's own IPO approached, he now had an opportunity to do something about unfair business as usual.

His ally was Kagle, who looked at every deal as a morality play, pitting the little guy against the big, the underdog against the unfairly privileged. He too had long burned with resentment about the way investment-bank clients had access to highly sought-after shares that they quickly flipped for unearned gains. As wealthy as he now was personally, he had not lost any of the indignation about unfairness in the system, and he too had waited years for a chance to do something about it. The eBay IPO was the perfect opportunity: Why not offer shares directly to eBay's user community, the thousands who were clamoring for shares? Omidyar worked on persuading Whitman and the rest of the executive staff of eBay, while Kagle worked on his partners, playing upon the call to action most favored at Benchmark: "We need to break the rules on this, guys."

Kagle met unyielding opposition, however, in Bruce Dunlevie, who had been an investment banker at Goldman Sachs for three years after getting his MBA. Though he had been bored at the job, he had left with a conviction, held no less strongly than Kagle's populist credo, that the investment bankers were necessary to make markets liquid in the aftermarket.

"I like to distinguish between day traders," Kagle explained to Dunlevie, "which I think *is* bad—they *will* come and go, they *will* be gone with a crater. But the individual investor, I think, is here to stay over the long term."

"Because the information is just going to get better and better," Kevin Harvey broke in, agreeing. "I was showing Bruce the chat board on Yahoo—it's unbelievable the dirt that you can dig up. You can find out *anything!*"

How about selling eBay shares through individual-investor banks like Schwab, Kagle suggested. "It gives you a much more stable, diversified investor base. Because what I see is even in these ones we've done most recently, the institutions flip and trade out of these things really fast when the valuations run." But Schwab did not permit buyers of IPO shares to cut and run. "If you buy on an IPO, you cannot sell for the first forty-five days, or else you can't buy in the next time. So they have a much more structured process for getting people to invest for the longer term, which I think is a sensible thing, too. It just feels to me it will be a healthier environment for investment. Besides, who understands eBay better? The bankers, or the people living in it?"

"I think," Dunlevie countered, "part of the rationale in this is your personal, deep-seated resentment of the fact that institutions make money on IPO's." But what happens when a large investor like Bowman Capital, which did not care from whom it bought the IPO shares, later wanted to sell a million-share block? "He can't do it at Schwab, more often than not." Only the market makers at a Goldman Sachs or a Morgan Stanley were willing to supply the capital, take on the risk, and buy those shares in order to create aftermarket liquidity.

"But they make money on the inefficiencies—that's why they play in those markets," said Kagle.

"This is what bothers you!" said Dunlevie, laughing.

"I know it!"

"If somebody wants to get out of a million-share block, and I'm willing to take the trade at twenty bucks a share, and nobody else is, then I'm going to make all the money I want to."

"I think that's fine," said Kagle. "But I think if the market is made up of more smaller trades, everybody is going to be better off and it's going to be more efficient. And people are going to be in less of a situation where one institution wants to get out of your stock, and you're hammered by that. If Fidelity runs away from some stock that they've got a twenty percent position in—"

"They're still going to do that, Bob. Institutions are going to continue to buy your stock, and they're going to buy it in comparatively larger size than any one individual. At the point of time when I decide to get rid of my million shares, and the only guy who is the market maker can't make it, then your stock is really going to go down a lot. Somebody's got to step in and make that market. That's a value. That's *creating* liquidity. That's *more* efficient, it's not *less* efficient."

The discussion ended without resolution.

■

EBay decided to have the customary bake-off among the leading investment banks, but Kagle and Omidyar continued to lobby for offering a portion of the IPO shares directly to the eBay community. In May Kagle reported that one of the investment bankers provided data about retail shareholders versus institutional shareholders that confirmed everything he had been saying: It's better to have individuals owning your company's shares. "The individuals hold better, they don't sell on earnings disappointments, they hold for longer periods. Yahoo, for example, is three-to-one retail to institutionally held, right now, today. Which was some really compelling shit, in a big way."

Dunlevie's voice went into high, humorous mode: "That's why their valuations are so high!"

Someone asked whether direct sales to individuals would eliminate secondary demand that sent the price up after the IPO. It had already been discussed at eBay, Kagle said. "Ten-share maximum.

There's no way anybody's going to be sated on it. And you can't afford to offer 'em any more than that, because if they take you up on it, it's huge. We're going to limit it to, like, the two hundred thousand people with the highest reputations on the site, or something. We're going to have to limit it. There's no way we can offer it generally to the community. I mean, you have to do it in a fair way. It's got to be totally defensible and fair."

Beirne had a question. "What'll be interesting is, when you get the exposure of eBay up, and you drive hundreds of thousands of people to the experience that haven't been there before, does the quality of the experience go down dramatically?"

"That's the biggest risk in the whole thing," Kagle said. "In fact I can argue with you guys very persuasively that keeping this low profile we've had in the company has been absolutely the healthiest thing to do. Absolutely the healthiest thing to do. We've already broken the systems a couple times, in spite of that. So we've been barely able to manage the traffic operationally so far."

Kagle said there had been a second benefit. "This organic growth has led to this very nice set of community values; people are honest, people treat each other fairly, there's not a lot of scamming going on in it. And if you turn up the volume way high, the woodwork gets filled with a lot of weird guys, and the whole tone of the thing could change. So that's a risk."

"What are you doing to make sure the systems don't melt down pre–public offering?" asked Beirne.

"We've hired three strong directors in the engineering department in the last three weeks. Good guys."

Harvey, the software guy in the partnership, pressed Kagle to be sure that the engineering department did not hide "the real ugly internal stuff."

"Oh, yeah."

"I mean, a rising boat here makes all the—I don't know what the metaphor is—makes all the girls look pretty."

"Close!" Dunlevie offered as a mock compliment.

■

Kagle and Omidyar suffered defeat in their campaign to offer shares in a nontraditional way that would give the community members the benefits of the first gains. "One of my most significant personal failures," Kagle moaned.

Dunlevie's counterpart in the internal debates at eBay had been Meg Whitman, who prevailed with these arguments: Many community users were inexperienced investors. This could be a frothy market. We could get in a situation where those people are all losing money rather than making money on the offering.

These arguments held particular power in the wake of the market's drop in May 1998, leaving investors queasy, and again in late August, shortly before Whitman and Omidyar were to begin the road show, pitching the upcoming eBay IPO to institutional investors. EBay and its bankers could not have chosen a worse time.

The road show was an antediluvian practice, akin to a medieval horse market in that its main purpose was to permit prospective buyers, managers of large funds, to stand close and physically check the condition of the teeth and hooves of the goods for sale. The heart of the road-show presentation was a canned introduction to the company's business and financials that followed PowerPoint slides and ran about forty-five minutes—superficial to the point of being of no discernible use to any investor—followed by a short question-and-answer period.

Everyone who attended eBay's road show had the opportunity to read the printed prospectus, which ran seventy-five pages with another thirty-five pages of appendices and offered far more depth than a short oral presentation could. But institutional investors wanted to check the teeth in person.

Another aspect of the tradition endured that should not have: Instead of buyers coming to meet the company's representatives for a single presentation, the representatives had to travel to the buyers, wherever they happened to be and at whatever time they wished. That meant the same presentation was repeated, up to eight times in a single day, for several weeks. Why was this necessary? Because it had always been done that way, that's why.

Whitman, Omidyar, and Gary Bengier, eBay's chief financial officer, prepared the slides, refined their presentations with the aid of a $4,000-a-day consultant who did nothing but coach executives prior to road shows, and rehearsed their spiel until they could recite it

backward. With the lead underwriter, Goldman Sachs, offering qualified reassurance that eBay would remain unharmed and the IPO
would get done ("as long as there isn't a complete meltdown"), they
headed to the airport to catch a plane to Baltimore to do practice
runs for the BT Alex.Brown sales force.

When the eBay delegation enplaned, the Dow was down a little
bit, and by the time they arrived in Baltimore, it had closed down another 155 points. Whitman thought, "Meltdown! Meltdown!" The
next day, as Whitman, Omidyar, and Bengier went through their
pitches, the market plunged another 250 points. The audience
looked preoccupied, and when their eyes did focus on the eBay
speakers, it was with an accompanying look that said, "Are you out of
your mind?"

Goldman Sachs kept saying, You'll get out, you'll get out. On September 10 the eBay contingent was back home to give another warm-
up presentation to some West Coast clients of Goldman who were
willing to come to Goldman's San Francisco office.

The contrast in setting between eBay's utilitarian office in San
Jose and this office in downtown San Francisco was stark. The fine
woods employed in a chinoiserie motif in Goldman's elevator
vestibule alone gave the appearance of costing more than eBay's entire suite of cubicles and PC's. The aircraft-carrier-sized conference
table that occupied the dark interior room in which the presentation
was given made Benchmark's look the size of a rowboat. Around it sat
thirty-two upholstered chairs, filled mostly with men who were sepul-
chral in appearance. All but one wore a suit.

So too did Pierre Omidyar, who did not look himself. He was the
first to speak, and he smiled winningly, but after he gave a thirty-
second introduction, his role was completed. Whitman then took the
podium and explained why she left "a six-hundred-million-dollar division, managing some of the great brands in the world, to come to
eBay." She walked through fundamental consumer appeal, profitable
business model, barriers to entry, growth. She was poised, well-
prepared, animated, and witty. Bengier, who was forty-three and had a
salt-and-pepper beard and an engaging smile, appeared to be no less
at ease when he ran through the numbers. When your business enjoys
88 percent gross margins, the financials are anything but dreary.

What the attendees could not see, nor could any of those interested parties who assembled for identical briefings over the course of the next three weeks, was Omidyar's dry take on the world of institutional investors and the absurd aspects of the road show, which is to say, virtually all aspects of the road show. He was thirty-one, utterly unacquainted with this world, and utterly uncowed, too.

When Goldman Sachs had told him about the road-show schedule, Omidyar had insisted that Goldman pick up the tab. That was not how things were done; the client was to pay for all travel expenses, Goldman had tried to explain ever so patiently. Omidyar's manner remained unremonstrative, and he continued to smile, but he was adamant: You want to be the lead underwriter? Then you'll have to pick up our expenses. He had other nonnegotiable demands for Goldman, which the bank tried to push back on and got nowhere. When the head of underwriting turned pleadingly to Whitman, she shrugged as if helpless and smiled. From then on, the inside joke whenever Goldman asked something of eBay was, "Sorry, Pierre says no."

Omidyar entertained eBay colleagues with daily dispatches from the road, accompanied by digital photos. The humorous accounts told of racing in and out of planes, hotels, and stretch limos ("Before I could get my seat belt on, or even find it, we were there; our first stop was practically across the street from the hotel"), laced with wry asides about class privilege and the comic assumptions others make on the basis of appearances.

In Houston, the eBay team of three jumped out of a chartered jet into a waiting limo. "The driver says, 'Hi, there, howya doin',' to each of us. He says to Gary, 'Oh, you must be the Man.' Meg is not amused. '*I'm* the Man.'" Boardroom tables so large you could reach only a quarter of the width across ("Exchanging business cards was a real problem"). The monotony of listening to the same presentation eight times a day. (Even by the end of day one, he reported, "By this point, Meg's excellent presentation is beginning to sound a little familiar.")

He watched the money class with the detachment of an anthropologist (still innocent of the knowledge that he would soon become a paper billionaire himself): "I put a penny down on the carpet, wondering if any of the portfolio managers would stoop down to pick it up. Nah. I guess 'a penny saved is a penny earned' doesn't jive with 'I make more money on the stock market in the time it would take me to pick up a penny off the floor than most small countries make all year.' Oh well."

To keep themselves entertained through the numbing repetition of the same transitions, the same jokes, they began a contest to see which of the three of them was the first to work into an answer the fact that 80 percent of eBay's active users at any given time were re-peat users. Even if no one in the audience were to ask, "What's your repeat customer rate?" the fact could still be worked in, Omidyar re-ported.

"How do your customers pay you?"

"Well, since eighty percent of eBay's active users at any given time are repeat users . . ." was an all-purpose opening.

■

While the road show ground on, institutional buyers were supposed to put in their orders, but the demand did not materialize. On Sep-tember 18 Whitman met with Lawton Fitt, Goldman's head of capi-tal markets, who attempted to be reassuring. Fitt said that investors liked the company but were bewildered by the market's decline since midsummer. They did not know whether they should get out entirely. Whitman looked at Fitt, whose body language was not nearly as pos-itive as the words that issued from her mouth, and thought, Oh, God, if the IPO were to be pulled—as Healtheon's had been (in August more IPO's were delayed or canceled than in any other month in the decade)—and she had to do the road show all over again later, she'd have no choice but to commit suicide.

■

After the close of trading on September 23, Whitman, Omidyar, Jeff Skoll, Fitt, and other Goldman personnel assembled in a Goldman office, and back in California Bob Kagle patched in through a con-ference call. The moment had arrived for the pricing meeting. Insti-tutional investors had been told the range for this offering would be $16 to $18 a share and had made their decision whether to participate on that basis. The meeting was to decide where, within that range, the shares would actually be priced for their initial sale. That day had been a good one on Wall Street. The Dow had closed up 257 points; Amazon was up 17 points, Yahoo, 14. This was encouraging. The eBay offering was now oversubscribed twenty times over. There was still time to reprice the shares higher than the range that had been set. This was done only rarely and would entail notifying all of the buyers to see if they wished to go ahead with their orders at a higher price. Fitt, however, argued against going beyond $18 a share, reasoning, "We're in a market environment that I don't think anybody understands."

Kagle asked her, "Would moving the goalposts have a positive effect?" Pricing above $18 might be read by investors as an indication of strength, and draw more investors, not fewer.

Fitt did not agree. "People resent it." And who knew where the market was headed? "We may have a spectacular market tomorrow, but in a few weeks the market could retrench."

Omidyar was against pricing higher, too. "I don't ever want to see the price again." If the stock traded up and they left money on the table, fine. That would be "sharing a little bit of our success." Skoll reiterated the point: Let's be conservative about the price. Eighteen dollars was the agreed-upon price, what Fitt called "eighteen with a vengeance."

That night the institutional buyers took legal possession of the shares, and the IPO was complete. Then the investment world waited to see the first trade the next morning.

Before trading commenced, Mary Meeker, Morgan Stanley's head Internet analyst who had been beaten out in the bake-off with Goldman Sachs for the eBay IPO and who had every reason to withhold her approval, surprised Wall Street by issuing a report recommending eBay as an "outperform." (Onsale's Jerry Kaplan, when asked for his reaction to Meeker's enthusiastic praise of eBay's business model, predicted that eBay's revenues would disappear altogether; person-to-person auctions would go the way of e-mail services and be available for free as a means to draw traffic to sites.)

When Whitman, Omidyar, and Skoll returned to Goldman's trading floor at about ten-thirty on the morning of September 24 to witness the processing of the first trade, Lawton Fitt approached them and said, "You've got a good problem. We don't have any sellers." Three and a half million shares had been sold in the offering, and no one had yet volunteered to yield his shares up for a flip. "We're trying to find the range where we can find some sellers." It took another hour before the first trade was done, at $54. At that price, Whitman estimated that half the people in the company were paper millionaires.

For Benchmark, which had purchased its share of equity when the company's valuation was much lower ($20 million) than it was when offered by the underwriters at the initial public offering price ($700 million), the gains were even more dramatic. Unless the price collapsed over the course of the trading session, the value of Benchmark's original $6.7 million stake in eBay was now about $416 million.

During the previous week, Whitman had pressed Kagle to join the eBay group in New York so he could be there, too, when "EBAY" crawled across the digital ticker for the first time. He had plane reservations set but at the last minute decided reluctantly to cancel, concerned that the CEOs of his other companies would think he had gone too far in giving eBay his attention, to the detriment of their own interests. Staying in Menlo Park, he fielded congratulatory calls all day from his entrepreneurs, who complained only half-jokingly that the eBay IPO set an "impossible bar" for the rest of them to best. He reassured each of them that their companies were sure to shine, too.

The Benchmark partners did not say much among themselves or exchange high fives. But when Bruce Dunlevie and Kevin Harvey, who were standing together by the assistants' workstations, saw Kagle come out of his office, the two extended their arms and bowed silently in his direction, in "We are not worthy!" fashion. Andy Rachleff walked by later and permitted himself an understated confession: "I'm feeling a little giddy."

Kagle and Dunlevie's administrative assistant, Marissa Matusich, felt *extremely* giddy. Her exultant screams kept the office apprised of eBay's trading prices. When a friend called her, Matusich already had done the arithmetic. "Meg is worth a hundred million and the entrepreneur seven hundred fifty million!"

From New York, Whitman called her husband at the Stanford hospital.

"Is there a Quotron handy so you can see what's happening?"

"No, Meg, there's no Quotron." He didn't seem keen to find one either. "I'm doing brain surgery in a moment."

Keith Krach, Ariba's CEO, called Kagle to offer congratulations. What was eBay worth now? "One point eight bilski," Kagle reported.

"That sets an awfully high bar," said Krach.

"Your day will come, too."

Odds were against any other company coming close to eBay's performance, however. At the end of the first day, the share price had held up; it closed above $47, giving eBay the fifth-highest first-day gain in the market's history.

Down in San Jose, eBay employees abandoned their cubicles and formed a giant conga line, a snake of conjoined, joyous, singing, delirious adults that wound through an ordinary-looking office in an ordinary smallish office building in an ordinary-looking business park.

In New York, Whitman, Omidyar, and Skoll looked on as the NASDAQ ticker showed a market now wholly consumed by trading of this stock; all ten visible slots on the electronic ticker filled identically:

EBAY . . . EBAY . . . EBAY . . . EBAY . . . EBAY . . . EBAY . . . EBAY . . . EBAY . . . EBAY . . . EBAY . . .

In San Jose delirium reigned for almost two hours. As the building rocked, another tenant called to complain and demanded to speak with the director of facilities. "He can't come to the phone right now," the receptionist apologized. "He's drunk." (This was the receptionist's little joke; the company was still too small to have a director of facilities.)

The eBay contingent in New York flew back and the next day came up to Benchmark's office for an informal celebration with the partners and staff, munching snacks and sipping champagne on the terrace at the end of the day. Dunlevie and his colleagues embarrassed Omidyar with we-are-not-worthy bows. Omidyar and Skoll were effusive in thanking the Benchmark guys for their contributions. Whitman entertained everyone with stories of the road show, of New York, of handling the calls of congratulation—and of not wanting her sons to know about the money. Anyway, "It's all paper."

Whitman's former boss at Hasbro had just called her. When she'd resigned fewer than nine months before, he'd told her that he couldn't fathom why in the world she would leave Hasbro for an unknown, on the other side of the country. Today he had called her and said, "Now I get it."

14. Techniqued

If a family has three dozen children, odds are that few of them will receive individual attention at the weekly family meeting. This was especially so when another dozen prospective adoptees were under active consideration. The partners' meetings on Mondays usually lasted four to five hours, including a working lunch, which was not a lot of time if two, three, or four hours were devoted to consideration of new deals or listening to presentations from entrepreneurs seeking funding.

After a little more than three years, the partnership's investments totaled $150 million and the value of those investments, calculated conservatively, was $1.6 billion. In the difference between the two figures were stories of dramatic growth in not only eBay, of course, but also others: Scient (a $3 million investment valued at $31 million at the end of 1998); Impresse Software ($3.8 million now worth $12.6 million); and Ariba ($3.9 million now worth $18.2 million). The partnership was doing well and had $250 million of gain on paper for portfolio companies other than eBay, most of which were readying themselves for IPO's in which their values would shoot many multiples higher.

If any given partner were asked on any given day what the current value of Benchmark's gains was, however, he would have had only the haziest of ideas. This was not because of a feigned avowal that "it's not about the money" but because there was nothing in the accounting that held interest or demanded action. The quarterly reports were prepared by Benchmark's chief financial officer and sent off to the limited partners, but Beirne, Kagle, Rachleff, Dunlevie, and Harvey had neither the interest nor the time to monitor the scoreboard. Instead, what was talked about was the wayward child—and at any given time, the portfolio had one or two—the company that had stumbled off the path and now was deep in muck and could only be pulled out with a collective rescue effort by Team Benchmark, if it was not too late (and if it was too late, it was the other partners who had to persuade the sponsoring partner to let it go).

■

Dave Beirne displayed a short-story writer's gift when it came to opening with an arresting line: "I'm working very hard to make sure Paul Wahl stays as the CEO of TriStrata. Very interesting game."

This was late November 1998, three months after Wahl had arrived and one month since TriStrata's chief technology officer had resigned, despite Wahl's and Beirne's efforts to persuade him to stay.

Andy Rachleff had not heard anything about Wahl's unhappiness. "What happened?"

"He's in it now; he's not threatened to leave or anything, but I'm spending a lot of time with him to make sure he's happy."

With a tightness in his voice, Beirne continued, "There's just a lot that isn't what it was made out to be."

"Any other people leave besides the CTO?"

Beirne shook his head silently. "And they're building a great team. Building a great sales organization. I've got to decide how aggressive we need to be with Young and Atalla. I'm damn close to angry. Over the price."

He paused, then continued. "You know, we don't even have a deal with Price Waterhouse, what we thought was seven to fourteen million dollars revenue. We had a deal, kind of, but we don't. They're not obligated to do anything."

Kevin Harvey recalled that the Price Waterhouse guy he had spoken with at the time Benchmark was considering the investment had alluded to the deal not being complete.

"Said they had a deal," Beirne insisted.

"No."

"Yes, he did. I asked him. He signed the agreements. The addendums never got signed, as to what we really had to do to produce. No, I asked him the question. I asked the guy in Europe, too."

"Where is John Young on all this?" Bruce Dunlevie asked. Young, a former CEO of Hewlett-Packard, was TriStrata's chairman of the board.

"I don't think these guys know. I informed the board at the last board meeting that we don't have a one-time pad implementation, we have a *pseudo* one-time pad implementation. Perkins got all pissed-off."

"At that fact?"

"At that fact. Started with the messenger, which I didn't take, and then got pissed-off at the fact. Then Atalla told him, 'We always said it was based on the one-time pad, there is no such thing as a one-time pad implementation. The technology is based on the theory of a one-time pad.' Perkins said, 'Oh, what's the difference?' Well, the fuckin' difference is we have every cryptographer on the planet up in arms, every one."

Prospective corporate customers did not care whether TriStrata had a genuine one-time pad technology or not. "If you say to Shell, our technology is ten times better than anyone else's, gives you ten times faster management capability than anyone else's, and you may get broken into five times over the next twelve months, can you live with that? All of them would say, hands down, no problem, great—where do I sign?

"But we have not said that. We've said. It's theoretically unbreakable. Can never be broken." Beirne was so agitated, his speech fragmented.

"All these red flags are all over the place. And this guy Bruce Schneier. Who is the book I was reading on cryptography? The guy who is the guru on cryptography? His website is all about TriStrata. He is just ripping this company apart. So every time [a prospective customer] goes to do due diligence, the first thing they find is this guy, the god of all cryptographers, saying, 'It's bullshit. And if it's real, release it so all the cryptographers can look at it.' "

Beirne had asked Bruce Schneier to take a look at TriStrata's software during the whirlwind of due diligence prior to Benchmark's investment, but John Atalla had refused to permit access, arguing that the software was not ready.

TriStrata had yet to release its software because Atalla wanted to continue to tinker with it. "Paul is all over Atalla, saying, We're going to release this fucking thing. And John has not agreed to do it yet, but I think it's going to come down to, Paul's going to say, Either release it or I walk. That's where I think this has to go."

Beirne felt badly for Wahl. "Because it was on my credibility he took this job. I feel more sorry for him than I do for me."

"I don't understand," Bruce Dunlevie said, "why he has to ask Atalla's permission to do that, while he's the CEO."

"He *can* do it, Bruce. He's trying to maintain some harmony, keep the guy engaged. He doesn't want Atalla gone."

"Why not?"

"Why not? Because the guy's a legend in security. He is."

"He's going to be a pain in the ass forever."

"Yeah. Well, again, Paul may get there."

Wahl planned to fire Atalla junior. "That's a very hard thing to do, to go to the founder and say—"

"John's been okay with that?" Kevin Harvey asked, surprised.

"John's getting okay with that, he will be. I think Paul's handled that right.

"So I'll keep you up-to-date. I don't feel like going to the company right now and saying we want to pull our investment back out, but I've thought about that."

"If Wahl leaves," Harvey began, "you should—"

"I'll give him my fuckin' office, that's how bad I feel. And I'll either make a company for him or we'll get him involved in another one. This guy's a good man. And he is working his ass off. He's there at seven o'clock in the morning, he's there till eleven o'clock at night, he's working on the weekends."

Beirne had spoken with Wahl a few hours earlier, telling him that the two of them had to get to the bottom of Atalla's claims for Tri-Strata's encryption software and find out whether TriStrata had a marketable product or not.

No one spoke for a long time.

At best, Wahl would have to orchestrate a public relaunch of the company, with technical claims that were much more modest than they had been. "It's going to have to be brilliant," Beirne said. "We have the product ready to release, but it's never been tested by the world of cryptographers.

"I can see Perkins finding out what the real deal is and just kind of floating away."

"Disappearing," Bob Kagle said. "I'd say there's a reasonably high chance of that."

"And just so that we're all clear from a strategic perspective," Beirne said, "I will go visit him and make sure that his ass stays in that chair. If we're staying involved, he's staying involved. 'Cause he has a major credibility issue. All these guys do."

Kagle offered his sympathy to Beirne. "It sounds like a tough situation, but sounds like you're doing all the right stuff."

"I feel bad I got him in it."

"Won't be the last one," Kagle said.

Andy Rachleff laughed ruefully and repeated the line.

Harvey said to Beirne, "We'll be nice to you if you're nice to us when it happens to us."

■

Wahl stayed, and for another six weeks TriStrata disappeared from the view of the other Benchmark partners, but Beirne had to work daily to keep Wahl and TriStrata from flying apart. Not just Wahl stayed but so too did Atalla junior, who decided he deserved a more senior position, a significant raise, and the ability to work full-time from a home in the Napa Valley. And all this while, Wahl could not persuade Atalla senior to release his grip on the software so Wahl could push it out the door.

Just before Wahl told him that Atalla's claims about the technology could not be substantiated, Beirne had lined up for TriStrata a $10 million round of financing, at a $200 million valuation. Beirne's partners were as mortified as Beirne had been when he told them that another TriStrata director wanted to withhold from the new investor the discovery that Atalla's software was something less than Atalla claimed it was.

"Pretty unbelievable," Beirne said to the others after summarizing the director's position. "Wow."

"Out there, huh?" said Kagle.

Beirne did an impression of his fellow board member: " 'I don't think we have to disclose any of this—the fact that the cipher doesn't work.' " Then, in his own voice, "I said, 'We're going to get ten million dollars from this guy, and you're telling me you don't think we need to disclose this?' He goes, 'I don't think it's material.' "

"Holy shi—," Kagle began.

"I said, 'I'll tell you right now. At Benchmark, we're not going to be associated with that. We'll tell them all the positive, as much of the glass being full as possible, but there's no fuckin' way we're doing *that*.' "

Beirne called the investor, explained that he could not accept the money, and withdrew the financing.

■

"Were you ever in a fight when you were a kid?" Beirne mused after a weekend dominated by the endless crisis at TriStrata. "I used to be in a lot of them. You know that feeling—shaking—after you're in a fight? That's the way I was here yesterday. I haven't had that feeling in fifteen years. It was just unbelievable."

Beirne had finally gotten Atalla to permit Bruce Schneier, the cryptography expert, to come in and take a look. Three other cryptographers had been hired as consultants as well. Their opinion: TriStrata had a decent cipher, but not the breakthrough that Atalla had led Beirne and Wahl to believe they had. Even if it was comparable to DES (Data Encryption Standard), the prevailing cryptographic standard, it had not been open to public review and pounded on for five years by the crypto community, as DES had.

It required every bit of Beirne's powers of suasion to keep Wahl from resigning. If the news on the technical front was not dispiriting enough, Bill Atalla continued to make demands, which in turn led to a confrontation between Paul Wahl and Atalla senior—and Atalla prevailed. And then John Young, the chairman of the board, had expressed misgivings about Wahl as the CEO. When Beirne expressed his surprise at this sentiment, Young had said, "Hey, Dave, John Atalla told me that if you weren't happy with the way things are going, he'd be happy to give you your money back. He'll personally buy you out of the company."

"I'll take your bet. I want to implement it *today*. I'll call John Atalla immediately."

He'd called Atalla and told him he would meet with him that day. Then he called Wahl to tell him that he'd keep Benchmark's money in if Wahl were to stay, but if he wanted to leave, Beirne would pull the investment. Then Beirne called Perkins to let him know what was unfolding. Horrified at the prospect of a showdown that would irreparably cripple the company, Perkins got Beirne to agree to call off his meeting with Atalla; Perkins went instead and told Atalla that driving Benchmark out was tantamount to committing corporate suicide.

More calls, more negotiating, and by the time everyone went to bed that night, Wahl had agreed to stay on as CEO and had extracted from Atalla senior an agreement that Atalla junior could be terminated at Wahl's sole discretion at any time.

The picture of Beirne that Perkins may have been left with at the end was of a guy who enjoyed brinkmanship. In fact, Beirne had been in pain during the entire crisis and now was emotionally spent to a degree he had never felt since becoming a venture guy the year previous.

"If you just take it as business, I guess you can get through that stuff without getting your emotion wrapped up in it, but it's not just business for me."

■

The thought that Kevin Harvey could not shake was how Benchmark had been rushed into investing in TriStrata in the first place—despite John Atalla's initial plea to "make the numbers work," subsequently the company had simultaneously claimed an outrageously high valuation *and* had played hard to get. "They said, 'A hundred million, and you can't have it.'" He repeated himself: "'A hundred million, and you can't have it'! This for a company that shouldn't have been funded at five. We got techniqued."

■

When TriStrata finally released its software in March 1999—six long months after Wahl had joined—it downplayed the cipher that had attracted the attention of the press the previous year. "I think maybe we got a little too excited about our algorithm," Wahl told *PC Week*. TriStrata planned to license DES and other well-known encryption technology, permitting TriStrata to extricate itself from what Wahl delicately called "a religious war."

It was soon after this, however, that newly hired consultants discovered major problems when they dug into the tests that TriStrata used to measure the speed of its encryption and decryption software. When Wahl heard that the one thing that had kept him from bolting—the encryption technology—was not marketable, he succumbed to Siebel Systems' long-standing courting and resigned. Beirne thought he had successfully coaxed him back to TriStrata, but two weeks later Wahl was gone for good, moving to Siebel in nearby San Mateo as its chief operating officer (and leaving not only TriStrata but the world of start-ups, having gone to a company that had $400 million worth of paying customers the previous fiscal year). Once again, TriStrata's financing—and very viability—was endangered.

The company now was out of cash and Atalla had to put in a million dollars immediately so it could make the payroll. But at the same time, there were a few corporate customers that seemed tantalizingly close to buying. Beirne listed for his partners three customer prospects who all showed signs of being excited. "There's a technology here. The question is, do you feed this thing a little bit, or just kill it?"

The other partners remained silent.

Beirne went on, in a voice that was barely audible. "I'd love to kill it and I'd hate to kill it."

"You know that emotion is exactly the emotion you feel when it's time to shut it down," said Andy Rachleff. He and Beirne's other partners all had faced similar junctures before; this was Beirne's first.

All of the other TriStrata board members had looked to Beirne to vow that he would single-handedly keep the company solvent, and he had demurred. "We had a brutal board call the other day. John Atalla basically saying, 'David, I can't believe you'd do this to this company.' I said to each of them, 'Hey, guys, we own only six percent of the company. We've a ton of money in it.'" Beirne had passed the challenge on to the founder, John Atalla, saying, "You're worth twenty million dollars, you own your home outright, you're seventy-five years old. I don't know what you're planning on doing with your money the rest of your life. But if you believe in this company, with the amount that you own in it, I'd put a couple million dollars in it to see if it will continue to live. If you don't believe in it, I understand that. But don't ask *us* to put more money in. I can't get my partners to do that."

Tom Perkins, who had invested as an individual, not as a partner of Kleiner Perkins, had begun to respond, but Beirne held him off. "Tom, don't go there, if you can't get Kleiner to invest in this company, either." Perkins went silent.

■

The Benchmark partners tried to find any glimmer of long-term hope for the company. "Have they sold anything to anybody? Do they have a revenue customer?" asked Bruce Dunlevie.

Beirne silently shook his head no. "Next version of the product comes out in July. All kinds of pilots set up. Really big customers that are really excited about it. But . . ." He paused for a long time. He said he'd spoken with the TriStrata sales team about precisely this problem, which of course gravely jeopardized the company's ability to attract new investors. "I said, 'Guys, help yourself.'" He whispered: "'Get a purchase order.'" Loudly: "'Show *something!*'"

Andy Rachleff judged TriStrata's straits to be hopeless. A company that had to rely entirely upon a next version of its sole product when no one was buying the current one was headed for death.

"The frame of reference that everybody has except you," Dunlevie said to Beirne, "can be put in a thimble, right?" No partner other than Beirne had spent time with the company; no one else had met Wahl; no one had seen the company's pitch. "I don't think we can be terribly helpful to you on the merits of the argument."

"I thought about having them come in and do a presentation today. But this company does phenomenal demo. It always has. That's what Tom [Perkins] said: 'Why don't you have them come in and present to your partners?' I said, 'Tom, it's not about demo ware. We know it's the best demo on the planet. Everyone gets excited. But no one *buys* it.'"

"I'd shoot it in the head," Dunlevie said unsentimentally. "You've got better things to do with your time."

Rachleff agreed. "You'd be amazed how much better you'd feel."

"I'm worried about the reputation hit for us," Beirne said.

"Companies go out of business," Dunlevie said. "Part of your reputation is, companies fail."

"I only want us to take the high road on this," Beirne said, still reluctant.

"The market's talking. The dogs aren't eating," said Rachleff. "When did we invest? Last June?"

"Yes."

"There were a number of customers that were imminent back then?"

"Ten-million-dollar supposed signed order from Price Waterhouse."

"Right."

"There sure are a lot of signs," Rachleff repeated. He wasn't concerned about Benchmark's overall reputation being badly damaged. "The amazing thing about our business is, everyone forgets the losers—they remember the winners."

"I'm not worried about the personal."

"I understand. The collective. But given the number of winners that you're associated with, and the firm's associated with, it won't be an issue."

"Part of hitting home runs, you strike out. Babe Ruth struck out," offered another partner.

"You know how many strikeouts John Doerr has had?" Rachleff asked Beirne. "Does anyone care? Will we win because of that? No."

"That's not the issue," Dunlevie broke in. "The issue is John Doerr knows and Dave knows. It's hard. It's really hard. The only person who cares is you. I've been there. And you're going to care *forever*. You've got to let it go. That's the best advice I can give you."

The room was quiet.

"You'll never take it lightly," Dunlevie added.

"All those people—that's the thing," Beirne said, thinking of the ninety employees on the TriStrata payroll.

Rachleff pointed out that in a portfolio, the emotions that Beirne would experience would always be biased toward the end of the spectrum representing pain. "The amazing thing is it hurts more on the downside than the good feelings on the upside."

"That's my experience—three orders of magnitude," Dunlevie quickly agreed.

"Yeah," Rachleff said, and then redid the ratio of intensity of pleasure versus pain. "One-X versus fifty-X."

"Anytime anything good happens to me? I wear my Opus T-shirt," said Dunlevie. When he and Rachleff had been junior venture guys at Merrill Pickard, Opus Systems, a manufacturer of Sparc workstation clones and one of Dunlevie's companies, was doing extremely well and preparing for its IPO when, out of the blue, Sun Microsystems decided to curtail its licensing program and kill off Sparc clones. It meant the end for Opus, but the company lingered in terminal pain for two long years before it finally died. Dunlevie had refused to issue do-not-resuscitate orders, and his Opus T-shirt was his memento of the experience.

"I've got mine saved, too," said Rachleff, laughing.

"'Kay," said Beirne, bringing the discussion to a close noncommittally. This was the painful task he had to address as a venture guy. The next month, when Beirne learned that John Atalla had peremptorily dismissed the CEO that the board had appointed after Wahl's resignation, Beirne, Perkins, and the rest of the board of directors all arrived at the same conclusion: Atalla would not permit a role for outside directors. The investments remained in place, but the board resigned en masse.

15. Go Fast or Go Home

In January 1999, in the midst of a major remodeling of Benchmark's offices—transforming them from once-posh back to posh—Louis Borders paid a visit. He and the five Benchmark partners squeezed into a small office that served as a temporary conference room, twisting their chairs this way and that so that the door could be closed.

"We haven't seen you since we visited the facility," Kevin Harvey said welcomingly as Borders took his seat. "That was unbelievable."

"Right place, at the right time, huh?" Borders said. "That was a big investment a year and a half ago, but now it makes a lot of sense. Then, it was kind of crazy."

The validation that Borders referred to did not come from Webvan's balance sheet. The distribution facility was still incomplete, and the company would not launch its service for another six months. But one could see signs everywhere externally, after strong e-commerce sales in the just-concluded holiday season, that consumers were becoming increasingly comfortable ordering goods on the Web.

The growing popular acceptance of online buying had not gone unnoticed in the stock market. Investors' appetite for Amazon, which had succeeded in shaking its books-only origins when it added music and video sales, seemed insatiable. Its market cap had zoomed from $19 billion on Monday the week before to $25.6 billion the previous Friday (and shot to $30 billion that Monday, the day of Borders's visit).

Webvan was in good shape, Borders said. "We'll have eighty-five million dollars in the bank after this month, and really everything's paid for. So we're sitting unbelievably pretty."

In fact, now that work on the Oakland distribution center was nearing completion, Borders had decided to adopt a new strategy going forward, which he had already tested out on Dave Beirne—who was adamantly opposed. Borders had no legal obligation to obtain the Benchmark partners' blessing; he was there simply to hear what they, with their experience, thought of his newest inspiration.

"We think our business model is great," said Borders, who always used the first-person plural when he referred to himself. "But there's a way to build throughout the United States, for seventy-five to eighty percent of the United States, within one year, and then go backfill with the more difficult groceries and fresh perishables and home-meal replacements, which is absolutely the endgame with this business, but it's hard to build and it's slow to build."

He passed around copies of a handout that had rows listing projected numbers of customers, revenue, and earnings, arranged in two columns. Column one represented the current plan, in which Webvan would build additional automated distribution centers like the first one in Oakland that would provide the full range of groceries and prepared foods directly to the home, and column two represented projections if Webvan were to build immediately an "ambient" distribution center—that is, a warehouse without refrigerators or freezers, that could ship out via freight carriers nonperishable grocery items and a full range of other consumer products to small neighborhood depots that Webvan would build in cities across the entire United States, where Webvan's own delivery trucks would complete the "last mile to the home" as Borders liked to say.

Everyone stared intently at the numbers.

"What kind of products do I order from column two?" Andy Rachleff asked Borders. "I understand what we order from column one."

"Media products. Electronics. Higher-ticket, no heavy food items—no low-priced food items. General merchandise."

"So we think of column two as Amazon, delivered? Books? Movies?"

"General merchandise," Borders repeated, without being pinned down to specifics. The actual product mix was not important. The question, to him, was how Webvan could acquire customers more quickly than it would if it built out distribution centers like the one in Oakland, each one of which would only serve about forty thousand customers, "which is kind of like zero in the Internet space."

Rachleff was puzzled, however. "So if I'm a customer in column two, why am I using Webvan versus a catalog or somebody else or an existing website?"

"It still goes back to my belief—people will want *one* person coming to their door. And the reason you would do that is because it's many products into one tote. So it's one vendor. Just like businesses want to go to fewer vendors. And the scheduling is going to be extremely convenient to the customer."

"But isn't FedEx convenient 'cause they'll just leave it on your door?"

"Well, sometimes. But then you have to go and sign for it; it's a total hassle. You have to call 'em and track it down where it is. And then returns is a big problem that people have."

"We buy a lot of stuff at home via the Web, from a lot of different vendors," Rachleff said. "And I guess I don't see the impracticality of that. UPS delivering CDs and books from Amazon and something else from eBay and something else from somebody else. I don't see the inconvenience of having multiple people deliver, or therefore the benefit of having one person deliver everything. As a consumer—as mother-in-law research—I just don't get that. I get column one, incredibly. I don't get column two."

What column two—one warehouse with nonrefrigerated goods serving the entire country—was all about could be summed up in one word: Amazon. This came out as Borders defended his plans. "Should we fold up tent because Amazon's out there ahead of us? We should go *after* them; they have the right business plan. We have the last mile."

"I had thought," Kevin Harvey said, "the idea was offer groceries and high-frequency things to your home, and then evolve into offering these less-frequent SKUs 'cause that's real easy for you to handle."

"That's what today's current plan is," Beirne said.

"What's wrong with that one?" asked Harvey.

"Too few customers," Borders answered.

Bob Kagle had a question for Borders. "Are you worried at all, Louis, about the service *dis*advantage you're going to live under with the ambient model? If I can find some dedicated merchant and know that I can get same-day or next-day or two-day air out of them, why would I be willing to live with this land-based solution? There'd have to be some compelling reason."

"In urban environments, FedEx doesn't leave things on the doorsteps of urban environments. So the scheduling is one thing. And instant returns."

"I think the negatives far outweigh the positives in doing this," Beirne said. "I think we should stick to Webvan today, get to five major markets, and then go national."

The interest in trucking goods cross-country from one centralized warehouse quickly faded.

"As I think about one vendor, why isn't that FedEx?" Harvey asked.

Borders's manner of speaking was calm and slow, almost without affect, and he explained his position without defensiveness. "If fifty percent of retail is going to be on the Internet within ten years, which I think it is, then that's going to be an awesome number. And customers are not going to be getting eight and ten packages a week, they're just not going to put up with that. The paper and cardboard and the tracking and the calling up. FedEx bringing four packages from four different vendors is not going to be a solution. Think of the volume that FedEx is doing now and multiply by about twenty, in terms of cubic volume."

"It would seem to me that FedEx has so much plane infrastructure out there," Harvey said, wondering how Webvan could begin to compete. "If I'm FedEx right now, I put together an e-commerce offering to get a little bit of return mechanism, maybe even go to some cached warehouses of some kind. But that seems easy. It seems to take them from where they are to where they need to be to do this isn't that much. But they're nowhere near able to pursue the competitive-to-Safeway business."

Harvey reasoned that Webvan faced a choice: owning fewer customers, who shopped more frequently, or more customers, who shopped less frequently, and the strongest base of customers to have would be the former group. Product lines could be added in the future; Webvan's customers would avail themselves of whatever else Webvan chose to offer simply because of convenience.

"We buy all our CDs and games and stuff like that at Price Club," Harvey said, "just 'cause of convenience." A frequent customer was much more valuable than an infrequent customer.

Beirne agreed. "When we expand the Webvan offering, configured today, to more like Wal-Mart than just grocery-drug to begin with, we'll crush anyone in our way. 'Cause we'll own that customer."

"It may be kind of late, though." Borders would not back down. "I think we may be too late to compete with Amazon nationally right now anyway. They have a twenty-five-billion-dollar market cap. They are on a *roll*. I don't think we bring anything [with an ambient warehouse] that is that much more to the consumer than they do."

Like a five-person wrestling tag team, but without prior rehearsal, each of the Benchmark partners took a turn trying to pin the phantom of instant national delivery to the mat. It was Dunlevie's turn. "Louis, you and I had lunch a couple months ago and talked a little bit about this. I think Webvan done right, in the local community, wins. I can't think of anything that can compete with it."

Beirne had a sudden thought: Would there be a way, he wondered aloud, of starting a companion business that would provide scheduled home delivery for Amazon, Microsoft, Yahoo, AOL, and other e-tailers?

"Amazon is not going to be your partner in this," Dunlevie said.

"But they may," Beirne insisted. "Amazon to your door? They can't do Amazon to your door."

"Amazon to my door is the way it works now."

"But not delivered by someone that represents the company with a call center that's handled by the company, that handles all your returns, scheduled delivery."

"I'm not buying it. I'm just not buying it. I have yet to return anything to Amazon. They do order consolidation. And they deliver it when I'm not there, which is the way I want it."

"You've got to be a top one percent user of Amazon, probably," Beirne said. Not only was Dunlevie a frequent buyer, voracious reader, and avid logophile, his partners maintained a standing joke that they all were Dunlevie's opposite—gum-chewing illiterates who struggled through *Sports Illustrated*. A few weeks earlier, Bob Kagle, handing Dunlevie a Christmas gift, a reprint of *Colonel Hawker's Shooting Diaries,* had said, "The way I picked this book is, on the first page, there were sixteen words that I did not know." And Beirne had quickly quipped, "That means there are sixty-four that I don't know." (Kagle had also presented Dave Beirne with Tom Wolfe's *A Man in Full,* with the inscription "Thanks for your courage.")

If Webvan hewed to its current start-with-groceries strategy, Borders pointed out—and if everything went smoothly and Webvan was lucky—then in four years, the company would have a grand total of one million customers, a paltry number.

"But we'll own them forever," Beirne said. "And no one else can offer what we offer."

Dunlevie wondered, "What's that? A fifty-billion-dollar-revenue company?"

"If we have a great success," Borders said, "we'll be a five-billion-dollar company in four years. But we'll be a nonplayer on the Internet."

Andy Rachleff laughed. "It's a shame you don't think big, Louis."

Beirne had a new suggestion: going back to Borders's own aggressive timetable of building clones of the distribution center in Oakland, launching the construction of a new center each month. That plan would make Webvan a $10 billion–revenue company in five years.

"And wildly profitable," Beirne said, growing more animated as he envisioned its reach. "We own national at that point. We're in every major market. We're the biggest e-commerce company there is. And because we own a new space all by ourselves that no one can compete with, the valuation on that business, guys . . ." He left the sentence unfinished.

"The problem with that is we'd have two million customers." Borders remained unimpressed. "I think someone will run over us if we only have two million customers."

Beirne and Kagle asked simultaneously: "How?"

"Amazon will have forty million customers in five years."

"But they won't have them," said Beirne. "We could take them."

Rachleff asked, "How can someone else build the service? Who's going to build the facilities to have the equivalent number of customers that you do?"

"I don't want to be left with the food buying," Borders said, without answering the question. "'Cause the food part is like a Trojan horse."

"But once you've got the food, you're going to hollow out all the other guys."

Borders paused for a moment and considered, "No one's ever built a ten-billion-dollar company in five years."

"Even close," Rachleff agreed.

"Even close," Borders repeated. "So that's a gargantuan challenge."

"Being differentiated will give you access to capital that you won't have if you're competitive," Harvey said, offering still another argument why Webvan should not change course.

"How does Wal-Mart or Sears get into this business?" Rachleff asked. "It's going to be at least two years, from April, before they can have their first site."

"Wal-Mart will eventually offer a fortune to buy this company, and it will be probably too late," Beirne said. "If we can do the revenues we think we're going to do out of this business, as a first mover, in a totally new category—it's staggering. If Amazon is valued at twenty-five billion—"

"Twenty-seven billion," Dunlevie corrected, having just checked the latest quote before the meeting.

"Twenty-seven billion, with two hundred fifty million in a quarter? Fuck, we're going to blow them away!"

"I don't know of a business that has the competitive advantage of Webvan of the first column," Rachleff chimed in. "That's the thing that's so striking. And that's not the case in the second column."

"So it's your consensus, it's very clear, this is a bad strategy?" Borders asked.

"Well," Dunlevie answered, "part of what you're hearing from us is generic. It's a knee-jerk reaction to the fact that we've been on the boards of hundreds of small companies, and the ones that focus, statistically, win at a much higher rate than the ones that try to do two or three things at once. So, no matter what the second idea was, you'd have that bias coming in. But I think you're also hearing that we are *so* excited about the Webvan idea. It's highly differentiated; the value of a customer is going to be super higher, and it becomes an execution issue, 'cause nobody can compete with you, as Andy says—whereas the other kind of feels to me like something I already got, frankly. I don't mind getting two or three packages right now. When it gets to be forty, I'll worry about that. But most of the dollar volume I spend is on stuff I want to get from Webvan."

Borders neatened the papers in front of him, getting ready to go. "Okay! Message was very clear." He laughed a little bit.

"Food for thought," Kagle said, attempting to soften the unanimity of the partners' opposition to Borders's plans to change course.

Beirne was eager to let Borders know that his partners had not been coached about what to say to him. "As you know from this group, I came back and told them what the topic of conversation was, but I didn't tell them what to say, 'cause they wouldn't ever say what I told 'em to say."

Borders explained that he planned to take the question up with the board and make a final decision in a week or two.

"Louis, if you pull off just column one, it's going to be the most successful venture ever," Rachleff said.

"I'm worried that that's not true. I guess that's where it's all coming from."

"I think Louis is on the right issue, for sure," Harvey allowed. "I think you *do* have to service more customers in a faster time frame in the current plan. I just don't think this is the right way to solve it. That'd be my feedback."

"Okay, gentlemen, thanks for your time." Borders made ready to go, but the Benchmark guys wanted to leave him with words of encouragement, so the end was protracted.

"You can't understand how exciting this is," Rachleff said to Borders. "For us to say this is going to be the biggest—"

"You can do it!" Kagle added.

"Okay, gentlemen, thanks."

■

"Man, does he think big!" Rachleff said admiringly of Borders, after he had departed.

"He's way smarter than I ever thought he was," Harvey added.

"This guy is *smart*," Beirne said. "But I tell you—remember the discussion that started when we financed the thing? We're back to it. Just because it's big doesn't mean it's a good idea."

"Boy, he's not necessarily off it, either," said Rachleff.

"Oh, no," Beirne agreed. Borders had arrived saying, in effect, "We're doing it!" and had left without indicating a change in position.

"We had very little impact," said Harvey.

"You've got to come up with an alternative way for him to solve his customer problem," reasoned Kagle.

"We convinced ourselves immensely," Harvey said, laughing at himself and his partners. "He was, like, 'Thank you for your input.'"

"I think he was kind of hoping you guys were going to agree with him so that I would shut up," Beirne said. "Do Myers-Briggs on him, he's a total introvert. Takes the data, walks around the block, maybe even for three days, and then comes back with the answer."

"He was taking notes on the good points," Kagle observed.

"What was interesting there is managing the relationship," Beirne said. "It's been such a positive experience, but there have been so many times that it gets to the borderline where I know I'm really pushing him. And you don't want to turn it off, you don't want him not calling anymore."

"Funny thing," Harvey said. "He's thought through very well why he wants to do something other than option A. But he's not thought through option B well at all." Maybe it was Amazon's market cap that had distorted his thinking.

Bob Kagle didn't think so. "I think he's worried about being pre-empted by some other approach."

"Sure he is," Beirne explained. "Wal-Mart's one of the biggest companies in the *world*. They put their sights on this, we've got a megacompetitor."

"You think that's likely to happen?"

"Yes. Totally. And if I'm Amazon and hear about this business, I come down and buy it right away. Think about it. This is the biggest risk to Amazon."

"I don't believe any of these are game-over strategies," Harvey said. "I think they'll all continue to do well."

The more that Beirne talked about it, the more critical he was of

Borders's wish to shift to a national warehouse of nonperishable goods. This was worse than Borders's original idea to have cafés as part of the neighborhood depots. "I hate this that much more. I think we're just going to screw it up. We're going to sit there with this service here [in Oakland] that works, that people are going to love, and not have expanded it."

"Boy, the order of the day is to just get that first one to work," said Dunlevie.

■

During the previous year, Louis Borders had checked in with Beirne almost every day. Now he hadn't called for a week. Perhaps, Beirne thought, he had pushed Borders too hard, and instead of seeing Beirne's partners as well-intentioned voices of experience, Borders instead had seen them as defensive tackles, piling on. Moreover, when Borders learned that the two other outside Webvan directors, Sequoia's Mike Moritz and e-Trade's Christos Cotsakos, agreed with the Benchmark partners that he should focus on the home-delivered-groceries strategy for the moment, Borders must have concluded that Beirne had rallied all parties to oppose his new idea.

Beirne felt ill. All the goodwill, all the close consulting had evaporated. He set up a dinner with Borders to talk things over, and then Borders sent word that he couldn't make it. Now what should Beirne do? Let time pass and hope Borders would get over his upset, or try to talk it out with him?

Beirne couldn't wait. "Louis, I need to have a conversation. Just Louis and Dave. Because I can't sleep. I love ya, I've enjoyed working with you as much as I've ever enjoyed working with anybody. We're now building one of the most important companies I think there is. I think relationships are all about communication. I want to apologize 'cause I think I've pushed you too far. And if I have, I'd like to get together and just make sure we're all on the same page, because I'm going to continue to throw myself on the tracks over this one. But I've promised you from the first day I met you that if we as a board agree to something, you get my one hundred and ten percent support."

Borders said he didn't know what Beirne was talking about— Beirne had worked himself into a state for no reason. "Hey, Dave, I don't think this relationship is even close to damaged. I think it just gets better. In my past company, I didn't have any board members. I had no one like you. You've kicked my ass from the first day I met you. And I love it. I want you to do more of it, because it makes me smarter, it makes us hone our plan even better. This company is a much better place because of the drive you've put into me. Please continue."

16. One Monkey
Don't Make No Show

Assembled at a lodge on the Pacific for the company's first all-hands off-site meeting, eBay's entire workforce—just 130 souls—took up only a small portion of space. It was remarkable how this tiny, young company—young in all respects, but especially in terms of the median age of the gathered employees—could have commanded the financial world's attention the way it had two weeks previously.

Later, critics of the company would sneer at the company's earnest talk about "the eBaysian way" or "eBaysian values," phrases that were much in evidence that day. If one were so inclined, one could draw a parallel between the church retreats of seventy years before in the same lodge and the eBay retreat in 1998. But the two were not really alike; the eBay crowd, even at its most earnest, brought along lots of irony, too. When Jeff Skoll led the company in "The Vision Song," to the tune of the *Flintstones* theme, it was postmodernist silliness. It was what kept the parts of eBay's belief in the world-changing aspects of person-to-person online trading ("capitalism for the rest of us") from sounding too cloying.

Omidyar read to the group one of the many "Dear Pierre" letters that he received from eBay users who were now making a living by selling items on eBay ("Hello from Indiana . . . You've made our life so much better, and I just cannot thank you enough"), and the group applauded for a long time. Steve Westly, eBay's vice president of marketing, who had joined from WhoWhere after eBay had gotten funding from Benchmark the previous year, stood up and with Old Testament fire preached against the false idolatry of "market cap."

At that point, the group was subdivided into three small groups to generate specific discussions about improving communications, respect, and morale, an agenda that brought on rapid onset of Dilbertian boredom. Animation disappeared from faces. Not all aspects of life in eBay were different from those in the rest of the organizational world.

When everyone gathered again as one group, energy returned. The program was turned over to Burning Questions. One could ask any question—absolutely any question—of anybody, and then that person got to ask the next one. The first question went to Omidyar. What *did* the name eBay stand for? Before Omidyar was permitted to answer, the moderator asked the audience to try to guess the answer.

"Echobay."

"Electronics Bay Area."

"E-commerce for the Bay."

"Pig Latin for 'b.' "

Omidyar looked down at his shoes, smiling, then looked back up. "I'm really embarrassed. We have two answers to that question. One is the official answer. And the other is the real answer." The audience laughed. "The official answer is eBay is Electronics Bay; we grew up here in the Bay Area and like to think about it as the Electronics Bay." But the real answer was that he had started with Echo Bay. "Why was it Echo Bay? 'Cause I thought it sounded cool." But when he went to register the domain name, "echobay.com" was already taken. "So I said, 'Gee, how about a shorter form of that? Why don't we just make it eBay?' "

Omidyar, exercising his right to ask the next Burning Question, turned to Westly, who his colleagues knew was an active Democrat who had once run for the party's state chairmanship. "Steve, what I'm dying to know is, When does the race for the governor of California kick off for you?"

Westly never lost an opportunity to exhort the troops to redouble their efforts, so he answered by declaring, "When the team here gets the stock to a hundred dollars"—a number that was three times its current price—"I'm running for governor." This was greeted with laughter and applause for his cleverness in dodging the question. There was no way, even if every single one of them were to devote every cell of their being to the task, that they could move the stock up an incline to such an unthinkable place.

■

The headiness of that first day of the IPO had been replaced by guilt for having toted up paper wealth—which was evaporating with alarming speed. EBay's stock, originally priced at $18 a share and closing on that first day above $47, had subsequently slipped. The day before the retreat, it had closed at $36; the day after, it slipped below $30. It was a good thing that it had not been repriced higher on the eve of the offering, after all. Perhaps the stock would slip below its offering price.

Pierre Omidyar had tried to prepare everyone for the worst in advance. Before the IPO, when he and Whitman rehearsed the road show in front of all of eBay's employees, he had begun by saying, Let me tell you what we're about to enter here: financial markets that are incredibly volatile. He showed slides that illustrated the volatility of Yahoo's and Amazon's stock. In the month of June, Yahoo's market cap had jumped by $4 billion. Do you think Yahoo was actually a really different company on June 30 than it was June 1? Probably not. He showed some stocks that had tanked. Here, too, the lesson to be drawn was, these companies were also unlikely to have been all that different at the time they hit bottom from before, when their stock was doing well. Don't get crazed about the stock market. Let's keep our heads down, staying focused on building a great company.

Now, when eBay's stock had plunged almost 40 percent, Omidyar gathered the employees together again and said, Remember what we told you? Who thinks the company is any different now than when it was at forty-eight? Put your head down and focus. That's what we do for a living.

Mid-October turned out to be the low. Muzzled by rules intended to prevent hyping of new issues, the analysts who worked for eBay's underwriters had been forbidden from commenting on the company, but on October 26 the blackout expired. Jamie Kiggen, an analyst with Donaldson, Lufkin & Jenrette, got attention for posting a six-to-twelve-month target price of $100. That day the price jumped almost 50 percent, from $50 to $73 on that news alone.

The few number of shares circulating intensified the trading activity. Only 3.5 million shares, or 10 percent, were in the hands of the public; in the two days in which the price went up 65 percent, nearly 17 million shares changed hands. The demand was coming from institutional investors, what Bob Kagle referred to as "huge institutional appetite."

■

Benchmark Capital owned just a hair larger than one fifth of eBay after the IPO. Seventy percent of those shares would be distributed to its limited partners, but for the moment they remained in Benchmark's hands. Neither it nor the limiteds were permitted to sell until the expiration in four months of the "lock-up" period imposed by the underwriters. In the interim, the value of its eBay stake fluctuated with the market's whims; Benchmark enjoyed no sanctuary from the volatility.

On the Monday that Jamie Kiggen's price target was issued, the partners were caught by surprise as much as anybody. As they returned to the conference room after a bathroom break ("Bio-break!" someone would declare, bringing a halt to the meeting), Kevin Harvey arrived with news: "EBay's at sixty-nine!" It had closed at 50 on Friday.

"Holy Christ," said Dave Beirne.

"It goes up from here," said Bruce Dunlevie, a comment that would have been sardonic if made by someone other than the resident bull.

Harvey turned his voice to a Crazy Eddie high pitch: "It's insane! Up forty percent in a day. There must be some serious mo investors."

Andy Rachleff walked in. "Seventy-two! Marissa just told me. She keeps the watch."

"Can we sell now?" Beirne asked, drawing laughs.

"If you want to leave most of the money on the table, you can," Dunlevie said.

"Yeah, I'm a pussy." Beirne laughed too.

Kagle hadn't yet returned from the break; now Harvey said to the others in a stage whisper, "Bob says, 'Never, *ever* sell a share.' Well, Bob," he continued, as if Bob were present, "what if it's valued the same as, like, GM? Can we sell then?" Everyone laughed.

"If you're stupid," Dunlevie deadpanned.

■

The next day, on October 27, eBay announced better than expected quarterly earnings: $2 million excluding special charges. Investors, inured to red ink among the hottest Internet stocks, regarded $2 million as whopping. CFO Gary Bengier told analysts in a conference call that he thought a surge of traffic on the eBay site was attributable to the publicity surrounding the IPO. "We do not expect this unprecedented level of publicity to continue," he said.

But a virtuous cycle had begun. Publicity fed higher visibility and higher usage, which fed more publicity. The higher the stock climbed, the more free attention eBay received. At the end of October Whitman said that the boost in traffic that accompanied the stock run was much greater than the increase that came from the publicity accompanying the IPO.

When the stock closed at $82.50, the papers noted that Pierre Omidyar had become a billionaire on paper. It was not a milestone mentioned by him. He gathered the employees once again. Three weeks ago the stock was at $18, he said. Now we're at $82.50. It's just like what we said: It's really volatile. Don't get crazed. Don't go buy your Porsches, don't go buy your resort home. We've got to focus on the long term.

Keep your head down—and, he could have added, don't pay attention to the critics. *Barron's* published a harsh, dispassionate analysis under the headline "Wall Street's Love Affair with eBay Could Be a Fling, Not a Long-Term Romance." At $82.50, the company's market cap was $3.2 billion, high even by Internet standards—it was $1 billion more than Netscape's. It was triple the capitalization of Sotheby's and ten times that of auction pioneer Onsale. EBay's most recent quarterly revenues were $12.9 million, yet its market cap was equal to that of Times Mirror ($729 million revenues for the same quarter) or to the Dillard's department-store chain ($826 million). The article gave Jerry Kaplan the customary opportunity to get in a dig. "They've done a terrific job," he began diplomatically, but "justifying the current stock price is a different question."

Investors shrugged off the naysayers. By November 9, the stock had exceeded Kiggen's price target, closing at 103. Passing that milestone only whetted investors' appetite, and the next day it was at 131, almost double the price level that had provoked *Barron's* to outrage only the week before.

Others piled on. *Slate* writer James Surowiecki pointed out that eBay's price-to-sales ratio was 500 to 1, compared with Microsoft's 20 to 1, and asked rhetorically, "Speculative froth, anyone?" He was comparatively polite. In an attempt to be heard, other critics cranked up the volume. Christopher Byron, a columnist writing for msnbc.com, said eBay showed him the rules had changed so fundamentally that the game had ceased to have any meaning that he could understand:

> For someone who has covered the day-to-day events of Wall Street for 30 years now, there is, I must confess, something at once awful yet fascinating at bearing witness to a Goldman Sachs–underwritten stock that comes to market at $18 and within six weeks is selling for $126. It's like watching every mesmerizing, discombobulated absurdity you can possibly think of, all rolled into one colossal Ur-event— like watching Mark McGwire step up to the plate blindfolded and hit 400 home runs in a row.

EBay was "a company with trouble written all over it," Byron said. Barriers to entry in the Internet auction field were nonexistent. The good stuff that people wanted to sell would go to specialty sites, and eBay was going to be left only with junk. The underwriters were engaging in "full-frontal, right-in-your-face stock hyping." How else could they say, only six weeks earlier, that the price was worth $18 a share, and now say, Oops, we made a mistake, it's really worth $130. "I don't think so," said Byron.

The market agreed. It wasn't worth $130—it was worth more.

■

At the weekly executive staff meeting, Whitman said she did not want to convene still another employee meeting to remind everyone about the stock's volatility. If members of the executive staff spoke informally about it with the members of their respective departments, it would save her having to walk through the warnings again.

"I think it's okay to acknowledge we all have families who are all very excited—it's reasonable to be happy and enthusiastic," added Omidyar. "But you still have to do your job."

Steve Westly was pleased to report that his group was putting in long hours: Half a dozen had worked the previous evening until nine, and another three until eleven. Some members of Gary Bengier's staff had stayed until eleven-thirty. Westly did not ever want to see a slackening of pace; remember that *Red Herring* article, with photographs of Netscape's parking lot at night, pre- and post-IPO? Six months after the IPO, the place was empty.

"Oh, yeah. There's not chaos in the halls here," Whitman quickly said. She had not meant to imply that she thought people were slacking off.

But since the others had mentioned it, there was something else she wanted to say about the previous evening. As she had walked by a cubicle, she overheard an employee speaking with someone over the phone: "Yeah, yeah, yeah. I think the institutions are buying big, which is why the stock is going up." She recounted what she had done: She'd pointed her finger like a gun at the miscreant, getting his attention, then walked on without saying anything. "He probably thinks he's going to get fired today." Reinforce with everyone, for their own sake as well as the company's, she said, they cannot say anything—who, how, when—about the price.

■

The performance of venture capital funds is measured by the gains in the portfolio up until the moment that shares of a given company are distributed to the fund's investors. By November, it began to dawn on the Benchmark partners that if the market held until the time of distribution, eBay might become the all-time venture capital home run. They asked acquaintances at other firms what the previous record holder was. Given that funds do not publish their performance data, the record was arrived at anecdotally, not statistically. Kleiner's

@Home and Sequoia's Yahoo were the two that seemed to be the incumbent leaders. The best gain for a partnership was said to be $600 or $700 million. If eBay's trading price was anywhere north of $111 at the time of distribution, it would represent a billion-dollar gain for the partnership. This seemed wholly possible; it was well past $111, having reached $150.

On a gain of $1.5 billion, $1.05 billion of stock would be distributed to the limited partners, to sell or hold as they wished, and $450 million would be retained by Benchmark itself. Each partner's stake was about 18.5 percent, or more than $85 million each, for the single investment. All of the partners would split the gain equally.

Yet the Benchmark partners had discovered, ruefully, that the biggest venture win did not help them sleep better at night; perversely, it served only to intensify self-imposed pressure. No one wanted to be receiving more than his own companies' gains were contributing to the pot. This was most visible in Dave Beirne, the newest arrival and the one who was most open about the desire to pull his own weight, but Bruce Dunlevie, Kevin Harvey, and Andy Rachleff felt it, too.

Bob Kagle could not take much pleasure in the event either, imagining, as he did, whispers that the eBay success was a fluke, akin to picking up a winning lottery ticket. He found himself working all the harder after eBay, to silence criticism that he had not actually heard but that he could imagine, beyond his hearing. One monkey don't make no show, he'd say.

Of all the partners, Kagle was the least prepared to celebrate eBay's remarkable post-IPO run, steeped as he was in the history of financial manias. On November 23, as eBay stock hopped weightlessly upward still again, rising almost a third in value in one day, Kagle held his head and moaned. "This is mania. This is nuts." He called Howard Schultz, the founder of Starbucks, whom he had recruited to eBay's board for Schultz's expertise in building a brand. The two agreed that nothing good was going to come of this. New eBay employees would receive options based on the current stock price; how were they to remain motivated when the stock collapsed and the options were under water? "This is tulips in 1600!"

He got together with the other partners. Dave Beirne pointed out that if eBay stock were to still trade at a high number at the time of distribution, then Marissa Matusich, Kagle and Dunlevie's assistant who had worked with Kagle for ten years, would become a millionaire. "That's why she's out of her shoes over it."

"It would be really nice if we could somehow lock in some of the gains for the staff," Kagle said. "'Cause it's always that first million that matters. The first million is the biggest million you ever make."

He thought a moment. "You know, the stock could get cut by two thirds and it won't change any of our lives," he said, referring to the partners. But that wasn't the case for the staff. More reason to worry about the stock's price.

■

At the partners' meeting, the guys traded stories about how the stock mania had infected their own relatives.

Bob Kagle said his mother, the retired AC Spark Plug worker, had left him a phone message. He had given her his allotment of "friends-and-family" eBay stock that the underwriters provide to each of the principals in an IPO.

"She said, 'Yeah, this eBay—I'm thinking about selling some of it and putting it into Computer Literacy, which I hear today is going public at ten bucks a share. Why don't you call me and give me some advice on that.'"

"And eBay is the first stock she's ever owned?" Kevin Harvey asked.

"Right. So I said, 'Mom, can you answer a few questions for me? What are the quarterly revenues of Computer Literacy? What are the quarterly profits? Do you know anything about the senior management?' She said, 'I get the point.'" The others laughed.

Kagle continued, "The problem is in half of America, nobody is"—his voice shifted comically higher for emphasis—"asking those questions!"

"Get her into some day-trader sites," Bruce Dunlevie suggested helpfully.

"That's where my dad has gone," Harvey said, seriously. Harvey had given him his friends-and-family shares, which was the first stock he, a professor of mathematics, had ever owned. Harvey shifted into his father's voice, commenting on patterns he wanted his son to see in graphs of eBay's price movements.

Dunlevie said his wife "finally got going on eBay." She had asked that he pass on to Kagle the following: "She doesn't know how much stock we're going to get or anything, but she suspects we'll probably break even now that she's buying so much stuff."

She had no idea what the biggest venture gain in history would mean to the household finances. The others were amused by her lack of curiosity.

■

The run continued. A month later the stock was above 300, then fell back to 241 on the last day of the year. It was the best-performing IPO stock of the year, having gained 1,304 percent in a little more than three months.

In early 1999 it bounced wildly, falling to 181, then within a week zooming up to 303. The stock split three for one in early March and continued to rise so fast that the postsplit price resembled the presplit price. Closing at 171 in March was the equivalent, presplit, to 513—and a long, long way from 18 in September. Kagle had an extended talk with Whitman about preparing for when something "took the air out."

"What's it like recruiting when the stock price is so high?" Rachleff asked Kagle.

"Really hard." The options offered to new employees were certain to be valueless, as they would depend on the stock ascending still higher. "I mean, it's such a ridiculous level now. There *is* going to be a big fall here. So the question is sort of when and how."

Bruce Dunlevie laughed and scrunched his face up in an expression that seemed to indicate he did not regard what Kagle was saying with complete seriousness.

"You can laugh . . ." Kagle said.

"You said that a couple hundred points ago," Beirne reminded him. Kagle had cried wolf too many times during the run-up to have retained any credibility.

The eBay phenomenon rested on revenues and earnings that kept improving each quarter. On an absolute basis, the numbers remained puny, but on a relative basis, they positively glowed. The company had ended 1998 with a large jump in revenues, from $19.5 million the preceding quarter to almost $34 million; and earnings had almost quadrupled, to almost $6 million.

The stock surged in April, in anticipation of release of the first quarter's earnings. It reached the presplit equivalent of 628, then held there after the numbers were released and showed revenue growth and profitability had continued. The critics had expended all their ammunition a few months back, when the stock had produced apoplexy at one fourth its current value. What was left to say that had not already been said—and said too early, as it turned out?

EBay's executives were as frightened of an impending fall as Kagle was, but in addition they were superstitious, regarding even mention of the stock as a bad omen. On the day that happened to be the one in which eBay's stock passed the 200 milestone for the first time after the stock split, when Omidyar called for Kagle, Matusich had answered the phone and said, "Pierre! Two hundred! All right!" But Omidyar had sounded very ill at ease, stammering that everyone at his end had been in meetings and hadn't paid any attention.

The math was rather simple, however. Omidyar's holdings were worth $7.5 billion, and Whitman, on paper, was worth $1.4 billion. There was fine print, which stipulated that her options would not be fully vested for another three years. That said, having a stake that was worth, even momentarily, more than a billion dollars in a job she had only occupied for thirteen months made her what had to be the best-paid hired hand ever, anywhere.

The insatiable appetite for eBay stock had fattened Benchmark's own gains. It had had to delay distributing shares because of complications from a secondary stock offering; in the meantime, eBay's market capitalization brushed $26 billion when it hit 209. By April, at the time of a partial distribution, it had fallen back to 175, giving it a market cap of $21 billion. Benchmark's $5.1 billion share, after distribution to partners, would place $1.5 billion worth of stock into the pockets of the five general partners. Scott Herhold, who covered the venture capital industry for the *San Jose Mercury News*, wrote, "Even in the athletic world of Sand Hill Road, where venture capitalists like to boast about hitting home runs, Benchmark Capital's investment in eBay Inc. is a ball that has left the ballpark and is still bouncing down the street."

The run also had been good to the eBay Foundation, which Omidyar and Skoll had founded in mid-1998 with what became 321,000 shares, whose nominal value at the time of the IPO had been $1.8 million but by April had jumped to $56 million. The local paper suggested that the rest of Silicon Valley follow eBay's model. The company was credited with having "turned upside-down the assumption that philanthropy can only follow success, not lope along with it." If philanthropy were to lope along in step, however, its endowment was susceptible to immediately losing value if the company that was its benefactor hit a bad patch of weather.

17. Off the Dole

O n the day after eBay's IPO, when Pierre Omidyar, just back from
New York, stood on Benchmark's terrace, he observed that the
world had imputed strategic savvy to the company that it did not
really have. "Our system didn't scale," he said, "so we didn't grow big
enough to attract competition. Everybody thought we were flying
below the radar screen on purpose." He gave a little laugh.

Up until early summer 1998, eBay's primary competition was Jerry
Kaplan's Onsale Exchange, which had launched in October 1997 and
had failed to attract a critical mass. When Bob Kagle introduced eBay
to Benchmark's limited partners at the annual meeting in early June,
eBay had an 89 percent market share. Kagle said that the company
anticipated major entrants, but "we think they don't get it. We think
they don't understand all the stuff about the community and what's
really special and unique about this." He also noted that in addition
to first-mover advantage, economies of scale, and definitive selection
in the various categories, eBay also enjoyed another advantage: Users
faced high switching costs. "After you get this reputation built up online," Kagle explained, "you've got all these people who have dealt
with you, you've got seventy-five people who've said good things
about you. That's a pretty fundamental thing."

Nevertheless, the attractiveness of 85 percent gross margins made
the person-to-person auction business too irresistible for eBay to re-

main unchallenged. Kagle and eBay's executives had long discussions about preparing for the arrival of entrants who would be much larger than eBay.

In June, Excite launched its site, Classifieds 2000. It was a scare, but after a month Kagle told his partners, "Excite? Nowhere. No traction. Three thousand listings, and going down."

One potential entrant was Yahoo, which eBay, anticipating this, had approached about a possible joint pact. But Yahoo, standing on top of the Internet world, was not interested in sharing equally with a pipsqueak like eBay, and brushed it off.

Amazon was another potential entrant, and eBay had sought to avert competition from that quarter, too. In August eBay had proposed to Amazon that the two companies jointly offer links to used-book auctions, cobranded on both sites. The Amazon board had been receptive and invited a delegation from eBay to come up to Seattle and present a proposal to Amazon chief Jeff Bezos and senior executives. EBay executives flew up and thought a deal could be hammered out. Kagle told his partners what eBay said to Amazon: Your customers win, our customers win, we'll do it 50/50, but the traffic is higher on your site, and you'll get more customers out of it than we will. Let's go do this!

Bezos said, Pssssssshhhh. This is too strategic. We're going to crush you. And we're going to figure out how to get Yahoo and Microsoft and us together to crush you.

To permit the image to sink in, Kagle fell silent for a moment, and everyone was quiet for a few moments.

"Meow," Beirne said, cracking everyone up. "Nice visitin' ya!"

Kagle shook his head in consternation. "We spent a lot of time figuring out exactly what was the win-win scenario, right? They didn't want any part of it."

■

Nothing more was heard out of Seattle the next month, but Yahoo soon joined the battle with eBay on its own. This constituted the sharpest challenge eBay had ever faced.

Yahoo's entrance was frightening because it had massive traffic, 28 million captive eyeballs a month to expose to its own auction advertisements—and it was willing to offer listings for free, in order to prime the pump. It seemed as if Yahoo was willing to pay whatever opportunity cost it had to in order to promote its auctions because Yahoo had figured out that moving from an advertising-based business model to a model based on e-commerce transactions was a matter of the utmost strategic urgency. Whatever it took, whatever the cost, Yahoo seemed determined to make auctions work.

Fellow eBay board member Scott Cook told Kagle that he couldn't recall ever being in a situation before where there were so few possible responses to a competitive threat. EBay could not match Yahoo in offering free listings; listing fees composed almost the entirety of eBay's revenues. Only 1 percent came from advertising, and that was deliberate, a result of Omidyar's championing doing the right thing and not putting irritating banner ads in the faces of users. Kagle had sung Omidyar's praises to anyone who would listen; when eBay had 250 million page views a month and could have easily quintupled its revenues by welcoming banner advertising, Omidyar had made sure that the company had not, in Kagle's words, become "greedy and screw this thing up." But now, with Yahoo giving its listings away for free, eBay was in a tight spot. It could redouble its work marketing to particular collectible communities, areas that required specialized expertise that Yahoo was unlikely to be able to assemble quickly. But other than that, there weren't many levers for eBay to pull.

Kagle tried to come up with more ideas. How about tracking the rate at which Yahoo auctions were completed, he suggested.

"We're already doing that," Jeff Skoll said. Assuming that at least one bid would make a given auction successful, eBay's tracking of Yahoo's auctions showed that only about 18 percent were being completed, compared to 70 percent of eBay's. Skoll took little solace in Yahoo's low completion rate. "They're smart, and they're going to figure things out."

Kagle thought Yahoo would soon be ready to sit down to talk about working with eBay instead of against it. "We should wait until they have enough experience to have figured some things out—but before they've had success—and go back to them, eat some crow, and have another discussion."

Kagle and Meg Whitman talked about the possibility of getting Yahoo to sit down and talk. The number of listings Yahoo had remained paltry compared with eBay's, and its completion rate never climbed upward, but Yahoo never signaled a willingness to talk. It persevered on its own. EBay did get a compliment paid by Yahoo's Jerry Yang, though: "I think they've taken a concept that most people didn't really understand, including ourselves, and executed in almost every way perfectly."

Fortunately for eBay, AOL, another juggernaut, did not choose to add its own auctions; it was content to sign an agreement in early 1999 in which eBay promised to fork over $75 million over four years in what was described as a "traffic deal," giving eBay a "prominent presence" on its sites and an agreed-upon number of page views. But the arrangement could also be described as something else, closer to a perfectly legal protection racket—with a $75 million payment, AOL agreed not to get into the auction business itself, so that was the price eBay had to pay in order to prevent something bad happening to its fine establishment. Considering its vulnerability—eBay only had 2 million registered users versus AOL's 16 million—eBay actually got a bargain for its money.

■

Danny Shader, thirty-seven, was a great business-development guy, the person who did deals with other companies. He had done the deals for Collabra, a software company that Bruce Dunlevie had backed when he was at Merrill Pickard, and for Netscape after it acquired Collabra. When he told Dunlevie in the spring of 1998 that he was planning to leave Netscape, Dunlevie suggested that he become eBay's biz-dev guy. If he had joined eBay then, six months before eBay's IPO, he would have gone from being a mere millionaire to a multimillionaire within the year, and he would have been the person in the middle of the talks between eBay, AOL, Yahoo, and Amazon. But he did not want to join someone else's company; he wanted to start his own. What it would do exactly, he had not figured out. But Benchmark was eager to host him while he sorted out potential ideas, and so too was Kleiner Perkins. So when he left Netscape he became an entrepreneur in residence at two venture firms simultaneously.

There is no single form of charisma, that ineffable quality that draws in others. One variant, which Dave Beirne possessed, involves projection of physical power. Another, Danny Shader's, was based on being the nicest extremely smart person you can remember meeting, someone who inside of thirty seconds effortlessly gets strangers to open up and talk, while he nods with an expression of interest on his face that says, This is fascinating! He also had experience and business sense that was not expected of entrepreneurs in residence. When Shader walked by an office doorway, a Benchmark partner would wave him in, show him a deal that was being mulled over, and get Shader's thoughts; he could tote up pluses and minuses in a business plan quickly and acutely. The partners enjoyed having him around; so did the administrative assistants. Everyone loved Danny.

So the Benchmark partners were especially pained to see Shader struggle in his quest to come up with a viable idea for his own start-up. He would take up an idea, get excited, dig into research, then two weeks later discover it was hopelessly flawed—or have a Benchmark partner point out that it was a dead end. As soon as he'd discard one idea, he'd find another, wholly different one and run with it for another two weeks, with the same dismaying end result. Months passed in this manner.

One of the more exotic ideas was a business to be built on what Shader called "industrial DNA." Drawing on recent research advances in materials science, the business would sell to overseas parts suppliers unique identifying tags with molecular signatures that could not be counterfeited and that would attest to the authenticity of the parts' origins. In a week Shader became an authority on the problem of shoddy imports in the auto-parts industry, but Bruce Dunlevie, who was the first line of review, was unable to see the business potential of industrial DNA, and it too died on the vine.

One day, out of Shader's hearing, Bob Kagle told Kevin Harvey, "This may be because I've got weird data points or something, but Danny seems to be an incredibly clearer thinker about other businesses than he does about the ones he's looking at prosecuting. It's the weirdest thing to me. Whenever he's looking at some other deal, I'm getting tons of insights out of him."

"You kind of have to be that way to get something goin'," Harvey said, thinking back to his own experiences as a software entrepreneur. "That's why guys who are too-critical thinkers have a tough time getting the business started, 'cause 'it was never possible.' "

After going through an adrenaline rush and postrush crash on the twelfth or so idea, Shader was not his usual ebullient self. He complained to Harvey, "I feel like I'm a ward of the state"—referring to the $10,000 a month that Benchmark paid its entrepreneurs in residence. "How do I get off the dole here and start earning my keep?"

His sponsor, Bruce Dunlevie, was not concerned. "Let it drift awhile," he told Shader. "Maybe there's a fish down there somewhere." Dunlevie was right: Shader found what he'd been looking for, and as it happened, it was an idea that would be of great interest to eBay, too, whom he took it to for its blessing before presenting the idea to the other Benchmark partners. EBay did not merely like Shader's idea; it wanted to coinvest.

In mid-September, Shader was given a slot in the weekly partners' meeting. Only Dunlevie and Kagle knew what he had finally come up with. When he came in midmeeting to begin his presentation, he was given an affectionate welcome that only a family member would receive—teasing that began before he even opened his mouth.

Dave Beirne: "As Don Valentine would say right now, 'Why the fuck should I give you any money?' "

Shader, without waiting a beat, shouted out, "Because we're going to enable about sixteen billion dollars' worth of transactions to occur."

That was good. That was very good!

Holding a pen as if ready to write a check on the spot, Kevin Harvey asked him, "How much money do you want?"

Shader smiled and launched what the partners would later say admiringly was one of the best presentations they'd ever heard. EBay had a problem, and Danny Shader proposed a solution. The average value of items sold at eBay was $40; this was true when items were sold for a fixed price on Internet bulletin boards, too. "There's something about forty bucks," Shader argued, "that has to do with the fact that's the price above which you start getting nervous about lack of recourse." He proposed a business that would provide eBay traders with escrow and payment services—"a branded infrastructure for safe and convenient person-to-person commerce." It would make people comfortable putting up more valuable items for sale; it would greatly increase eBay's revenues, since its listing fees were tied to the value of the items sold; and it would solve a nagging problem—eBay was not getting paid for 2.5 percent of completed auctions, a problem that, given eBay's high margins, would mean, if solved, a big boost to earnings.

The proposed new company would eventually be called Accept.com. Shader explained that in offering escrow service, his company would temporarily hold on to the money that a buyer sent in until the buyer had received and formally accepted the goods.

"Awesome cash implications of that," Harvey said. "The float!"

"That's an Aha!-*less* moment," Dunlevie corrected. The others laughed. "That's exactly what I said last week. Tell him."

Shader's associate explained, "With escrow regulations, you have to put all the money into a non-interest-bearing account 'cause you have to be essentially the neutral party."

Harvey got excited again when Shader explained Accept's plans to take in credit card payments.

Bob Kagle, mimicking Kevin Harvey's jokey mantra of understatement—"this Internet thing could be big"—told everyone his own insight: "This credit card thing could be big!" The others laughed. "The way I see this is," Harvey continued in the same spirit, "credit cards"—he drew a large circle in the air, then he drew another, "Internet." Combined? "Big!"

After Shader and his associate left, the Benchmark guys marveled at how far Shader had come with this newest idea after stumbling with so many duds.

"I lost steam on him when he was going through fifteen different things," Harvey said.

Dunlevie broke in to confess that he too had felt some weariness when Shader was investigating his fourteenth deal.

Harvey said he had regained steam seeing the way that, through all the twists over the months, Shader "got a bunch of guys to follow him around. Showed a lot of leadership."

"He's made some very tough decisions here, too," Dunlevie pointed out. Six weeks earlier Shader had told the associates of an existing escrow-on-the-Internet start-up that would be folded into Accept, "I'll take provisional control of the business. I won't join the company. I'll take responsibility for putting the plan together. And *if* we decide there's a business, and I can get it financed, then I'll join the company. But I want you to fire four guys now."

Hearing that, Beirne was impressed. "I was going to say he's got the talent to recruit; his passion will get him great people. His issue, I thought—until hearing that—would be, Is he tough enough? Is he really going to be able to make the hard decisions?"

Harvey said of the Accept deal, using the partners' ten-point ranking scale: "On escrow, I'm a 5; on credit cards, I'm 8."

"Yeah," Kagle concurred. "That makes it a totally different deal. EBay will love that."

Dunlevie, the Accept advocate, declared his vote on the deal was 7, and passed out strips of paper, which were quickly filled out and returned.

"Seven or above from everybody." Deals never received such uniformly high votes. "That's scary."

That afternoon, Shader went up the street to present to the partners at Kleiner Perkins. The next day he was back in the Benchmark office, reporting that he had expected the Kleiner partners to bare their fangs and "dog pile," but they had been pussycats. The only concern they had registered was that this would "only" be a hundred-million-dollar business. Shader laughed. "A hundred-million-dollar business seems substantial to me."

Swiftly, in October, Accept received $5.2 million in equity financing, at $5.1 million pre-. Danny Shader was the CEO and had Benchmark *and* Kleiner Perkins as his venture backers, each receiving 20 percent stakes. *And* his company was poised to make eBay, which had its IPO while Accept was being formally set up, even more successful than it already was. For Benchmark, this was going to be a double win.

But the relief that the Benchmark guys had felt when Shader had come up with a good idea had blinded them to the complications that lay beneath the surface. When the idea for Accept had been pitched to Meg Whitman, she was in the midst of the road show. She wasn't able to give it attention until after the IPO and the distractions that followed had abated, and eBay did not turn out to be a coinvestor— Benchmark and Kleiner Perkins had balked at eBay's wish to invest at a 50 percent discount to what they themselves were paying.

A week after the IPO, when Whitman took a second look at Accept, she was unhappy with what she saw and she unloaded on Bob Kagle. "If we're eighty percent of the revenue sources for this business for the next two or three years, I don't understand why this is an independent company. Help me understand why this is an independent company."

"Look, Meg," he said, "you need to dial the terms and conditions of this deal so that you feel like it's fair for both companies. That's the only advice I can give you here."

While Kagle reported to the partners Meg Whitman's perspective, Dunlevie had Danny Shader's, who was extremely frustrated that Whitman was now insisting that Accept agree to work exclusively with eBay. "Danny's perspective is that after the fifth time that she said 'We have to have an exclusive,' he had said, 'I'm not sure we're an independent company if you have an exclusive.' "

Kagle came to eBay's defense. "I think it mostly does stem from the fact that some of these elements [like credit card payments and shipping services] are strategic to them."

Dunlevie returned to speculating on the psychology of eBay's executives, which he believed was the real obstacle in Accept landing the deal it needed with eBay. "It's hard, psychologically; in the flush of this IPO, you tend to conclude that you're worth a hundred million because of your indomitability, prescience, and omniscience, and every guy that comes through the door now is a knucklehead. It's not a unique phenomenon."

Kagle frowned. "I didn't hear any of that. I would say that she's thinking about it rationally."

"Danny said that that meeting was one hundred and forty degrees different than the ones he had before the company was public. It's human nature, right?"

As a conciliatory offering, Kevin Harvey said, "It sounds like the opening salvo of a negotiation on both sides."

■

The negotiations between Accept and eBay dragged on for weeks, and within the partnership, Dunlevie and Kagle, maintaining gentlemanly tact, pressed upon the other the viewpoint of their respective portfolio companies. Dunlevie had dinner with Pierre Omidyar, after which Kagle saw in Omidyar a receptiveness to Accept that had not been there before. But Whitman remained, in his word, "spooked." He spoke with her over the weekend.

Whitman had suspicions about Accept.

"Meg, what would that be?" Kagle asked gently.

"I don't know. But every time I've been in these situations, I haven't trusted my gut and I've learned to regret it."

Kagle did not push her any further. Experience told him that for a merger to work, the chemistry had to be just right. "No shotgun weddings," he had always promised entrepreneurs before they signed the Benchmark term sheet.

Meg Whitman turned over the negotiations to eBay's business-development group, and meeting every third day, the subordinates made progress.

Dunlevie reported to his partners that eBay was still heaping on "a lot of 'I know this doesn't make sense, but I want it anyway' conditions. They're fussy."

Harvey, thinking about what eBay's market cap meant to the partnership's portfolio, jokingly interrupted: "I think they're awesome!"

Dunlevie continued, "I just keep telling Danny to do whatever eBay says."

A month slipped by, then another one, and still no deal. Now Kagle was pessimistic about a deal so "long in the tooth" being completed. EBay was making noises about buying another company, i-Escrow, instead of doing a business deal with Accept.

To Dave Beirne, the answer then was for eBay to simply buy Accept. He asked his partners, "What do you think they'd sell this company for?"

"Emotionally, probably eighty to one hundred," said Rachleff. There was no wholly objective way to arrive at a value of any early-stage company, but in this case the emotions of Shader and several of the people he had recruited, who, like him, had passed up shots at senior executive positions at eBay and, as luck would have it, options that had turned out to be worth multiple millions of dollars, made it all the more difficult for the entrepreneurs to see their own start-up as worth anything less than a very large number—like $100 million.

"Yeah, I'd say a hundred," agreed Beirne.

"Which is hard to justify given that—" began Rachleff, before Beirne cut him off.

"It *is* strategic for eBay. Big-time." It was almost more important that Accept *not* serve Yahoo, whose auction site had very poor customer satisfaction, than that Accept serve eBay. Purchasing it was the only feasible way, given Shader's refusal to do an exclusive deal, to keep Accept from bailing out Yahoo. Beirne concluded, "I think you can argue one hundred."

Kagle disagreed, however. Accept was at least six months away from launching a service. "If this turns into a buy-the-company thing, it's going to be buy i-Escrow for five million bucks, or buy these guys for a hundred. I'm not sure you want to push it very hard right now."

The next week eBay seemed poised to move forward, not to buy but to strike a deal. Frustrated that every deal he had proposed to eBay had been shot down, Shader had finally said, Tell me what deal you want to do, and had given eBay a Monday deadline to respond. Monday night, Jeff Skoll called him and said, "I want to get your fax number 'cause I'm going to fax you a proposal. And I'll Federal Express it by separate cover. But I want you to get it right away." Shader gave him the fax number, but no fax came.

The next day Skoll called him back to say, "We're not going to send you a deal because we've done a deal with i-Escrow. So you guys are out."

Surprised, Shader said, "But I thought you called to get my fax number—you were going to send me a proposal."

"Sorry, we've changed our mind," Skoll said. "We've enjoyed talking to you guys."

"Jeff, this doesn't make any sense to me still. Why can't we do a deal with you guys?"

"We think we have a better deal with i-Escrow."

When Shader reported back to his team, they were, as could be imagined, stunned. After months of enforced idleness, waiting for the eBay deal that was to be the foundation for the business, they found themselves not just where they had started, but further behind. If they were to try to take their offer of escrow and payment services to Yahoo, they would be chasing an auction business one tenth the size of eBay's. Unexcited by this prospect, they decided that they had no choice but to tear up their original business plan and try to figure out another business, quickly.

From eBay's perspective, i-Escrow was obviously the best choice. It was already up and running and would give eBay a competitive advantage in the present, without a six-month delay. They also felt, Bob Kagle believed, that Benchmark had been trying to strong-arm eBay into buying Accept.

Dunlevie was aghast to hear that was eBay's view. He turned to Kagle. "The Sunday night before Accept's presentation, you talked to Meg, and she said, 'Yeah! We'd be interested in doing a deal with them,' right?"

"Right. You know why the i-Escrow thing happened? You had two companies vehemently, aggressively telling one another they didn't have an option. That's all they kept telling each other. Accept kept telling eBay they didn't have an option. EBay kept telling Accept they didn't have an option. So eBay went out and showed them that they *did* have an option!" He laughed. "If I'd been put in that box, I don't know, I might have done the same thing."

Continuing the eBay thread, Dave Beirne said, "I think they're going to have to learn how to be a very powerful company, and they haven't figured it out yet. I think they'll look back on this six or twelve months from now and think they fucked up."

Kagle told of a conversation he had just had with Whitman. "You know," he had told her, "it's not that long ago we went through this discussion on the other side of the stick, with Yahoo." He was referring to when Yahoo had spurned eBay's offer of working together on a joint auctions deal. "Where our reaction was Yahoo thought they could do it all—they had all the power and they had all the control. And it doesn't look like that now. Looks like they were foolish for not figuring out a way to actually do business with us. And maybe that's a lesson *we* need to learn."

Kagle went on to say that he had not been willing to press the case aggressively. He knew, after all, that as an investor in Accept, he was not perceived by Whitman and the other eBay executives as wholly disinterested. "I'm used to fuckin' pounding on the table"—he brought his fist down hard on the table to illustrate, a gesture that, despite what he had just said, he had never made before—"but I'm just squeamish about that here because I know what they're thinking." He regretted that at the very beginning he had failed to see that the negotiations would run into trouble; he had thought that both companies would naturally see the "win-win for everybody."

Only two things could have made a bad situation worse: Amazon launching its own auction services, and Amazon purchasing Accept. Both events soon came to pass.

18. Communist Capitalism

When the Benchmark partners got together, most days, most of the time, their conversations were interrupted by jokes, laughter, word play, self-confessed foibles, and still more laughter. They positively reveled in one another's company.

They even found ways to laugh when they were spread across two continents. One meeting day, Kevin Harvey called in from Barcelona, where he was attending a conference. His voice came through clearly on the speakerphone, which was placed in the center of the conference table. Harvey's business judgment was regarded by his colleagues as the best in the group, but a well-read student of other cultures he was not. When Harvey said, "You guys should come to Spain," his partners sitting in California waited expectantly for him to elaborate in a way that would be entertaining. He did not disappoint, sensing how to play his designated role of Babbitt abroad to comic effect.

"Spain is way underrated. Spain's up there with France and Italy." He paused. "This is good eatin' here."

Bruce Dunlevie asked gently, "Have you been to El Prado, Kev?"

No, El Prado was closed, Harvey reported. He hoped to get to it after he delivered his speech. But not to worry, he had picked up a little bit of knowledge at another museum. "The history of Spain, I think, is really cool. You know, the Moslems were in control for a long time."

"They ruled," Dunlevie confirmed.

Andy Rachleff elaborated: "For four hundred years they slowly washed down the continent and saw the future."

Harvey offered up a theory. "It seemed like one of the things that really blew it for Spain was, in the 1500s, they evicted two hundred fifty thousand Moslems, and crushed their economy."

"I *hate* when that happens," Bob Kagle interjected.

"Bad executive decision," said Harvey.

■

When Dave Beirne came to Benchmark in 1997 he was the first partner to join since the partnership's founding two years previous, but he joined shortly after the departure of a founding partner, so the number of partners had effectively remained the same. Maintaining a steady state was not in Beirne's nature, so it was not surprising that it was he who in early 1998 had broached the subject of adding a sixth partner.

Accustomed though they were to making decisions rapidly when considering investments, the Benchmark partners approached the question of expansion with trepidation and moved at a glacial pace. In terms of economics, adding a partner would immediately decrease the earnings of the others: Unlike a law firm, where additional partners could bring in additional clients, in a venture capital firm like Benchmark's, the pool of capital that it had under management was not tied directly to the number of partners. In the short term, the pie would remain the same and the individual slices would become smaller. An additional partner would have to offer the prospect of either being, or being capable of becoming, as able an investor as the incumbents so as to avoid diluting everyone else's earnings.

The cultural fit had to be just right, too. It was this issue that the partners would spend the most time agonizing over. The five Benchmark partners felt keenly the closeness of a basketball team; in moments of private vanity they liked to think of themselves as the Chicago Bulls in the early nineties, but it wasn't apt—this was a team that was knocking down wins but without a single dominating presence like Michael Jordan. So maintaining the chemistry that permitted all to feel that the others brought out their individual best was regarded as paramount, even if it meant Benchmark could not expand.

In passing, Bill Gurley's name came up in the course of an unrelated discussion in February 1998. Gurley, thirty-one, had been a research analyst on Wall Street before switching careers and becoming a venture guy, joining Hummer Winblad at just about the time that Beirne had joined Benchmark.

"Gurley?" Beirne stopped the flow of conversation to ask the others, "Is he someone we would ever consider here?"

Beirne was unaware that Bob Kagle and Kevin Harvey had already talked at length between themselves about Gurley as a possible partner at Benchmark.

"He's awesome," said Kagle. "That's my feeling."

Beirne added his own high praise, which was that the attention Gurley received as a sought-after speaker at industry gatherings had secured for Gurley "a lot of mindshare."

"We should try over the next year to do a deal with him, and get to know him better," suggested Kevin Harvey.

Kagle was enthusiastic. "I think we'd all like him if we spent more time with him."

"You think he'd be a good investor?" asked Bruce Dunlevie.

"I do, but the reason I do is because he's a rare combination of highly intellectually curious and humble. I think he really is open to questioning his own thought process and what's really working, what's not working."

"It's like being around an academic," said Dunlevie. "He's got so many ideas spouting forth, I really enjoy talking to him. My fear is that he'll outthink it."

"Yeah, that's a possibility."

"This is more a balls than brains business, as we've said many times. I think having too many brains can hurt you at some level."

"Does he understand enough about how a company operates to add any value?" Harvey wondered. "Is he a good judge of people, which is more important, I think."

"He's a good guy," Kagle said, "a good human being."

Harvey said that must be the case—Gurley was from Texas, too.

"I think he's pretty competitive, too," Kagle said. "We could go to a basketball game with him, a few of us, like a Stanford game or something, if you want to do that." Gurley, who was six foot nine, had played college ball at the University of Florida.

"Wouldn't that be a little obvious?" Harvey pointed out. Half of the venture world would be in attendance in the small Stanford arena, and for Gurley, who had no known ties to any of the Benchmark partners, to appear at the game in their company would draw attention. The resulting gossip would put him in an awkward position. The discussion about Gurley faded as quickly as it had appeared, without any action taken.

■

Two or three times a year the boys decamped for a partners-only off-site meeting for a couple of days and nights to take up a big strategic topic that required a sustained discussion, free of interruptions, which a regular partners' meeting could not provide. The Benchmark tradition was to eschew resorts and repair to either a small ranch near the sea that Bruce Dunlevie co-owned with one of his entrepreneurs, or a larger, thirteen-thousand-acre cattle ranch that the entrepreneur, Dunlevie, and Kevin Harvey had recently purchased together, and where Harvey liked to hunt.

Dunlevie had a new idea for the partners' next off-site: Instead of heading to one of the ranches, how about enrolling at snowboarding school? He passed out brochures.

"I did this in Tahoe," Beirne said noncommittally.

"I want signed waivers of everybody that I won't be held responsible for any broken bones, cartilage damage, ACL tears, hip breakage," said Dunlevie.

"I'm not seeing the risk/reward here," said Bob Kagle, looking skeptically at the brochure. He laughed. "I'm not. My knees are still intact."

"Unlike a deal, this needs to be unanimous," Dunlevie said. "It's like hiring a partner."

"How about if I do the filming?" Kagle asked.

"No."

"Think of it this way," Andy Rachleff said to Kagle. "It's your chance to be on par with everybody's skiing."

"So who's actually snowboarded in this group?" Harvey asked.

"I did," Beirne said, the only one. "One day."

"How was it?"

"Ouch."

"Was it fun?"

"It's very cool when you get going. The fact that all of us are as tall as we are does not bode well."

"I'd love to try," said Rachleff.

"I'm a definite maybe," Kagle said.

"All it is," Beirne said, as mock encouragement, "is pain."

Kagle remained unenthusiastic. "There's a million things I'd rather do."

"Now you know how I feel about fishing," Rachleff said.

"I will not be the boat anchor," Kagle said gamely. "I'd be happy to go and have some fun. But I'm having trouble getting up off the couch these days. Getting up off the snow, on a board?"

"We're talking snow-bunny babes for teachers, Bob," Dunlevie pointed out helpfully. He assumed a new voice: "Bob, what amazing pecs!"

Beirne offered a better impersonation of a twenty-something Scandinavian ski instructor: "Bob, I've never seen anybody hit the ground that hard." Everyone, including Kagle, laughed hard, as Beirne continued: "That was awwwwesome! You bounced!"

■

Benchmark's self-proclaimed "fundamentally better architecture" was based on a bedrock tenet: equal partners, without hierarchical separation, with equal votes and equal compensation. They had used it brilliantly from the beginning to differentiate themselves from the rest of the firms on Sand Hill Road. But by year three, as the five felt "overwhelmed by opportunity," as Kagle put it, the fundamentally better architecture began to seem to some of them a fundamentally less efficient architecture, preventing them from hiring some associates to do some preliminary screening and due diligence. Yet even the partners who brought the subject up would express ambivalence about a change that would alter a distinguishing cultural feature of which they were proud.

Bruce Dunlevie brought up the subject of associates when Andy Rachleff complained that too much of his time had recently been scheduled in meetings that partners had asked him to sit in on with entrepreneurs, where his point of view really was not needed. How about an associate?, Dunlevie suggested. "Somebody who is smart. Somebody who you bring to a meeting and they add value to it. I think there are associate candidates who exist in the world that we could recruit to do that. So, A, are you proud to have them in the firm, and B, do you get leverage out of them?"

"My retort to that is, I'd rather spend that time recruiting a partner," Rachleff said. "Because I think we dilute our story—the one great thing about our fundamentally better architecture is you always get a partner, you always get a decision maker."

"I hear that all the time," Kevin Harvey agreed. "Right now, if we were to add another partner, we'd have more deals getting close to the decision point and more meetings. I don't think delegating all of the due diligence and that stuff is the answer."

Dave Beirne was interested in trying out associates. "You don't have to delegate *all* of the due diligence. We all run companies, guys, we know what management's about. I just think there's an awful lot that falls through the cracks, which we could have done by someone who we think is really smart that gets you closer to the answer."

Harvey was skeptical. He had not met any impressive associates at other firms, and he was concerned that if the partners hired one, they would ultimately feel obligated to promote a mediocre person to full partner.

"Bob and Andy were associates," Dunlevie pointed out.

"I think that was a different age," Rachleff said. "It was a very much less competitive age. I had the time to make mistakes that I don't think is afforded to us now."

"The major thing that would help," Harvey said, turning the focus back to the present problem, "would be us being more ruthless about using each other's time. That's the only solution."

"You know, that doesn't always promote the best-quality thinking," said Bob Kagle. "Having somebody else to bounce this off when it's early really helps you figure out whether it goes to the next step. At least I, and I know you, Bruce, are like that, too."

"Oh, yeah, I can't think by myself. But I think the larger issue is one of leverage. We are *not* getting to all the deals on the list. If an associate finds one good deal a year, that's awesome leverage, unbelievable. Twenty-million-dollar gain for a hundred-fifty-thousand-dollar salary."

Beirne saw no threat to Benchmark's core strength. "It's about the team, the best team in the business. People are saying Benchmark, they're not saying Andy or Bob."

"The second we have an associate," Harvey said, "we don't have a different architecture. We have the same fucking architecture."

"No, we don't. We're a totally equal partnership."

"And the associate?"

"No! That person is an associate."

Andy Rachleff laughed at Beirne's sophistry. Beirne tried to explain: "An associate doesn't sit on a board, they don't make an investment decision, they're not a partner."

Whatever they're called, Harvey said, they're not equal. "A huge change in our firm. Massive. If you don't see that, you need to think about it more. 'Cause it is a massive change."

"I do see that."

"I know you're off the red-eye," Harvey said, offering that as explanation for Beirne's logic-defying stance. The others laughed.

"You don't have to kill me today," Beirne said. The two slapped high fives.

"It sounds like you guys"—Rachleff was referring to Beirne, Dunlevie, and Kagle—"are redoubling your effort to go after an associate and not after—I believe, in better respects—pursuing a great, young partner."

"Why can't you do both?" asked Beirne.

"'Cause you don't have enough time. If you're going to go take on another project outside of doing deals, why not spend that on finding a great thirty-two-year-old partner?"

"Hopefully," Beirne said, "we're recruiting partners all the time. When we're meeting great people, I assume we're sizing up at some level, could they fit our firm?"

■

Only two of the five partners—Kevin Harvey and Andy Rachleff—were strongly opposed to the idea of hiring associates, but as time passed, theirs was the position that prevailed. More and more, discussion turned to the question of hiring a sixth partner, which brought out the partners' desire to find someone whose strengths would complement their own individual weaknesses, making the firm stronger. But almost another year would pass before the search would narrow and Bill Gurley's name would come up again. When Kevin Harvey had looked at Newwatch, he had shown the deal to Gurley, but Benchmark had turned out to be the sole investor, and the opportunity of getting to know Gurley better had evaporated. The Newwatch episode had not caused Harvey to rule Gurley out, however, if Gurley were to be interested in a move. Harvey invited Gurley, a hunter too, to go along with him one weekend to hunt game and see how the conversation happened to go.

Golf is a game well-suited for acquaintances who want to spend time together—but not too much time. The enforced intimacy of a two-day hunting trip is quite different, however, exhausting as it does the polite pleasantries that would suffice for conversation elsewhere. Gurley did not know Harvey personally, and professionally, Harvey was a rival, so the two felt they had to tiptoe around some large enclosures that tacitly seemed to be off-limits. But the trip turned out to be an efficient means of speeding up the getting-acquainted process. By the end of two days of lots of hunting and almost nonstop talking, each had gotten to know quite a bit about the other.

Harvey returned to Menlo Park impressed. To the other partners, he ticked off a number of Gurley's strengths, as he saw them. To begin with, "A very good guy, personality-wise."

"Brainpower?" Kagle asked.

"Great. Very smart guy. Very analytical, which we're not. I think that could be a dimension that's positive for the firm." Harvey made fun of his own way of making investment decisions instinctively and justifying them with no more explanation than a shrug.

Kagle described Gurley's approach: "He goes, Why?"

"He does like to talk about the why. Which could be useful for us."

"Painfully useful," said Beirne.

"But he's not one of these analysis-paralysis guys. A guy who does five deals in his first year is not an analysis-paralysis guy. In fact, if anything, I think he's not that discerning. I think he's done a lot of deals. What Bill doesn't have, and we take for granted, is operating experience. Bill doesn't know what hiring people is all about. He wants to learn it all. He's a total learn-it-all guy. He was asking me questions: 'How do you spend your time? How do you recruit? What do you look for? What do you ask people? What do you do?' "

"He's pretty humble," said Rachleff.

Beirne agreed, and added, "He does a very good job at the shows. He doesn't just stand in the back and not talk to anybody—he's out talking to everybody."

"How old is he?" asked Kagle.

"He's thirty-two."

"He's a mature thirty-two, too."

Harvey had also been impressed by his willingness to chase a wild boar down a steep cliff. "He is kind of an animal," Harvey said with manifest respect.

"I love that," said Kagle.

Jumping over the cliff had been too much for Harvey. "He thought I was kind of lazy 'cause I didn't want to," he said.

What Gurley did not know about the venture business he would soon learn, suggested Rachleff. "I tell you, I'm a much better sales-man since I started working with Dave. You guys rub off on me, and I'm sure you guys experience the same thing. I think differently since I've been here. I take more risk."

"I think," said Beirne, "we all evolve every year. Just what we learn from our CEO's, our company experiences, and from each other."

Rachleff pointed to Bruce Dunlevie, his old colleague at Merrill Pickard. "He had a huge impact on me before Benchmark. And you three have had a huge impact on me since. I've got to believe it's true for whoever comes into this firm."

When they had discussed the addition of a new partner in the past, they had always said to themselves that they should not settle on someone who was merely as good; it should be someone who "takes us up a notch." Now Beirne asked how would Gurley take the group up.

"Intellectually," Kagle said immediately. "He's smarter than most everybody in this room."

"He's definitely smarter than I am," said Beirne. He pointed to Kevin Harvey. "This is the smartest guy in the room. So—"

"Right," Kagle continued. "I think that Kevin would mostly appreciate Bill over all of us." When Kagle had a conversation with some-one, he was disappointed if he did not "come away feeling like I've learned three or four things. When I interact with Gurley, I'm strug-gling to keep up a lot of times, and I like that, I like what that does to me, and I like what that would do for us. I think if there is a dimen-sion on which we're lacking now, I think a little more intellectual horsepower doesn't hurt us."

Dunlevie and Beirne, the two who had had the least amount of contact with Gurley, said they would set up a breakfast meeting and gather some impressions.

■

When Bruce Dunlevie and Dave Beirne came into the office after meeting with Gurley—who now knew that an offer was a possibil-ity—Dunlevie said he was no longer worried about the view that Gur-ley, a venture guy for only two years, was on training wheels. "I think he's a pretty complete package now," Dunlevie said. "I think his hu-mility can lead one to maybe conclude more of that than is actually the case."

"He was in big-undersell mode with us," said Harvey.

"That's his style," said Rachleff.

"He thought that each of us was pretty humble and conscious of the shortcomings of the firm," Dunlevie said, "with the exception of Dave." Everyone laughed. Gurley was a perceptive guy.

Beirne tried to defend himself. "I could have bullshitted him and said, 'We think fifteen years from now we may be a pretty good firm.' " The others laughed, trying to picture such humility. Beirne protested, "That doesn't work for me, guys!"

Kagle, who had been enthusiastic about Gurley at the first passing mention of his name, now had a small concern after his last meeting. "We sometimes think we need a little more schmoozing. I think that's the pejorative way to think about it. What I think we need is a little more capacity that makes an instant connection to other people that they don't know. I think Dave's actually the only one in our partner-ship who is outstanding at that. And Bill is a little bit like the rest of us on that."

"For sure," Harvey agreed.

"He's not you-meet-the-guy-once, you've-just-got-to-be-with-him," said Kagle. "I don't think he grabs people emotionally and connects. And I asked him this, I said, 'Do you connect easily, Bill?' He said, 'My girlfriend would say no.' "

"See, I don't think Dave connects," said Harvey. "I think he impresses."

Beirne pointed to Bob Kagle and said, "*You* connect."

"Yeah," Harvey said, looking at Kagle, "you connect emotionally the easiest of the five of us. I think with Dave, they feel the power, they kind of want to be in that. They have fear." The others laughed.

Gurley had asked Beirne what he was most concerned about. Beirne had told him: "Screwing up the Chicago Bulls. Every one of us will be happy to be the sixth man. You start. But when it comes down to it, if we lose the dynamic, the cost is just unbearable for us. 'Cause it works."

Beirne said he also had told him, " 'You know our stated intention is to be the next great venture firm.' He said, 'I think you guys already are.' And that's when Bob and Kevin did this whole humble thing. I said, 'I'm not going to play that humble bullshit.' I said, 'We're not out saying we're there, but, man, we're working hard enough so that we can be.' And he said, 'Well, I'll tell you as an outsider, you guys have done it.' "

"So he's passed the test of applying appropriate suction," Harvey observed.

"I don't think he did any of that," Beirne said.

"No, he didn't. He's a pretty no-bullshit guy."

"He is such a *big* dude that his presence is pretty compelling," said Beirne, in the unaccustomed role of shorter person looking upward. But Gurley seemed so shy that Beirne wondered if he could be a charismatic leader on a board of directors.

"It's through thought leadership rather than force of personality," said Kagle. "It's a different style, I think."

"If you talk to people about him that know him well," Harvey said, "he's a high-impact player on people."

"I think what he'll have to learn from us, frankly," Dunlevie said, "is how to shoot more from the hip, how to tune his instinct at the expense of his intellect."

Beirne was in the position that a new partner, whoever it was, would be in: a nonfounder. "It's a good thing I'm as confident as I am, because it's a hard thing to walk into."

"It took a long time to integrate you," Harvey admitted. "I mean, you felt that. We all felt that."

"I actually think the integration of fifth partner in was the hardest we're ever going to have. For me, and for you guys. You had someone who was a nonfounder. I was the first one in that was not a founder. And everyone that comes in, it should get easier."

"The founder thing, I think, is something that you might have felt a lot more than we did," Rachleff said. "I don't think that means anything to us."

"I'm not talking about founder as in status. I mean, you guys started this together. It *is* a difference. You'd already been doing this for a few years together. You knew how one another thinks. There's sign language that goes through any organization. You have it with your assistant, I have it with my assistant. You guys had it between one another. The first couple of meetings, you sit there, you guys are talking in very short sentences that meant an awful lot. I'm sitting there going, what the *fuck* are they talking about?"

The candidacy of "the Gurley Man" had advanced to the point where it was time to spend more time—Rachleff would meet him one-on-one on Friday, Harvey would have breakfast on Saturday, and a dinner was set up for Sunday. Gurley would be told that it would be with two partners, but all five partners would appear, a surprise that would underline the group's interest in his candidacy as a partner. Then the partners could come back and decide the following week whether to make an offer.

In the middle of the Sunday dinner Kagle pitched a hard fastball to Gurley: "We're in the elevator. Sell us on why we should have you join." There was sweet justice in a venture guy getting hit with the what's-your-elevator-pitch question; it was an expression that the Benchmark guys did not use, but it was the one question that entrepreneurs faced whenever they made the rounds of venture firms. On this occasion, Gurley stepped up and acquitted himself well. A bit later, when Harvey and Beirne found themselves with a moment to confer while standing in the restaurant bathroom, they exchanged nods: Gurley was TheGuy. When they went back to the table, they asked him to leave for a moment; the partners quickly confirmed their unanimous agreement to make an offer, and he was called back.

Kagle said to Harvey, "Okay, make him the offer."

Harvey turned to Gurley. "First, I want to know if you'll take it." This was the way Harvey preferred to seal a deal with an entrepreneur: to secure the agreement before bringing out the term sheet with all of the details. Here Harvey feared that if he brought out the terms of the partnership offer, Gurley's analytical bent would lead him to say, "Okay, I'll take this home and think about it." Harvey wanted him to show trust that the partners had put together a generous package that accorded him fully equal status from day one.

Gurley came through and, without asking to see the terms, accepted on the spot.

When *Red Herring*, a magazine that covers the venture capital industry, reported on Gurley's joining Benchmark, the story called attention to the unusual nature of the equal partnership. Kevin Harvey was quoted as crediting the structure for fostering teamwork and reducing political infighting. "We share in the governance and the economics," he said. "It's like a communist capitalist system." Art.com's Bill Lederer had likened himself to a capitalist among communists; with his tongue working against his cheek, Harvey flipped the formulation around—communists among capitalists.

19. "R" Toys Us?

In the spring of 1999 the senior executives of the Fortune 500, one by one, awoke with an identical epiphany: The Web would soon be either their company's bane or its salvation. It was less a manifestation of calm analysis than an outbreak of mass hysteria. Everyone—including unlikely companies such as Starbucks—felt equally threatened, and equally inadequate to the task of crafting new strategy for the New Economy. Lacking in-house expertise in e-commerce, many of these companies looked to the venture capital firms of Sand Hill Road, whom they had heard so much about, for guidance and partnerships. The venture firms, on their part, received the entreaties warily; these bricks-and-mortar businesses were the sworn enemies of the start-ups they funded.

In the first four months of the year, Benchmark had received lots of calls like the one from BP Amoco, the giant gasoline and petro-chemicals company. *You've got to help us dot.com ourselves!* For what? *We don't know. We're looking to you to find out for us.* Benchmark politely demurred in that instance, but others, including Goldman Sachs, Ford, General Motors, Whirlpool, GE Capital, and the National Basketball Association, got in the door and had at least an initial conversation, and in some cases many conversations, with Benchmark partners about possibilities.

Some industries offered much clearer opportunities for terrestrial companies to reinvent their business than others. Financial services were well-suited for a transition because the "product" is an intangible service involving information bits. Other industries were less suited because they were burdened with complex distribution channels—like automobile manufacturers, which were tied to multi-hundred-billion-dollar vested interests in the form of automobile dealerships. And some industries, such as fast food restaurants, sold products that were perishable and appeared to preclude the Web entirely.

Other criteria for evaluating Web initiatives included the value-to-weight ratio, which is high in the case of watches and diamonds and low in the case of iron and lumber (or furniture; nevertheless, Dave Beirne had championed a Benchmark investment in a furniture-via-the-Web start-up that became Living.com). "Dollar density" was the phrase Bill Gurley used to refer to the same criterion.

After turning away for sundry reasons a majority of the invitations to explore partnerships, Benchmark still had many prospective partners, including the illustrious investment-banking firm of Goldman Sachs. By April, when the noise from these exploratory talks reached a crescendo, Dave Beirne was levitating, excited by the arrival of this moment for Benchmark, which was on the verge of receiving equity stakes in newly formed Fortune 500 dot.com subsidiaries not for the capital that Benchmark would contribute but for its ability to serve as the ultimate matchmaker, bringing old and new together. Unable to sleep, yet flushed with adrenaline-fueled energy, he was at the office before six o'clock every morning, eager to get started on the day's calls. Just as Herb Allen had been the power broker for the traditional entertainment and communications industries, Benchmark now was in a position to be the broker for the new Internet economy.

A giddy sense of limitless possibility characterized phase one. Phase two, negotiating terms of a joint dot.com venture, turned out to be a lengthy process. The old world had come to Benchmark's door, but after the initial conversation Benchmark was expected to reciprocate the favor and get on a plane and help sell the idea to the more resistant among the staff at the corporate home office, wherever that happened to be. The partners found themselves in reversed roles; now it was they who were in suits, flying to the East Coast, working on PowerPoint presentations on a red-eye, headed to meetings with companies to explain why they should do business with

Benchmark. The Goldman Sachs deal alone consumed about one third of all of the partners' time over a two-month period, the most amount of time spent on any single deal in Benchmark's history.

What Benchmark learned painfully was just how slowly those sclerotic businesses born in the pre-Web era moved. The very reason that start-ups had an advantage over these incumbents—speed in execution—was the same reason that the old companies acted so slowly, even when the task was to organize a new entity that would be free to compete without organizational drag. As the negotiations stretched out, the West Coast discovered that there was far more opposition to collaboration on the East Coast, within the prospective partner's ranks, than had initially seemed to be the case. Even the corporate change master who had approached Benchmark originally, the person who had professed that he had seen the light, that he *got it*, got a shaky hand when given a pen to sign.

After eight weeks of courtship, Henry Paulson, Jr., Goldman Sachs's CEO who had seemed so ready to commit to founding with Benchmark an entirely new online banking service for high-net-worth individuals, balked in the end. "What if there were to be another Meg Whitman?" he asked Dunlevie.

What would happen, that is, if the head of this new Goldman Sachs entity, which would be structured like a Silicon Valley start-up, and its CEO, given an equity stake similar to that given to other Valley CEOs, was very successful, went public, and its CEO—like eBay's Whitman—became extraordinarily wealthy? Wouldn't the other Goldman Sachs partners become envious and demoralized?

Dunlevie did not try to argue that that would not be the case. He instead focused on the numbers: a $30-billion-market-cap business; Goldman Sachs would own 75 percent of it, which would mean a boost of $22.5 billion to the parent investor's market cap. Yes, the CEO would own 10 percent of the new company, and consequently have a net worth twice that of the wealthiest partner. But you would have added that $22.5 billion in shareholder value.

Yes, yes, Paulson said, but he reiterated his concern that the assets on the other side of the fence, that is, the Goldman Sachs partners stuck on the Old Economy side, would deteriorate in value as envy set in. Dunlevie, who had been a Goldman Sachs investment banker once himself, had no way of demonstrating that Paulson's fear was unfounded. The old-and-new combination, with radically different compensation structures, was an experiment that had yet to be run, and in the absence of contrary evidence, Paulson was probably correct. In the end, Goldman Sachs passed.

For Benchmark's partners, to have worked so hard on a deal with a partner with a gold-plated reputation, addressing a business that by its nature was perfectly suited to the Web and a hugely profitable opportunity only to have it fall short of consummation, was a considerable disappointment. The Goldman Sachs deal, like almost all the others in that spring's talk of "the dot.comming of America," died in negotiations.

■

The one deal that moved ahead while the Goldman Sachs deal died involved the toy business. A year before, in the summer of 1998, Toys "R" Us was preoccupied with fixing the base business of toy retailing. Bob Nakasone, the recently hired CEO, was busy identifying problems in the company's eight hundred U.S. stores. The Web received little attention, but by September, unease had crept in. As the Christmas season rolled on, the newcomer eToys generated all the buzz, and Toys "R" Us's stores began to be affected visibly. Its own website, hastily thrown up, did not go online until November. Based on poor technology, it was quickly overwhelmed by the traffic and broke down. The company had to take the site offline before Christmas because it did more harm to its reputation than good to its top line.

In the spring of 1999 Toys "R" Us watched investors ecstatically talk up eToys as it prepared for its IPO. The bankers said that when eToys went public, it would have the same market cap as Toys "R" Us—and it was only one-four-hundredth its size.

The standard prescription in the diagnostic manual for ailing divisions called for hiring a star. But when Bob Nakasone tried to retain Ramsey Beirne to find a talented executive with the requisite e-commerce background, Alan Seiler agreed to take the assignment only on condition that Nakasone first agree to get venture capital involved. It happens, Seiler said, I know of a good venture guy to call.

Seiler's recommendation of Dave Beirne was the first time that

Nakasone heard of Benchmark. He soon heard of the company a second time when he tried to recruit Bob Moog, the Silicon Valley–based head of University Games, a supplier who had been in the toys-and-games business for twelve years and was well known to Toys "R" Us. Moog, like Seiler, had a precondition: that other investors become involved, and Moog had the same firm in mind as Seiler. Bruce Dunlevie was a longtime friend of Moog's from Stanford business school, and Dunlevie had served as a director of University Games for seven years. Nakasone and the company chairman, Mike Goldstein, flew from the home office in New Jersey out to California to meet the Benchmark partners and talk about a possible joint dot.com venture.

Where Goldman Sachs and the other putative Fortune 500 partners had dithered endlessly, Nakasone moved with dispatch. At the end of a two-hour meeting on a Wednesday, the CEO of Fortune 500 company no. 151 said, "I want to be in business with you guys. I'll fax you a term sheet tomorrow," which he did. Dunlevie worked on the draft over the weekend, and by Monday Toys "R" Us and Benchmark had reached verbal agreement on the deal. Two days later a public announcement was made.

That Toys "R" Us would have committed so quickly suggested that this was an organization that had the fast clock rate of a Valley company. It was not so simple, however. The following week, when the Toys lawyers sent the final term sheet, much had been changed, reflecting the desire of Toys' finance and accounting organizations to use the new entity for their own tax purposes. In Benchmark's eyes, this was a term sheet that had hair and complexity all over it.

While Benchmark was wrangling to remove the clauses that Toys "R" Us had just inserted, Bob Moog had to get to work without delay—there was little enough time to reinvent the site and become a credible competitor with eToys—and also with Amazon, which everyone knew was preparing to add toys—before the fall shopping season arrived. Toys "R" Us issued a press release announcing Moog as the CEO of Toysrus.com.

Moog set up a temporary office at Benchmark. Stopping by a Monday partners' meeting for a moment, he offered an entertaining story of Dave Beirne's sweet words of encouragement, when the two had met recently for the first time and were shaking hands: "Don't fuck it up."

■

Bruce Dunlevie was the Benchmark partner who went on the board of Toysrus.com. At Benchmark's 1999 annual meeting in early June, when about a dozen of Benchmark's limited partners gathered at the conference center a short stroll away from the Benchmark office, Dunlevie told the guests that it was too early to say what the outcome of the Toysrus.com experiment was likely to be. "It will be a very positive, signal event of the dot.comming of America, or it will be a large disaster." In the meantime, it had already triggered still more phone calls to Benchmark from other large companies that were interested in doing joint deals.

Dunlevie explained why this seemed to be a case in which it made sense for Benchmark to try to take on revamping a Fortune 500 company rather than sticking with its customary business of funding brand-new companies. The skills that would be required to do Toysrus.com right were highly similar to what Benchmark did: recruit the team, craft a strategy that makes sense, and execute it. "Does an eToys first-mover advantage and the looming Amazon threat make this a bad idea?" he asked, parenthetically cracking, "which we only thought about after we made the investment." He had reason to be optimistic: "It turns out that this is very, very different than Amazon books. The supply chain in toys is incredibly complicated. There are thousands of sourcing relationships. You don't just get to drop-ship them in Memphis. You've got to buy unit quantity—two hundred fifty thousand—in China, get them on a boat and to the United States and distribute it out to your stores, or in the case of the dot.com business, get it into your Memphis warehouse. This is very, very different, and far more complicated, and a source of great expertise at Toys 'R' Us."

This was one dot.com that would enjoy the superior cost position. No other company in the world bought more toys and games than Toys "R" Us. And most important, the dot.com business would have access to the parent's acquisition power—and the ability to get the items that were always in short supply every Christmas season. The other toy retailers would have to beg for what they thought would be a fair allocation, but Toys "R" Us could go to the manufacturer and say, I'll take every single one you make and pay COD. In the book business, if a product is in short supply, the publisher simply goes back to the presses, but in the toy business, the hot toys of a season cannot be produced and delivered fast enough.

Toys "R" Us's dot.com business would also enjoy the advertising muscle of an $11 billion company, which had spent $150 million the previous year on TV, print, and radio advertising. They had just begun placing "Toysrus.com" on every ad, providing a free ride at no cost.

Dunlevie was excited about the prospect of using customer "touches" in the legacy bricks-and-mortar business to pull people to the Web. Plans were being drafted to place greeters in the stores in neighborhoods where there was evidence of high Web usage. The greeters would offer to escort customers to a Web terminal set up in the lobby to show off the dot.com site and offer inducements to use the online business in the future.

"This is a very different mind-set from most companies that are trying to *protect* what they've got, as opposed to cannibalizing," Dunlevie said. "You have to decide you're going to eat your own business yourself, as opposed to having eToys or Amazon or somebody else doing it for you."

From the evidence Benchmark had collected over the course of recent months, it appeared that the number of big companies that were really willing to cannibalize their own business was small. The partners had talked to lots of businesses that claimed to have absorbed the reasoning presented in *The Innovator's Dilemma*, which showed the price paid by great firms that failed to adapt in a time of disruptive technological change. But very few of the prospective dot.com partners showed that they had truly taken these precepts to heart.

"You've got to do it the right way," Dunlevie concluded. "You've got to set up a separate company. It's not divisional—it's a subsidiary. The management team and the board of directors have to be fully independent and autonomous." The Right Way also meant the dot.com business had to offer the financial upside of stock options to employees and have unlimited access to use of the legacy business assets. The parent had to be ready for "one-hundred-percent self-cannibalization." The independence that Toysrus.com enjoyed would enable it to go public whenever it wanted to, without needing the assent of Toys "R" Us the parent. "We structured the deal in a way that they can't meddle."

In the vanguard, Toysrus.com seemed well-positioned to be the first success in the dot.comming of America. But perhaps thinking silently of those niggling legal issues that had not been fully resolved between Benchmark and Toys, Dunlevie ended his otherwise upbeat presentation on a jarringly ambiguous note: "Time will tell."

■

The telling began almost immediately, and it was not encouraging. Less than ten days later, Bob Nakasone met with Joel Anderson, the person who had overseen Toys "R" Us's earlier online efforts. Anderson told Nakasone that Moog was a disaster. Meanwhile, people in Anderson's group in New Jersey were jumping ship because they had been told that all would soon be leaving for California but the details of the offers had yet to be disclosed.

Nakasone's decisiveness, which had given Benchmark a deal within ninety-six hours of the initial meeting, surfaced again. He listened to Anderson, hopped on a plane for California, asked Moog to dinner, and then told him that he'd lost confidence in him.

Bruce Dunlevie had not heard what Nakasone did, having just left on a long-planned family vacation to Europe. When he landed in England, he picked up a message from Nakasone, who asked him to call as soon as he got the message, regardless of the time. Dunlevie called him as directed, even though it was 4:00 A.M. at Nakasone's hotel. Nakasone wanted to fire Moog.

It was Dunlevie's friendship with Moog that had kept Dunlevie involved with University Games; it was his friendship with Moog that had drawn him into the Toys "R" Us deal; and now it was his friendship that complicated the decision at hand. Moog had not gotten off to a fast start; that there was no denying. He was not well organized by nature, and had been rushed into starting work at Toysrus.com before he had had time to hand off his responsibilities running University Games. The guy had only been on the job seven weeks, Dunlevie pointed out, and was integral to talks with a number of potential partners, including AOL and iVillage. Changing horses now would mean the dot.com would stall. Nakasone agreed to think about it.

The next day he met with Moog again—and fired him. Then he called Dunlevie up and said, "Hope you don't mind, but I've let Moog go."

"It's your deal," Dunlevie reminded him. "We haven't closed this thing yet."

"We're partners, aren't we?"

"We are. You've got to do what you've got to do. As I've expressed to you, I think this is a net mistake. I'd rather keep Moog involved, at least on an external basis, until he can be replaced. As a result of this, we have nobody running this company."

"Having nobody is better than having somebody do a bad job."

Later that day Nakasone faxed Dunlevie a revised equity budget for the dot.com subsidiary. Instead of reserving 20 percent of the company's equity in a pool for distribution to the employees, it would now only be 10.5 percent. Nakasone said that he had Salomon Brothers do a study and they had assured him that the 10.5 percent would be sufficient for hiring three hundred people. Where Salomon had looked Nakasone did not say, but that was an equity budget barely adequate for a single CEO, let alone three hundred employees.

Dunlevie interpreted this as reflecting Nakasone's realization that if the stock options that had originally been budgeted were distributed, the executives of the new entity would likely become more wealthy than everyone else in the old business. It was the same realization that Hank Paulson of Goldman Sachs had come to earlier, and it exposed the difficulty of having two very different sets of compensation models placed side by side, the newer equity-based one being viewed as far more attractive.

Dunlevie met in New Jersey with Toys "R" Us's incumbent e-commerce honcho, Joel Anderson, who showed him a business plan for the dot.com subsidiary that called for $25 million in revenue that year.

Dunlevie was puzzled. "I thought it was going to be a hundred million."

"Oh, for that we would need access to the hot products. If we could just get our hands on Harley Barbie, Harley Ken, and Sega Dreamcast, I could easily do a hundred million."

"I talked to Nakasone on this very issue on Friday morning, and he said you can get whatever you want."

"Well, it's not really true." The dot.com subsidiary would only receive a small portion of those products that the parent received.

Dunlevie returned home to California and was attached, as he had been in Europe, to the telephone. In a conference call with Bob Nakasone and senior Toys managers, Dunlevie brought up the most immediate sore point, the internal pricing of merchandise. The latest document that the Toys attorneys had sent to Benchmark stipulated that the parent would charge an uplift of 5 to 15 percent for all products it provided the dot.com business.

This was the epitome of how *not* to do the dot.comming of America. Dunlevie was provoked to do something he rarely did: He lost his temper. Mildly. "This is bullshit," he allowed, and said he was going to join his family for dinner. "You guys can continue if you want to." He hung up.

Three minutes later, Nakasone called back. "C'mon, partner, let's get back at this."

"Bob, this deal gets worse the closer I get to it. None of what you represented is true. The organizational dispreference for trying to accomplish this is obvious to me." Nakasone unilaterally struck the pricing uplift, saying, "Everything you get, you get at cost."

They then turned to the other sore point, concerning the allocation of hot product. To Dunlevie, this issue was the touchstone for the deal.

"When we talked about this eight weeks ago," he reminded Nakasone, "you said [Toysrus] dot.com got everything it wanted. So what I'm telling you now as the only guy who seems to be paying attention to this is, I want *all* of the Sega Dreamcasts in dot.com. That's forty million dollars of business right there. The product's going to be in shortage. There are only going to be three hundred thousand shipped to the United States. Two hundred thousand are coming to Toys 'R' Us. I want all of them at dot.com. And if I create an inventory problem for myself, then I'll liquidate them through the stores. And I want the Furbies and I want Harley Barbie and I want Harley Ken."

"You know, it's just not that simple," Nakasone said, attempting to placate him. "We've already committed catalogs, which is a three-million-dollar annual business; store managers are already taking presales. What do you want us to do? On Christmas Eve, go into stores and pull things off the shelves?"

"I'm not talking about that at all. I'm talking about things that you can prespecify that are going to be in limited quantity, and therefore in complete demand, that Toysrus.com gets them all."

They spent an hour hashing out the issue, each unable to persuade the other. In the end, they agreed to put the matter on hold for the moment because they were not speaking the same language.

"Look," Dunlevie said, "the goal of the dot.com business is to cannibalize the stores."

Nakasone was silent for a long time before speaking. "That's not the goal at all. The goal is to complement."

"Okay, I'll correct my language. The end result is going to be cannibalization of stores. And you're going to go from eight hundred stores to two hundred in the next three or four or five years as a result of the Web."

Nakasone did not agree, leading Dunlevie to conclude that he wanted everything—the existing network of stores *and* a thriving online business—which was a natural-enough inclination but a delusional expectation if he really understood what the dot.comming of America entailed. This was hard sledding.

■

Bob Kagle reminded his partners that they would be meeting with Whirlpool later in the day.

"Another dot.comming of America?" Kevin Harvey asked.

"Yeah. Maybe our last one." Everyone but Bruce Dunlevie laughed. The others had heard only that a few problems had surfaced with the Toys "R" Us deal.

"It's not that funny," Dunlevie said, with uncharacteristic shortness. "I need help. I'm now the CEO of Toysrus.com."

The others looked at him in surprise; they had had no idea that the situation had turned so grave so soon.

"This project is just eating me alive. The complexity of the deal, coupled with a lot of Toys 'R' Us constituencies' pretty patent desire to really not do this, has caused this thing to go very slowly. Dispreference, not just inertia, in some cases. Everybody kind of walks the walk, but as soon as Nakasone says, 'Make it so,' and he goes away for two weeks, the lawyers don't do anything.

"My every inclination is just to say, 'Let's get the fuck out of here.' Which may still be what we end up doing. What causes me to hesitate on that is A, we've got a reputational issue, having had this announced. And more than anything, this poor son of a bitch needs us. If we walk away, he's going to get fired, I think. He will lose his job as CEO of Toys 'R' Us. He's not a bad guy. He doesn't know what he's doing here. His lip-service commitment to self-cannibalization, I think, is insufficient."

Andy Rachleff couldn't believe that Nakasone was now saying something so different from what he had said in the meeting with him, Bob Kagle, and Dave Beirne. "He said, 'We'll obsolete ourselves. And I'm happy for the new CEO to make many more times [what I do]'—all the things he's now going back on, he said to us."

Dunlevie returned to the sticking point of hot products. "I think without the favorable resolution of the allocation topic, we're not going to be able to recruit the right CEO. If you're not going to be able to go shit-can the base business, why do it?"

"Do you feel like you need *all* the hot product?" Kevin Harvey inquired.

Before Dunlevie could answer, Bob Kagle jumped in, making explicit the criticism implied in Harvey's question. Kagle addressed Dunlevie: "That's not really the fair or right answer, to have it all. The fair or right answer is to have a grossly disproportionate share."

Andy Rachleff chimed in his agreement. Kagle continued. "That is *clearly* the right answer. And taking your position right now can help you get there, I think, on that. But I can see their side."

"I think having something nobody else has is the best customer-acquisition tool in the world, right?"

"I think it's a great one," Harvey conceded, "but there's others as well. I think the brand's strong. Having more than eToys."

"Yeah," Kagle said, "if you could have some meaningful multiple of eToys, that would be a reasonable place to start."

Dunlevie defended his position. "In the land-grab business, every customer matters. We're going to want as many as we can get."

Kagle reiterated a compromise position. "If you got twenty-five percent? Total home run. Off the charts." Perhaps frequent buyers on the website could earn customer points that gave them the right to buy the scarce items.

Dunlevie reflected on his experience to date. "The depth of the problems, as I've peeled the onion back, in the past four or five days, has surprised me a little bit."

"Do you feel you've hit bottom on the problems, yet?" Harvey asked.

"I think so. With the possible exception of even more organizational inertia. How's the store manager going to react if I've got a greeter in the store, starting October first, who doesn't work for the store manager, who is wearing the Toysrus.com hat, as you come in the front door, who says, 'Do you have a Web connection?' And the customer says, 'Yeah.' And the greeter says, 'Don't come in the store. Go home and order there.' The guy's bonus is at stake; that's going to cause a riot."

"At the end of the day," Harvey said, "I think all you need is the brand and the supply. Then you can build a business. Despite all that stuff that will suck."

Kagle argued for a more conciliatory approach to the base business. "I don't think there has to be a religious war to trash the physical system either. I think you can focus on the benefits of the online business, and they can be complementary in some ways, for a while. You just have to get more of your share of the advantage. In other words, that greeter in the store? Doesn't have to say, 'Go home.'"

"I know."

Kagle continued with a sample spiel for the greeters: "Here's what we have; and if it's more convenient to order at home sometimes, we offer this as a service."

"My point is, I'm not sure of getting that done by Christmas. Think of the logistical complexity, of starting where we are now. If the site sucks, if we lose Christmas '99, how much value is the business going to have? I think we might not be able to go public in Q1 [first quarter] 2000 'cause we got outsold by eToys three to one. If that transpires, then you're in a death spiral."

"You've got to make sure the website works for Christmas," said Bill Gurley. "You've got to believe that here. How much do you think their back's against the wall? The parent."

"As they perceive it? Completely."

"So they know they're in a tough spot." Still, the inertial drag in a big company was the most powerful factor in the equation.

"Makes me think that this e-commerce start-up thing is looking pretty good," Harvey said, laughing.

Rachleff turned to Dunlevie. "What can we do to help?"

"What I'm most worried about, frankly, is the technology scalability. Then just running the business."

"How much do we own?" asked Harvey.

"Twelve and a half percent."

"I think that there's still opportunity. That's the sense I get. Forget the reputational thing. It's possible to clear this up and make this work. It's not reached the point where it can't be, yet. Although it may. The problem is, you're about to get hitched to the wagon."

"There's less to work with than I thought," Dunlevie continued. "It is really poor. We are adding at Toysrus.com about fifty items a day, and they estimate that eToys is adding two hundred items a day. EToys already has twelve thousand SKUs, and we have three thousand. So we do *not* have definitive selection, and won't for some time."

"You don't need full organizational commitment" from the parent company, Harvey argued. Just accept that that organization "will be a pain in the ass forever."

The Harley Barbie exemplified the problems. The new doll was produced in a three-way deal between Harley-Davidson, Mattel, and Toys "R" Us, so the only distributor in the world would be Toys. Out of 134,000 pieces, the dot.com business was only going to get 17,500, or 13 percent of the total. Dunlevie said he'd asked Nakasone, "Why don't we get them all? If you could monetize a dollar of revenue fifty-X on the Web, versus fifty cents on the dollar in bricks and mortar, that's two orders of magnitude difference; why not run it all through the dot.com?"

"What did he say?" Rachleff asked.

"He said, 'It's very complicated; you don't understand.' "

Dunlevie asked the partners what percentage of the hot items they thought should be guaranteed in the contract. Kagle and Harvey agreed immediately: 25 percent gets you there.

Kagle saw the strain in Dunlevie's face. "The other point we need to make, Bruce, is, if life is just too short for this? It is too short. And you don't have to go through this."

"I appreciate that. Thank you." On a lighter note, he returned to recounting the phone conversation he had had with Nakasone. "You should have heard it last night. I said, 'The objective is to cannibalize the stores, and a few years from now we're looking at a couple hundred stores—'"

"I think that's going over the top," Gurley said admonishingly.

"It's kind of clear—you got a little angry," Harvey pointed out to Dunlevie. Everyone laughed at the thought of the unflappable Dunlevie talking unusually wildly. Harvey pretended to be Dunlevie on the phone with Nakasone: "I want *all* the hot products. Die, motherfucker, die!"

"I don't think it's going over the top," Dunlevie said seriously about Toys "R" Us's need to cannibalize its physical stores. "I think it's what's going to happen."

"I don't think mentioning that helps you in your two-year quest," Gurley pointed out.

Dave Beirne, who was on the road, called in to the meeting and asked for an update on the Toys "R" Us situation: "So what's the bottom line?"

"Draw a few cards," Dunlevie said. "May shoot it. May go forward."

■

Six weeks later *The Wall Street Journal* announced that the partnership between Toys and Benchmark had collapsed. The story described the partnership as an "unusual marriage," but the end would have been better likened to an annulment. When the *Journal* ran a longer feature story about the breakup two days later, using it to illustrate the difficulties faced by land-based companies adapting to different rules in cyberspace, Bob Kagle supplied another nuptial metaphor when he explained that ultimately the deal had fallen through because of a disagreement about whether the venture capital firm would have a permanent stake in the Internet business or would instead be given a fixed payment, like a management consultant. "It was a bit like going into a marriage knowing that you had to contemplate divorce at some point," Kagle said. "The prenuptial agreement was a lot more difficult to negotiate than we thought."

The collapse of the Benchmark–Toys "R" Us alliance had immediate repercussions within Toys. The next week, CEO Bob Nakasone was forced out of the company.

This would have been the end to Benchmark's dot.comming of America experiment were it not for a parallel unrelated deal with Nordstrom, on which Bill Gurley was working as the Toys "R" Us relationship was fraying. A week after the split with Toys, Benchmark and Nordstrom announced plans to launch a new online site, Nordstromshoes.com, part of a joint venture in which Benchmark contributed $15 million, one of its largest investments ever. Nordstrom's existing website offered 200,000 pairs, but the separate dot.com subsidiary planned to offer 20 million pairs.

Negotiations had gone swiftly and smoothly, helped by the thirty-six-year-old executive that the parent company had placed on point and who would become the new unit's CEO. An avid skier and climber, he got along well with the Benchmark partners when he came down from Seattle to visit, and he declared that Nordstrom had chosen Benchmark not only for its e-commerce expertise but also for help in developing a corporate culture at Nordstrom "just as dynamic and hard-driven as a Silicon Valley start-up."

At the onset, Toys had said all the right things, too, but in Nordstrom's case the details agreed upon between the two partners had remained intact, free of CFO and attorney meddling on the part of the larger partner. The new subsidiary would have its own management team and its own board of directors, and the sourcing arrangements with the parent were clean, without any surprise gotchas.

Why, then, had Nordstrom executives been able to avoid falling prey to the fear that wealth generated by the dot.com side would create a rift between haves and have-nots, and why was it then able to follow through, organizationally, when Toys "R" Us had not? Perhaps a clue is found in the selection of that young executive appointed to head the dot.com. His name was Dan Nordstrom, and he was one of six co-presidents who shared the surname, a youthful group of brothers and cousins, all in their thirties. Although the company's shares were publicly traded on the New York Stock Exchange and the

CEO was not a Nordstrom, the family owned 35 percent of the company, wielding power that could obliterate organizational inertia. Ironically, given the problems that family ties had caused in a tiny start-up like TriStrata, the same atavistic feature from a precorporate era served here, in a large organization, to speed internal change.

20. Crash

A good business will attract good competitors. This eBay's executives knew in the abstract, but like the abstract concept of war, the theory necessarily bore a limited relationship to the thing itself. Yahoo, a well-financed foe, had dug in, seemingly ready to fight indefinitely with free listings. As eBay's own listings climbed ever higher, reaching 700,000 in September 1998 at the time of its IPO, so too did Yahoo's increase, staying fairly consistently at about 10 percent of eBay's. Yahoo's progress was not sufficient to close the gap between eBay and itself, but it was not insignificant either. By early December 1998, Yahoo reached 100,000 listings; by early March 1999, 150,000.

That was when rumors that Amazon was on the verge of launching its own auction site filled the air. In late March an Amazon spokesperson made the news official, explaining that more than one hundred businesses that sold toys, rare books, and memorabilia had been signed as "charter sellers" who were ready to stock the Amazon site on its first day. Amazon was also going to introduce an innovation, a free guarantee against fraud by sellers on all purchases up to $250.

Stock traders liked the news. The price of Amazon's shares jumped eleven points, and eBay's fell six.

On April 2, Amazon opened its virtual auction house, offering more than fifty thousand items, or approximately the same number that it had taken Yahoo Auctions two months of operations to reach. On April 5 the number had passed sixty thousand. In the same month Amazon acquired Accept, the company that Benchmark EIR Danny Shader had incubated. Considering that Accept had only been in existence six short months, the $175 million worth of Amazon stock that its owners received was a payoff that was more than respectable, and all the more so considering how the company's original plans had foundered when Accept could not work out an alliance with eBay and it had had to scramble to reinvent itself.

Nevertheless, for Benchmark, the sale was a bittersweet outcome because of the missed opportunity for Accept to ally itself with eBay, and it was bittersweet for Shader and his crew, too, because the sale meant that they had to move to Seattle. As for the Amazon stock that they received in the sale of their company, the temporary illiquidity of the currency left the sellers vulnerable to a drop in the market; the shares that had been valued at $175 million at the time of the sale in April were worth only $100 million in June when the details of the transaction were disclosed to the SEC.

■

Life within a company like eBay, a combatant on the front lines, was noticeably different from life within its venture backer, situated toward the rear. In Menlo Park, Benchmark's primary rival, "our friends up the street," was Kleiner Perkins, which was a competitor on some deals (like Critical Path, the e-mail-services-for-corporations deal that Benchmark had won; or Chemdex, a specialty-chemicals deal that Kleiner had won). But the intensity of the competition between the two was kept in check by the fact that on other deals they were co-investors (beginning with Silicon Gaming and subsequently including Impresse, Juniper Networks, Handspring, and most recently, Accept). As Benchmark's star ascended, Kleiner's John Doerr showed signs by late 1998 of having developed a particular dislike of Dave Beirne and Bob Kagle (after hearing secondhand about derogatory comments that Doerr had made about him, Beirne said, "I believe John Doerr wants me to die; I'm totally in touch with that"). But the two firms' relationship was further complicated by the fact that Doerr went out of his way to maintain a cordial relationship with

Bruce Dunlevie. Members of both firms had to talk with members of the other all the time, and this too made the nature of the mutual competition a genteel affair.

At eBay, however, there was no ongoing dialogue with the Enemy. In a way, eBay versus Amazon was a proxy war between Benchmark and Kleiner, as Amazon was part of Kleiner's portfolio and Doerr a director on its board. But this was a war fought in a different fashion from that of venture firms jockeying to advance their reputation. It had an urgency lacking on Sand Hill Road; its outcome would be decided in weeks, not years, or at least was experienced as if it would be; it was fed with daily loads of fresh data gathered from the field and arranged into spreadsheets and analyzed in real time; it involved platoons of troops who were guided by long checklists, dispatched on missions to study the Enemy and strengthen eBay's own offerings.

Just as it had done when Onsale first went after eBay, the company designated a conference room as the War Room, and three times a week Whitman, Omidyar, and the other members of the executive staff gathered for what was called "the Amazon meeting" to pore over data and plan responses. In the first weeks the room was either the main office's sole conference room, which accommodated only six people, or Whitman's office, where four was a crowd. In early May eBay moved across the street to more spacious, and freshly redone, offices in the same complex and the gathering could spread out in a more generously proportioned conference room (Omidyar had vetoed a move to space that had been found downtown in a large office building, which he deemed "too corporate").

A designated squad of eleven eBay employees had done reconnaissance and bought and sold items on the Amazon site over the course of a week and a half to see what could be learned. The buyers reported that bidding there was fast, quick, and easy, but the selection of items was so limited a visitor had to spend a lot of time searching for interesting items. ("Ah!" Omidyar joked. "Usage minutes up!") One staff member noticed that Amazon allowed a handy way to store a reminder about one's password; eBay did too, but the link was hard to find. His own mother had called him the other day, distraught because she had lost her password and could not get into her eBay account.

EBay was galvanized into immediately matching Amazon's free fraud insurance and accelerating plans to offer a thousand new categories and localized listings that made it easy to search for items available in one's own city. Bob Kagle had long pushed eBay to add a service he called "persistent search," which would allow a buyer to submit a request for a kind of item and receive e-mail when such an item was listed by a seller; now eBay added it, calling it "Personal Shopper." Out of the hearing of eBay, Kagle said, "Competition brings out the best. It may not be the most comfortable feeling for the participants, but it does produce a better result. 'Cause I *guarantee* you that the user experience at eBay will be better as a result of this— much sooner!"

Omidyar also took clear pleasure in the improvements eBay was making. "*Ex*cellent," he'd say at eBay's Amazon meetings, accenting and drawing out the first syllable. Whitman kept the pace of the meetings brisk but not so brisk that jokes didn't fly frequently. She and the team could exchange half-completed sentences; the working relationships were close, and that was helpful. Back in the fall, when Whitman returned from the IPO road show, she had commented on how strange an experience it had been, finding herself in nonstop meetings with one group of investors after another who were "nothing but white males" and how good it was to be home—this she said to nothing-but-white-male colleagues. But the eBay crew was not the love-to-hear-themselves-talk, feelings-impervious guys that constituted white-maleness; only when she stepped away from the eBay world was she reminded that her guys were different.

The atmosphere of an emergency was sustained even though a week after Amazon introduced its auction site, the number of listings slipped and then stayed static, for weeks. The Amazon meetings continued, and the data was scrutinized as carefully as if Amazon had 2.3 million listings like eBay, and not 55,000.

One thing that Amazon's entry had exposed indirectly, by contrast, was how eBay's customer service had not kept pace with the growth of its auctions. The service was badly broken, and frustrated customers tried to reach Whitman herself to complain when no one in eBay's customer-service department responded to their pleas. When she learned that her administrative assistant was fielding calls from irate customers, she told her assistant to put the calls through. In early May she got one from a customer who claimed he had sent twenty e-mail messages to customer service and had not received a single response. So while Whitman waited, her assistant called down to customer service to see if someone could be found to straighten the matter out. The phone rang but no one picked up. She tried another extension, and another, with no luck. The twentieth attempt succeeded in locating someone. Whitman told the story to the Amazon-meeting attendees without appending an editorial; the newly hired head of customer service took it all in, mumbled a promise that big changes were on the way, and let it go. But knowing that the CEO was personally fielding calls from angry customers when they could not find someone to speak with in his department would provide all the incentive he needed, and she knew it.

The Amazon meetings should have been called the Amazon-and-Yahoo meetings because even while Amazon seemed to stall, Yahoo's listings kept climbing. Its rate of completion remained low, less than 20 percent, but the raw number of listings passed 200,000 in April. "Why is that?" Whitman asked of the assembled group.

"There's always a group that likes RC Cola because it's cheaper," said Steve Westly. Free listings would always be cheaper than eBay's.

■

On April 23 the customary late-afternoon Amazon meeting was canceled at the last minute, preempted by a more pressing matter: negotiations to do a deal with the leading terrestrial auction firm, Sotheby's, which was also openly talking to Amazon, playing the one off against the other.

Whitman and Omidyar were in frequent communication with Bob Kagle, who was anything but encouraging of eBay's moving forward with Sotheby's. He told them not to be unduly worried about "Will we look like we're losing to Amazon if Amazon does this Sotheby's deal and we don't?" Sotheby's was not a must-have. A *sensible* deal with them? Sure. What Sotheby's could provide was credibility to move eBay's average selling price up and authentication services around art objects—that made sense to him.

But on the other hand, Kagle held that Sotheby's "was a very elitist brand. EBay is of the people, by the people, for the people. I think you risk changing the character and the tone of the eBay experience by affiliating with Sotheby's."

Kagle had to win over two people: Omidyar and Whitman. Initially, Omidyar did not see affiliation with Sotheby's as the threat that Kagle did, but Kagle rang his bell and got him thinking second and third thoughts.

Kagle told his partners that Whitman continued to lean toward Sotheby's. What would doing a business deal with Sotheby's say to the eBay community, Kagle wanted to know. "Are we enabling this person-to-person marketplace, or are we taking more than our fair share of the transaction, which I think is what most people would think Sotheby's does. In fact, Sotheby's is arguing to us, You guys are stupid. You're giving up money at the high end by charging low fees."

"To which I respond, Nope! That's our business!"

Kagle's position prevailed. Amazon did do a Sotheby's deal, and eBay announced the purchase of Butterfield & Butterfield, which occupied the midmarket segment of art auction houses. Newspapers played up the fact that a 4-year-old-company "swallow[ed]" a 134-year-old company, "the guppy eating the whale," and *Fortune* gleefully depicted the purchase as a repudiation of eBay's roots. (On a message board, one antique dealer wrote, "It seems that the 'junk' that brought Pierre millions is just not good enough anymore!")

Within eBay, the cultural differences between it and Butterfield were a source of humor in the days that followed the announcement, and eBay's twenty-somethings sat down with Butterfield's fifty-somethings to work out the details of the acquisition. Given their stock options, the former group was undoubtedly many times wealthier, at least on paper, than the latter, but their class identity lagged and they did not think of themselves as rich at all (just as Bob Kagle, a centimillionaire, was put off by Sotheby's culture of privilege). At an internal eBay marketing-group meeting, the young woman, two years out of Stanford, who was the primary liaison with Butterfield in planning a new, joint Great Collections page featuring art objects, told the group, "We're working on customer service for . . ." And after fumbling for a few seconds for a euphemism for customers who would be different from the usual eBay customers, she gave up and said, "um, rich folks." The room rang with laughter.

■

In mid-May, Amazon opened up a price war in books, offering *New York Times* best-sellers at 50 percent off. Most of the eBay executive staff members were glad to hear of it: another distraction from auctions. Every day Amazon seemed to enter an entirely new business: Investments in pet supplies and an online drugstore had been the most recent moves. But there was another view within eBay that held that the price war in books showed that once again Jeff Bezos was unpredictable, and he could bring woe to eBay without warning.

"Should we be spending any time trying to figure out what Amazon's next move is?" Meg Whitman wondered aloud.

"If I was making the case," Steve Westly said, pretending he was Bezos, "I'd say I'm not expecting much yet from auctions. They hit a plateau. They'll go up with another ten-million ad spend."

"They have a hundred people in auctions," said Gary Bengier, eBay's CFO. "That's a million dollars a month in head-count costs. They're going to try stuff."

"He could come in one day and say, 'Guess what? You're all going to be working on . . . pet drugs!' " cracked Mike Wilson, VP of engineering.

"Question is," Whitman said, "should we be doing anything in anticipation? Is there any way we can go to them and say, 'Can we take this off your hands?' " Remembering what Bezos had said the previous year when the eBay delegation had trooped up to Seattle, she then took back the thought; there was no way Bezos would consider such a possibility.

■

Date: 06/09/99 Time: 07:12:44 PDT
*** Noticed something different about eBay today? *** After several months of working on a new way to organize information on eBay—as well as incorporating your helpful feedback—we launched the new eBay site this morning! Many of you helped us by testing our beta (trial) site, which has been accessible to eBay members since April. And others of you even participated in focus groups, one-on-one usability tests, and surveys. . . .

So why did eBay make this change? If it ain't broke, don't fix it, right? Well, we wanted to make eBay easier to use for everyone, including newer eBay members, who may have had difficulty with the old site. The easier we make eBay to use, the more people are likely to bid on items and to create more business for our sellers!

When the new design was put in place on the morning of June 9, 1999, it marked the first significant change since the site had gone from black-and-white to color in 1997.

The spirits of the marketing group's weekly meeting that morning were high. The redesign of the Web pages had been a consuming project, with the focus groups and debates and planning and coordination with engineering, and finally it was done. Westly presented the weekly Gold Gavel Award, for making the most contributions the preceding week, to the two organizers of a group party held at a member's house the preceding weekend, which, besides being fun, had helped knit the new members in; of the thirty people in the room, more than half had been hired in the past six months.

As staff members reviewed the status of various projects under way, the only visible thunderstorm was coming from Amazon's direction. After two months of static listings, Amazon had made available to sellers a "bulk loader" that expedited uploading of many items at once. EBay had lagged in developing a bulk loader with the same ease of use. In the meantime, Amazon's listings had shot from 60,000 to more than 120,000. But Westly was not overly concerned about this blip. After getting a report about the imminent introduction of eBay's own new, improved bulk loader, he told the group, "We're going to leave the others in the dust." He smiled. "But of course in a nice eBaysian way."

The ebullience of that moment would not be sustained through the end of that day.

Date: 06/09/99 Time: 18:24:02 PDT We apologize, but we are currently experiencing system problems. Some of you may receive a connection error while this is ongoing. Engineering is working to get everything back to normal as quickly as possible. We thank you for your patience. Regards, eBay

Date: 06/09/99 Time: 18:55:28 PDT ** System Update ** We are so very sorry, but there have been additional problems with the system and it is not coming back up at this time. Engineering is working diligently to get everything back to normal. Unfortunately this is going to take longer than expected. We will keep you updated as we work through this. Thank you very much for your patience! Regards, eBay

A month earlier, when *The New York Times* ran a profile of Meg Whitman, the article mentioned that eBay's site had been afflicted with short outages recently. She had called Scott McNealy, chairman of Sun Microsystems, and had said, "Scott, I need a nanny for this system until the baby gets better." From then on, Sun technicians had been on call twenty-four hours a day, but the reporter noticed that the baby was still fussy—the site had been down for four hours in the previous week.

Now, when Sun got the call, it flew in its crisis-intervention team, who had been in Tijuana. Within hours, three hundred technical personnel from Sun and Oracle were swarming over eBay's engineering group.

Date: 06/09/99 Time: 22:03:01 PDT We currently have vendor engineers on site working with our engineers to resolve the problem. We will continue to keep you updated throughout this situation. As stated below, auctions will be extended per our "Automatic Auction Extension Policy." We sincerely apologize for this unfortunate inconvenience and thank you for your patience! Regards, eBay

In retrospect, it was easy to find the blind spot that Meg Whitman and kitchen-cabinet member Bob Kagle shared: more interest in marketing issues than engineering ones. It was not that either was blind to the technical problems that grew as eBay itself grew; but neither Whitman nor Kagle was willing to push everything else to the side and focus full attention on the problems.

After the outage she experienced on her second day on the job a little more than a year earlier, Whitman had augmented engineering's budget and thought the systems beast had been tamed. At the time, Kagle, watching as a director and informal advisor, was not convinced.

At Benchmark he had lamented that the weakness in eBay's systems "is the only thing that could get us at this company."

"You've persevered through that before," Andy Rachleff had observed, in a sympathetic voice, recalling Kagle's pushing eBay for the upgrade in systems that was put in place after Benchmark's investment decision.

Kagle was not consoled by the reminder that the systems problems remained. "It's something that really should be fixed."

"*Fixed* is a relative term," Rachleff corrected.

"Yeah. For a while." They shared smiles of resignation.

Kevin Harvey, a software guy himself, asked, "Is eBay on a new architecture now, or is it wire and glue holding it together?"

"They did the architectural changes that we talked about. It's more that every time we go up another factor of two, something else shows strain in the system."

He had seen it coming, but he had not stayed on it. When it broke, he did not blame others; he blamed himself.

Date: 06/11/99 Time: 02:00:13 PDT ***** SYSTEM UPDATE ***** Engineering is still working hard to complete the rebuild of the corrupted disk files. We will continue to update you as the recovery progresses. Thank you again for your patience and support during this difficult time. Regards, eBay

The glitch that had brought the system down apparently was related to a problem in Sun's operating system. Sun had previously made a patch available that fixed the problem, but eBay's engineers had not installed it. Still, eBay's redesigned home page was pulled and the old one restored, just on the off chance that it somehow was related to the outage.

Date: 06/11/99 Time: 13:53:28 PDT ***** SYSTEM UPDATE ***** Folks, we do apologize, but it looks like the system won't be up until approximately 16:00–17:00 PDT Engineering found additional corrupted data files. Although no data was lost, they are taking every precaution to ensure 100 percent viability before bringing up the database. Our deepest regrets for this delay, but we want to make sure everything is fully functional before bringing the system back up. Regards, eBay

Date: 06/11/99 Time: 17:37:01 PDT *** Important Letter from Meg and Pierre *** June 11, 1999 To our valued community members: We are sorry. We know that you expect uninterrupted service from eBay. We believe that this is reasonable, and we know we haven't lived up to your expectations. We want to earn back your trust that we'll provide you with this level of service. . . . We want to assure you that our highest priority today—as always—is your trading success. We also understand that keeping the site up and running is crucial to your achievement of this success. We cannot apologize enough for this disruption in our service and in your ability to participate in online commerce. . . . We have taken a serious look at our priorities because of this outage. We hope you will give us the chance to show you our commitment to your success and to keeping eBay up and running 24 hours a day, 7 days a week. Our goal: Uninterrupted service. No fancy bells and whistles. We just want to make it work. To help ensure this, we are working diligently on a hot backup system that should automatically limit the length of potential outages to less than an hour or so. We have been working on this system for many months, and it is almost ready. Sadly, if we had this system in place a few days ago, we might have avoided this outage. . . . We are refunding ALL fees for ALL ACTIVE auctions on eBay. We promise to redouble our efforts to make sure that another outage like this one will never happen again. Our sincere apologies, Meg and Pierre

On the following Monday, Bob Kagle opened the partners' meeting with a day-by-day review of the problems that engineering had grappled with over the course of the past week.

"Here's some really good news. The community is *totally* hanging in there. There's been no uptake in either Yahoo or Amazon since it happened. At all."

"Is this the most defensible business to be in or what?" said Kevin Harvey, amazed at users' loyalty.

The cheering would prove premature; Yahoo was already beginning to draw users away, and within two weeks Yahoo's listings would go from 250,000 to more than 400,000. But the market had not waited to tally the data before reacting. On the preceding Friday, eBay's stock had dropped 17 points, from 182 to 165. That Monday, as the partners discussed the situation, it was being crushed, losing 30 points, as investors reacted to eBay's warning that it expected to take a $3 to $5 million charge against earnings that quarter because of the outage. In two days, the stock lost 25 percent of its market value.

"I don't understand how one day [of outage] results in [a loss of] three to five million of forecast earnings," Bruce Dunlevie said.

Kagle explained, "In addition to that lost operating opportunity, you've got to give people relistings for X period of time for free. Just being good guys."

"Why do you think the stock is down so much? 'Cause that three- to five-million-dollar number was published? Or people are losing faith that the company can just keep the site up?"

"Keep in mind," Bill Gurley spoke up, "it's actually doing better [than some others]. I mean, Amazon is trading at less than fifty percent of its high right now. Almost all Internet stocks lost ten percent on Friday, almost all of them."

Whitman had asked that Kagle and Kevin Harvey join her that morning immediately after their partners' meeting to meet with senior executives from Sun and Oracle.

"She needs some coaching," Harvey guessed in advance, "just about technology. It's probably a legitimate thing in her mind that it's their fault."

"I was going to say the same thing," said Beirne. "This is all so new to her. It's like, the suppliers in her old business, if they didn't get the product there or something was screwed up in delivery . . ." there really were no excuses.

"In the technology business," Harvey said, "you live with bugs and you work with them; you assume they're there."

"Right," Kagle agreed. "I think the first step is to take responsibility for your own system."

The meeting with Sun and Oracle turned out to be free of finger-pointing. Whitman simply sought technical guidance from the vendors. But when the eBay contingent suggested that the outage had been caused by a system so complex that it was unique, the SWAT teams from Sun and Oracle shook their heads in dissent, as they thought of the systems at banks and at NASDAQ that they had been flown in to fix, too.

Ironically, Amazon provided indirect support for eBay's position. Instead of crowing that its systems were wholly reliable in contrast to eBay's, Amazon spokesperson Bill Curry said, "These are large, complex systems. There are things that are beyond anyone's control." What had happened to eBay turned out, upon inspection, to have been within human control. EBay should have had in place redundant processing; a mirrored site to test changes to the system; procedures that ensured that change orders that tinkered with the system were more closely supervised; the hot backup system ready ("hot" meaning it could be swapped instantly). With more experience, eBay would have been further along, but adolescence cannot be skipped.

■

On the walls of eBay's Amazon War Room, someone had posted the front pages of the previous Saturday's newspapers: the *San Jose Mercury News*: EBAY AUCTIONS FROZEN FOR 22 HOURS; the *Los Angeles Times*: NEARLY DAYLONG OUTAGE PLAGUING ONLINE AUCTION. Even though Meg Whitman had spent a harrowing weekend working with the SWAT teams from Oracle and Sun, she looked unchanged. When she walked in the room for the regularly scheduled Amazon meeting and overheard one of the managers report, before the meeting had begun, that "Amazon numbers are down!" she broke out in a grin, clenched her fist and pulled downward, and exclaimed, "Yes!"

Amazingly, eBay's listing numbers were coming back as fast as sellers could get back on the system—more than 300,000 new listings each day. Most of the day's meeting was spent puzzling over the data; could eBay's user base really be so loyal?

"You heard about the woman"—Steve Westly asked of Whitman and Pierre Omidyar—"who said, 'EBay, stop apologizing already. You're too feminine. Suck it up!'"

"I love it!" said Whitman.

Omidyar remained concerned that the user community did not have the data that showed that eBay's sellers had stayed put. "My recurring refrain is, Perception has an undue weight here. In our community—and I don't care what's in the press—but in our community, if there is a *perception* that listings are going down, it will become a self-fulfilling prophecy."

Westly had prepared a draft of a press release that presented data pointing to a downturn of listings at Amazon. Omidyar vetoed its release, however. "It's always better to emphasize our strength." Talking about defections, even to show their absence, would only serve to call attention to the issue.

EBay's users were remaining calm, Westly said, but the customized screen, My-eBay, had yet to be restored. Whitman, who had overnight been forced to learn a technical lexicon, explained it would remain off until continuing problems with "Oracle latching" were solved. It was really not an Oracle problem but a result of hasty re-assembly after the initial outage. "It's like when you crash a car," she explained. "There are parts all over the highway. You put them all back together, and there's a clanking sound. You know how the car will never be the same after an accident? Well, I've been assured that that won't be the case here." She laughed ruefully. At that moment there still were clanking sounds.

A week later eBay's listings reached 2.2 million, almost back to the preoutage level. In the same week Amazon's dropped 15 percent; the week following they dropped another 8.5 percent. Amazon had been given the perfect opportunity to pull eBay customers to its site, yet it had failed to do so.

Bob Kagle told his Benchmark partners that eBay was "throwing money like crazy now" at technology investments, which he was pleased with. "Meg's doing a good job. She's really dug in. She's now a technology exec." He laughed and thought for a moment. "These things can be blessings in disguise, no doubt about it. To have recovered as quickly as we did, and had the learning that happened in the last two weeks."

Within three months eBay's listings went from 2.1 million to 4.1 million.

21. Hoover Dam

As the final countdown for Webvan's June launch began, Dave Beirne returned for one of his periodic visits to the Oakland distribution center. The visits were ostensibly to check on progress but in fact seemed to be a source of fuel for the spirit. "I am so stoked!" he said as he climbed out of the car and met Gary Dahl, Webvan's vice president for distribution, at the central dock. It was not the financial aspects of the deal, but Webvan's ambitious reach to reshape the retailing landscape, that made it a sentimental favorite of Beirne's, even though he never would have confessed to it out loud.

Much work had been done since the eBoys visited the facility en masse. The mammoth kitchen areas had been filled out with equipment and were already in use, refining the routines of preparing pre-cooked meals as beta testing had begun the day before, delivering to households of employees—and investors. Beirne admired an enormous standing pot with boiling chicken stock and took a look at the blast chillers, which maintained temperatures as low as −40 degrees F., into which freshly cooked pasta would be plunged. He paused for a moment in the meat department and asked Dahl why the meat was being wrapped in plastic rather than paper like the local gourmet grocer's. "That was a big fight," Dahl allowed. "That was a battle we lost." The advocates of plastic prevailed with the argument that it was better to show off the quality of the meat, especially since customer concern about the quality of items that they could not personally select was initially likely to be high.

Produce was the one area that was conspicuously low-tech: a few rows of wire shelves, upon which were cardboard bins holding the day's fresh produce. Dahl pointed to the box holding heads of lettuce and explained that customers would be able to eat lettuce at dinner that had still been in the ground at the beginning of that day. Walking through the rest of the center, Beirne had exclaimed in unbroken succession, "Great!" "Awesome!" and "Incredible!" but here he gushed with febrile abandon. "Look at the quality!" The credit went to Borders, he said. "You can just feel Louis here—high-quality, thoughtful."

Beirne and his partners at Benchmark had not received their passwords yet, so they had not yet been able to place their first order in the Webvan beta test. On his way back to his office, Beirne called Borders and pretended that the missing passwords had been an intentional slight. Borders apologized for the delay. "You should have been my number-one man!" Borders said. "You should kick my ass."

"That's okay," Beirne said. "I'm coming back from a tour—it's awesome."

"It's coming along," Borders said. "It's coming along."

■

If Louis Borders had had his way, Webvan would not have been mentioned in the press by a single soul, right up until the day of the public launch. This reluctance was a mixture of personal shyness and calculated stealth, but by April 1999, *The Wall Street Journal* told him that it would hold off on a story no longer, and the only decision Borders could make at that point was whether to offer an interview. Dave Beirne put in a vote for cooperating, and Borders acceded.

What's most interesting about that moment were the metaphors that were used in the resulting article to talk about the Webvan experiment. One unidentified venture capitalist described Webvan as a "moonshot," a daring, high-risk venture, and the reporter wondered alternatively whether the company would end up becoming "the Internet era's equivalent of *Waterworld,* a disaster so epic it becomes an American legend."

Such comparisons were made casually, but they are worthy of a second look because they throw into relief how Webvan was actually quite different from either a big-budget space program or a big-budget movie. One obvious difference was cost: *Apollo 11*'s 1969 landing on the moon was the culmination of eight years of manned space programs that had spent $24 billion. The Webvan moon-shot was a bargain, by comparison. It would be headed for an IPO having only burned up $50 million in capital. Not all start-ups that launch untested technology can start off with an ante of that size—Iridium, for example, burned through a $5 billion investment before its creditors and shareholders learned that there were virtually no customers for $5-a-minute wireless phone service anywhere around the globe. Benchmark, as an early-stage investor, only had to put up $3 million, in Webvan's initial round of financing, to get a seat.

The business risks entailed in the Webvan experiment were also more palatable, at least conceptually, because of the way that Webvan's service, if it were to become accepted, would become a regular part of life for its customers. Louis Borders told investors that he calculated that the lifetime value of a Webvan customer, purchasing groceries alone, would be $40,000. In contrast with weekly grocery orders, lunar landing missions were rather rare—the last one, in 1972, took place only three years after the first—and did not meet the everyday needs of the masses. Most movies that do well at the box office have their run for a few weeks and then disappear until a video release. No one's daily routines are much affected by the question of whether *Titanic* did well and *Waterworld* did not. But if Webvan were to attract large numbers of customers that were willing to shift their shopping from Safeway—*and* from Wal-Mart *and* from Amazon (and their reliance on UPS *and* FedEx)—then that would have a conspicuous and enduring effect on the way people spent their time and money, day after day, week after week, month after month. Given Webvan's outsized ambition, this was an experiment that required comparatively small table stakes—Webvan still was a very, very large *small* business.

■

One week after Webvan's beta test began, Kevin Harvey asked Andy Rachleff—both of them lived in Portola Valley—whether he'd shopped on Webvan yet. Rachleff said no.

Beirne overheard the exchange. "You haven't shopped on Webvan yet? The fuck is that?"

Rachleff was apologetic. His wife had tried but could not reach the site. "There's a bug in her browser."

It didn't matter, Harvey said, because the company didn't deliver in their neighborhood.

"They don't?" Rachleff asked.

"They don't deliver on Sundays, either," Bruce Dunlevie added.

"Not yet," Beirne explained. "It's the first phase of the beta. This thing only has twelve thousand SKUs. Sorry!" He told the partners that Elizabeth Dunlevie had called his wife to complain that there were nine items that she had wanted to order that Webvan did not stock. "I almost called Elizabeth and said, 'Elizabeth!' "—he shouted with mock exasperation—" 'It's *beta!*' "

■

On the morning of June 2, under overcast skies, Webvan held a brief coming-out party for itself, inviting members of the press, assorted business associates, and Webvan employees to a ribbon-cutting ceremony, held in the Oakland facility's parking lot. The affair was a public relations pseudo event intended to provide a news peg for stories about the company's debut. But Louis Borders was so concerned that the competition not learn the details of the Webvan system that he could not bring himself to permit the guests to actually see anything; they had to remain standing in the parking lot, munching hors d'oeuvres. The produce stands flanking the podium were the only indication that behind the closed doors to the rear was food, not rolls of galvanized steel.

Borders wore a baggy dark blue sport jacket and a light green knit shirt and did not seem at ease at the podium. Reading from notes, he briefly recited some catchphrases such as "brand selection" and "outstanding prices," and then recalled nostalgically, "I remember the days when neighborhoods were dotted with delivery trucks." Webvan, combining the latest technology with the service of the past, would give customers "a lost and valuable resource: time."

Polite applause followed, but Borders had only been the warm-up act. No sooner had he finished than the headline attraction bounded to the podium: Oakland mayor Jerry Brown. The former California governor was dressed almost identically to Borders—dark sport jacket, black sport shirt, no tie—but he showed the politician's fondness for hearing his own public-speaker voice. Brown gripped the podium and, without notes, shouted out thoughts in short bursts:

"Oakland is going to reach out and change the way things are done! Can't wait to get back to the office and order."

He paused and then offered an aside: "I hope my Internet connection will be working"—this provoked a few nervous laughs—"and that it will be a fast connection. Because speed is everything."

He was rhapsodic in praising the technology that allowed someone to use on-screen menus to select desired items. "That is power! It's decentralization! It's the wave of the future. Thank you."

■

The question that remained unanswered was whether Webvan was timed well. The beta test, restricted as it was to friends, family, and investors, provided no advance data, and no market research was done. The only way to get an answer was to open the doors, figuratively speaking, and see whether people walked in. No advertising was launched; Webvan executives were concerned that if too many customers arrived at the site at the same time, the systems, which had never been stress-tested with real customers, might break under the crush. So the company simply removed the password protection on the website and waited for customers to show up and order.

It was a slow start. Two days after the ribbon-cutting ceremony, 200 orders were expected but only 125 came in. The system was designed to accommodate 8,000 orders a day. While waiting for demand to materialize, the company reserved Mondays for internal tests of "volume testing," which put through 1,000 hypothetical orders. Instead of picking actual goods, Post-it notes were used as substitutes and placed in bins, which then went out to the various substations, then into vans. The delivery people then drove out to addresses assigned by the computer and waited a certain amount of time to simulate delivery.

A number of initial minor glitches surfaced in the first days: Too few vans because the vendor was late in delivering the vehicles Webvan had ordered. Assignments of sequential deliveries that could never have been executed when promised without a helicopter. Parking nightmares in San Francisco that made it impossible for drivers to park legally and still make their deliveries on time. The driver who tried to take his ten-foot-tall van through an eight-foot-high underpass. That these sorts of problems were the worst of the headaches showed that Webvan was spared the real nightmare—a system that simply did not work. This was no mean achievement.

■

EBay had forcefully become acquainted with that nightmare, and its stock had taken a beating. On the day preceding the outage, eBay's shares had closed at 183; by the next day, they slipped to 165; the day following they were at 136. And eBay's technical woes were not over. There was a five-hour outage in June, a two-hour outage in July, and a nine-hour outage in August, which sent the stock down 10 percent, to 83, the next day. All Internet stocks had a tough summer, however. By August 4, the Dow Jones Internet index had dropped to 44 percent below its record close of April 13. Amazon was down 60 percent; Schwab, 52 percent; AOL, 50 percent; Yahoo, 50 percent. The NASDAQ composite index officially met the definition of "market correction," as it was off more than 10 percent from its high.

Bob Kagle remained certain that Internet stocks had much farther to fall; reality could only be kept at bay for so long. He gave each of his partners a copy of Edward Chancellor's history of financial manias, *Devil Take the Hindmost,* urging them to read it. Chancellor's account of England's railway mania of 1845 had made an especially deep impression on Kagle, who saw all of the similarities between the railroad, then hailed as a revolutionary advance without historical parallel, and the Internet. In both cases the technological change was as fundamental as its champions claimed, but investors' enthusiasm about imminent opportunities to reap fortunes moved beyond the reasonable. All businesses must earn a profit in order to be viable; Kagle refused to relinquish this simple truth. When Internet stocks bounced back for two days in August, Kagle shrugged; it was, he said, a "dead-cat bounce": Dropped from sufficient height, even a dead cat will bounce.

None of his partners owned up to completing their assigned reading, but Kevin Harvey, who had been one of the most stalwart bulls in the group, now said he had the same foreboding as Kagle. "Companies are buying companies with Confederate money," he said at one partners' meeting, referring to the inflated currency of high-priced stocks. "I'm not a flat-earther, but companies are sold for two hundred million today that would have been twenty before."

"You've gone to the dark side," said Bruce Dunlevie, horrified.

The bubble would eventually pop, Harvey maintained.

Bob Kagle reminded the optimists that in the venture capital downturn of 1983–84, annual returns had been in the single digits.

"Didn't have the ecosystem then," Dave Beirne asserted as rejoinder. "The whole Valley is built around entrepreneurship. It'll be hard to kill."

The present moment's worship of the entrepreneur might be a bad portent, Kagle suggested. "You guys believe when somebody is on the cover of a magazine, they've reached the peak? Tends to be midnight at the party."

Two years previously, Beirne recalled, everyone he knew had said to him, "You're at the top of your game; why be a venture guy? It's already crested—there's no more upside." Obviously, that would have been bad advice for him to heed.

Kagle did not agree. "It's like the 1840s railroads. What I'm seeing right now is an environment where every company you fund will have a dozen well-capitalized competitors."

"That's why I think the Internet thing is going to eventually crash," concurred Harvey.

■

What all of the Benchmark partners could agree upon was that the ability of a company to produce profits remained the touchstone for a true built-to-last company, even if investors seemed less than concerned. EBay was the company that all were most proud of, as it was that rarity, a *profitable* Internet company. Even when investors treated eBay's shares no differently from money-losing Amazon's—

and on August 4 eBay's stock was off 68 percent from its fifty-two-week high—eBay remained the brightest star among the many Benchmark successes for that reason.

Amazon's Jeff Bezos defiantly told the world that Amazon would be "unprofitable for a long time"; his bravado in pursuing growth above all else served to reassure investors that Amazon was on course. Webvan's Louis Borders, however, did not subscribe to the Bezos line. Borders publicly stated, "I don't see any reason why an Internet company should take five to ten years to be profitable," and in this way Webvan was philosophically linked to eBay. He predicted that Webvan's first distribution center in Oakland would be profitable within six to twelve months.

The only way that Borders could achieve profitability and at the same time pursue the grand vision of a national rollout was by enlisting the assistance of business partners. It was this task that Dave Beirne energetically addressed when Louis Borders was on the verge of resorting to scaled-down expedients in order to claim national distribution. Beirne and the other members of the board were able to convince Borders to hold off changing course while Beirne investigated a possible answer: enlisting Bechtel, the world's largest construction company, to replicate the Oakland distribution center. Beirne had a close tie with Fred Gluck, its former vice chairman, whom Beirne had recruited to Scient's board of directors. With a few phone calls, Beirne got an appointment to see John Carter and Adrian Zaccaria, Bechtel's executive vice president and president.

"We don't do retail," Carter explained, after listening to the Webvan pitch.

"Guys," Beirne said, "don't think of this as retail. You will be a major player in electronic commerce. This is the only play where you can actually do bricks and mortar *and* e-commerce. If this works, we build over five hundred of these in the next few years in the U.S., plus we go global. This is *huge*." Unable to elicit a visibly encouraging response, Beirne said, "I'm going to say something, and I want you to not laugh us out of the room: Webvan is every bit as important to Bechtel as *the Hoover Dam*."

The mention of Bechtel's glory, the company's first megaproject, the then-largest civil-engineering project in the United States—and one completed two years ahead of schedule and under budget—was a calculated play to Bechtel's vanity. It did not produce the desired results, however. Over the next weeks Bechtel moved agonizingly slowly in negotiations. When Webvan balked at signing Bechtel's standard contract, which in Webvan's view stipulated an imbalanced relationship that gave Bechtel all the advantages, Beirne used what he called the "take-away," the same technique he used when his Benchmark partners were being obstinate. He called Carter to say, "The opportunity is trading away. If you don't think Webvan is the most important relationship for Bechtel, that's fine."

"Dave," Carter pleaded, "your comment about Hoover Dam? We're on it. We're getting mobilized." As a gesture of penance, a delegation of Bechtel executives was dispatched to meet with Beirne, Borders, and the Webvan executive team. Negotiations were reopened and an agreement was announced in early July. Webvan placed a $1 billion order for distribution centers for twenty-six cities and at the same time announced it had raised $275 million in a private round of financing that gave the company a valuation exceeding $4 billion.

■

Dave Beirne didn't pause to worry about Webvan's prospects, at least when he was speaking with his partners. He forwarded to the others an e-mail message about Webvan order flow that he had received from Louis Borders two weeks after commencement of deliveries to the public. Beirne sent it with an excited annotation: "Scaling Without Advertising," but the scaling was decidedly modest. On a given day, Webvan was delivering a grand total of 382 orders. The average order had twenty-one items, adding up to only $75. (Borders predicted that the average order size would go up considerably when Webvan secured its liquor license.) What Webvan could show was that the basic system worked. It could not show that Bay Area residents were fighting one another to get in through the virtual doorframe.

Without advertising, there would not be much scaling. How best to communicate Webvan's offerings posed a creative challenge. The first print ad, which took up two full pages in the local newspapers, was taken up almost entirely with a photograph of a live lobster standing defiantly on the carpet in someone's living room. A man crouched near it, with fingers spread, about to pounce upon it, presumably retrieving dinner. In the upper left-hand corner was a brief explanation: "7:15 P.M. Fresh seafood is delivered free to a couple in Oakland." On the far right was more text, introducing Webvan's delivery service. "Whether it's cake mix, caviar, or live lobster, the selection and quality is amazing." (The caviar and live lobster seemed a far remove from Jerry Brown's breezy Power to the People introduction a few days before at the ribbon-cutting ceremony.) "All you have to do is unpack the groceries. Unless, of course, they unpack themselves first." Another print advertisement apparently was designed to appeal to the same high-income demographic group: A woman in a swimsuit is lazing on a recliner in a spa or tanning salon, with cucumber slices placed on her eyes—while Webvan does her shopping.

In the long view, the first advertisements were curiosities, not a medium from which Webvan's future could be divined. Even in the short view, those advertisements and the modest rate of order growth were not regarded by Webvan's venture backers and investment bankers as material, not when placed against the potential business that could be imagined in the future. In the July 1999 financing, Webvan's $4 billion private-placement valuation bore no relation to the valuation of traditional grocery stores. Winn-Dixie, for example, had a market value at the time of about $6 billion but operated eleven hundred stores. By such measures, Webvan's valuation was unsupportable. But by other measures, it didn't seem so high. When Benchmark was discussing whether it should invest in the round when Webvan had a $4 billion price tag, Kevin Harvey asked what was the present market cap of FedEx. It was $13 billion—a number that had nothing to do with Internet froth—and one could see that a case could be made for regarding FedEx as the comparable company rather than Amazon. But for the comparison to hold up, both customers and profits would have to materialize.

In August, Webvan filed registration papers for its initial public offering. This was an aggressive schedule, even by the standards set by other Internet companies. The most recent period for which it could offer financial results was the one that had ended on June 30, when its delivery service in the Bay Area had barely begun. Sales for the first six months of 1999 had only been $395,000; the actual cost of those groceries to Webvan had been $419,000; and the company had posted a loss for that period of $35 million.

In September, on the eve of the IPO, the company's stature grew when Webvan announced that it had recruited as its new CEO George Shaheen, fifty-five years old, the chief executive and managing partner of Andersen Consulting. Shaheen's decision to jump to Webvan implicitly conferred on his new home the credibility associated with the firm he had headed, a $9 billion company.

Shaheen arrived just in time to join the Webvan road show, bringing the forceful public persona that Wall Street demanded and that Louis Borders lacked. A professional CEO like Shaheen needed little time to acclimate: Just a week after joining Webvan, he smoothly articulated the company's potential business to institutional investors when the show arrived at the Goldman Sachs offices in San Francisco.

Custom dictated that the lead underwriter provide financial projections to the gathered investors, and Goldman Sachs's estimates of red ink for Webvan would give anyone pause. Revenues for 1999 would be $11.9 million, with net losses of $73.8 million; revenues would climb to $518 million by 2001, but losses would be $302 million. However, with $300 million in cash in hand, no debt, and the expectation of raising another $350 million from the IPO, it appeared that Webvan was financially well positioned to build out its centers nationally.

Louis Borders showed a slide titled "Enormous Addressable Market," which offered a listing of the annual revenues for three businesses—groceries ($449 billion); drugstores ($106 billion); home meals ($100 billion). And then Shaheen described how Webvan didn't merely reach the customer's door, but literally crossed the threshold and stepped inside the home (when the Webvan delivery person unloaded the totes), creating an intimately personal relationship with the customer that no other Net business had any chance of reproducing.

The Webvan vision appeared to cow skeptics in the room. The only questions that the prospective investors mustered concerned the picayune: How soon after ordering could the groceries be delivered? What percentage of orders are delivered when the customer is not home? How could online customers be induced to buy impulsively? The most substantive one posed in the session was this: What was to keep local grocery stores from adding technology so that they could deliver groceries, too? Shaheen had a ready answer: "They're adding cost to existing cost; the physical store becomes an albatross."

The Webvan road show proceeded on to other cities and the IPO would have been completed as planned were it not for an unexpected development. The Securities and Exchange Commission intervened and prevailed on Webvan to delay the offering. The SEC was upset that Shaheen had made comments about Webvan in an interview that was quoted in *Forbes,* which the SEC deemed inappropriate in the "quiet period" preceding an IPO. The commission was also upset that the contents of the road show had been disseminated publicly by Adam Lashinsky, a writer for *TheStreet.com,* who had listened in to a conference call version of the show.

The delay of the offering at the behest of the SEC, an unusual event, drew a slew of attention to the way that the democratization of investing had still failed to fully democratize access to IPO-related information. The restrictive by-invitation-only nature of road shows required by the SEC—which Lashinsky had breached—kept members of the general public from knowing as much as the privileged, the institutional investors. Lashinsky asked, "Why not throw the show open to the great unwashed, if only in a listen-only mode?"

With an amended prospectus that incorporated the financial projections and other information that had originally been provided only to the road show attendees, Webvan was permitted to refile its plans for an IPO. It turned out that the publicity had worked in Webvan's favor, piquing the curiosity of investors who had not heard of the company before the furor about the unquiet "quiet period." Instead of pricing the issue in the $11 to $13 range as had originally been planned, the offering went out at $15 a share, and on the first day of trading it closed at almost $25 a share. Its market capitalization was more than $8 billion, or nearly half of Safeway's.

At Benchmark, no party was held to commemorate the successful offering. The company had only begun to realize its founding vision, and Dave Beirne was too superstitious to allow premature celebration to jinx the venture. He swore aloud that Webvan was going to be a $100 billion company—in annual revenues, not merely market capitalization—but he also knew the risks related to execution that still lay ahead. Two years earlier, Louis Borders had declared that Webvan would either be a $10 billion company—or zero. His prediction was fundamentally sound; he had been off only by an order of magnitude. A $100 billion company. Or zero.

22. Built to Win

That only two years had elapsed between the time Webvan was added to the portfolio and its IPO was a sign of the tremendous acceleration in a young firm's life cycle. Even two years, however, was relatively long. Other companies in the portfolio that had been started well after Webvan took their first public bows at the same time or even before Webvan.

One of these was Red Hat, a North Carolina–based software distributor of the Linux operating system, at the forefront of the open-source movement whose internal code was freely published. The company had received a $2 million investment from Benchmark in September 1998 at a price of $20 million pre-.

At first glance it appeared that Red Hat was competing against Microsoft with the same hopeless odds of success that Netscape had. But Kevin Harvey took the view that Red Hat could avoid a frontal challenge to Microsoft's business model; he worked to reposition the company away from the business of selling packaged software in boxes (Harvey's old business) and move it toward providing support services and a central website for the Linux community. The only way Microsoft could compete with Red Hat, he would say gleefully, "is by abandoning five billion dollars of annual revenue, which they can't!" Exactly one year after Benchmark's investment, Red Hat went public, with its stock priced at $14 a share, giving it a nominal value of $935 million.

Just before the IPO, on the eve of the pricing decision, Harvey tried to persuade Red Hat's investment bankers to tell their institutional buyers who held large positions in Microsoft stock that Red Hat, with its alternative operating system, offered a convenient hedge in case Microsoft should take ill. He suggested that Microsoft investors purchase shares of Red Hat equivalent to 1 percent of their Microsoft holdings. Harvey was hardly a disinterested observer, but if one accepted his reasoning, it was conceivable that Red Hat could claim a market value that was 1 percent of Microsoft's $500 billion, or $5 billion, which almost looked unassuming and reasonable when placed alongside the larger figure.

Perhaps it was this rationale that found a receptive audience. In any case, on August 11, the first day of trading, Red Hat jumped from $14 to $54.50 a share, or a market cap of $3.6 billion. A month later it had passed $119—and the company was worth $8 billion. Benchmark's $2 million investment was now worth, on paper, almost $700 million.

Another Kevin Harvey company, the one started by his high school buddies that had entered the portfolio as Newwatch the year before, also went out quickly. It had gone through dramatic changes, receiving a new pseudo-Anglo name—Ashford.com—and adding lots of high-end luxury product-line extensions beyond new watches (antique watches, fountain pens, perfumes, leather goods, sunglasses). The "friendship risk" that Kevin Harvey and his partners had worried about before committing to the investment had been kept at bay; when the company's continued growth needed new executive leadership, Harvey and the board recruited a senior executive from Compaq as Ashford's new CEO, and the incumbent, James Whitcomb, accepted his new role as chief operating officer without blowing up either the company or his friendship with Harvey. When Ashford went public in September 1999, the market gave it a value of $600 million, exactly one hundred times its appraised value when Benchmark invested the previous year.

Other companies that had gone out earlier in the year prospered in dramatic fashion, even when the prices of other Internet stocks were diving. It was especially satisfying to the partners to see homegrown companies do so well. Ariba, the e-commerce company that helped businesses order supplies and materials, had begun in Benchmark's office when Keith Krach and Paul Hegarty, entrepreneurs in residence who had not known each other previously, decided to go into business together. Benchmark invested $4 million; Bob Kagle served as the director representing Benchmark and spoke frequently with CEO Krach as a strategic advisor (and morale-boosting buddy). Three months after going public in 1999, its market cap was $8 billion. Benchmark owned 14 percent, a chunk worth about $1.1 billion. Krach, who, like Kagle, had left the security of General Motors, was now worth on paper about $960 million.

The same week in June that Ariba went public, so did Juniper Networks, a manufacturer of high-speed Internet routers that was directly challenging Cisco. Benchmark had invested in Juniper in August 1996, at the urging of Andy Rachleff. The partnership's stake was small, only 2.3 percent, but this was another of many Rachleff bets in networking-related businesses that did exceedingly well. Juniper's market cap, at the close of the first day of trading, was almost $5 billion. (On the speakerphone the following Monday, Dave Beirne tendered his compliments: "Bob, studly on Ariba. Andy, studly on Juniper.") By early September, Juniper's value had climbed to almost $10 billion, giving Benchmark a stake worth almost $230 million.

Scient, the computer-services consulting company founded by Eric Greenberg, was another home-incubated company that shone brightly. It had added consultants to its payroll as fast as it could hire them, yet demand for its services continued to exceed supply. Investors perceived Scient's capacity "problem" as a rather nice one for a company to have and accorded it the highest market capitalization in its business; by early September, the company was worth $2.8 billion, and Eric Greenberg, thirty-five, was listed in a *Fortune* magazine article on "America's 40 Richest Under 40" as worth $355 million, immediately behind Michael Jordan ($357 million). For Benchmark's original $3 million investment in Scient, and the business and personal advice provided by Dave Beirne and his colleagues, the partnership owned equity worth about $400 million. With these and other stories from the firm's portfolio, Bob Kagle need not have worried that after eBay's success the world would view Benchmark as a one-trick pony.

A few other Benchmark-affiliated names appeared on *Fortune*'s 40 Richest Under 40 list: eBay's Pierre Omidyar, thirty-two, occupied fourth place, with $3.69 billion. EBay's Jeff Skoll appeared, too, with $1.35 billion, and undoubtedly regarded such lists with abhorrence that only Omidyar could match. Red Hat's cofounder Marc Ewing, thirty, had a net worth pegged at $775 million, a number that was already laughably too low by the time the magazine had gone to press.

The list also included the names of two under-forty venture capitalists, one of whom was Kevin Harvey, whose personal wealth was placed at $278 million. The estimate was not too far from the truth. In mid-1999 Benchmark had invested $267 million of capital, obtaining equity that had a current value of $3.9 billion. Recalculating after the summer's IPO's, the value of the portfolio passed $6 billion. After deducting the gains owed to the limited partners, each of the four partners who had been at Benchmark since its founding in 1995 had increased his nominal net worth by approximately $350 million, and that took no account of the dozens of portfolio companies that had yet to mature. The most remarkable aspect of Benchmark's investments was that the entire basket increased in value in a way that would have brought renown if merely a single company had done so. By January 2000, the collective value of the twenty-five investments in Benchmark's most mature fund, begun in 1995, had grown ninety-two-fold. Benchmark's limited partners, many of whom had investments in other venture funds as well as in Benchmark's, whispered a most astounding fact: Only five years after its founding, Benchmark's returns beat those of Kleiner Perkins.

■

The eBoys almost never mentioned the growth of their personal wealth. One of the rare occasions in which it surfaced was the day Bob Kagle asked his partners if they had seen a profile of another venture capitalist that had appeared in a magazine.

"Pretty nice piece," Kagle said. But he had been surprised to learn of his colleague's blue-blood Exeter background. He blew a raspberry. "Everything else in the article I was groovin' on. Especially the rock-band thing."

"God, our kids are in trouble," Dave Beirne said suddenly. He laughed, almost bitterly, and recited the private schools his kids were attending.

"That bothers me a lot," said Kevin Harvey, who had two young children himself. He and the other partners had become wealthy so quickly that most of the group's fourteen children were still young, and thus especially vulnerable to the ills that come with extended exposure to unearned wealth. Harvey thought for a moment and then concluded, "I don't know what to do about it." The other partners laughed uneasily at their shared predicament. Harvey continued, "I'm going to have kids like the kind I hated when I was a kid."

Kagle grinned. "I can see the bow ties and suspenders now!"

■

The Benchmark culture included a share-the-wealth ethos, and the largesse extended to the receptionist. When E-Loan, a Benchmark company that offered mortgages online, went public, "friends and family" shares were made available, and the young woman, who answered the phone and greeted visitors, picked up five hundred shares at the offering price and sold them on the first day of trading for a profit of $18,000. In such a time and place, one's nominal salary was the least significant portion of compensation.

■

Burt McMurtry, sitting one floor below Benchmark's office, had been in the venture business thirty years and had been Bob Kagle's mentor; now he shared his perspective on his experiences with plainspoken candor. His firm, TVI, had funded Microsoft, Compaq, and other notable technology companies, but it was not these that McMurtry wished to talk about. Rather, he wanted to talk about the companies that did not succeed.

He recalled that in the mid-1970s, having been in the business a number of years, he had become depressed because "out of ten startups, we would lose three or four—lose all our money. Maybe just get our money back in two deals. Then you've got two or three where you get one to five times your money. That leaves just one or two deals [out of ten] where you make more than five times your money." The high payoffs for one or two never erased the pain of those that did not survive: "You feel so responsible for the disasters."

Whenever he asked colleagues at other venture firms about their experiences, he was told that they had many fewer casualties than he did, which served to deepen his depression. But when he looked at the data that went back to the 1960s collected by Horsley Bridge, a fund that invested in many venture capital firms, he was surprised to see that the high rate of casualties he had experienced was in fact very typical.

The present moment felt altogether different, however; very few of Benchmark's start-up investments had gone bust. Of seventy-three investments made by July 1999, only three had gone out of business. To be sure, Benchmark was only four years old, and its first fund was still too young to construct an actuarial table. But to the extent that mortality tended to reveal itself early in the life of the typical start-up, it seemed as if venture investing in the late 1990s was fundamentally different, less exposed to the risk of failure, than it had been in an earlier era.

Or had the ready supply of follow-on capital—in private and public markets—merely prolonged artificially the lives of companies that would have soon perished were it not for the extraordinary infusions of life-sustaining fluids? As long as young companies could go public without having first achieved consistent profitability, they had yet to really establish long-term viability. This held true even though the mortality rate of public technology companies created between 1990 and 1998 was, as of 1999, only 1 percent. Most technology start-ups were acquired by other, larger companies. Such mergers, though a welcome "liquidity event" financially speaking, were nevertheless a source of frustration to venture capitalists who longed to build companies that had staying power. One could argue that after a merger the basic DNA was transferred and persisted, but that did not offer the same satisfaction.

Two generations of venture guys wished start-ups could remain independently viable. When characterizing the venture capital industry, Burt McMurtry summarized his feelings by saying, "This is a discouraging business—the number of long-term-player companies that are created is not big, even though the carriers of the knowledge move on." When the eBoys founded their own firm, they wanted to do better in this regard and resolved to instill a built-to-last culture among their portfolio companies, as well as adopting the motto for their own organization.

Despite the noblest of intentions, however, the crop of companies that were born circa 1999 had no more apparent chance to retain their original names and independent identities into dotage than those in the crop of 1969 had. Some examples: Accept was sold to Amazon; When.com, an online calendar service, was sold to AOL; Art.com, the online posters and framing service, was acquired by Getty Images; and Shasta Networks, a networking-equipment company, was sold to Nortel. How should these transitions be regarded? If a calendar service that few would use as a freestanding website becomes, after incorporation into AOL, a feature that potentially twenty million AOL users rely on, does the original investment represent a fulfillment or failure of built-to-last?

Bill Gurley, who joined the firm four years after its founding, had a different perspective from the others. At one point in the summer of 1999 the partners were contemplating an initial public offering for Benchmark Capital itself. One argument in favor was offered by Bob Kagle, who thought going public would be "more built-to-last." Kevin Harvey agreed with him, arguing that a public entity would help to curb what he feared would be a wave of partners "checking out" after completing the next fund. Gurley cast cold water on the proposal to go public, however, by asking, "Is it built to *win?*" He explained, "GM is built to last, but it's got so much bureaucracy, it's not going anywhere." Maybe "built to last" was not the right criterion to optimize on.

■

A willingness to experiment is praiseworthy, but it can be costly, too. In the summer of 1999 Benchmark received a lesson in the perils of mezzanine investing, which refers to investments in companies that are on the eve of an IPO. Having ventured far from its roots in early-stage investing to make its largest single investment—$19 million in 1-800-Flowers.com—the Benchmark partners thought they were making a bet on a low-risk, no-work deal that seemed likely to bring a threefold return in a few short months. All that was required of Benchmark was one fat check. But when 1-800-Flowers.com

debuted, the market's appetite for Web IPO's had momentarily evaporated, and the stock dropped 13 percent on the first day of trading. It remained below the offering price in subsequent months of trading.

Even without including Flowers, the average size of Benchmark's investments had climbed steeply. By midsummer, Benchmark's third fund, of $175 million in capital, was fully committed. The partners had run through it in only nine months, a frightening pace measured by customary standards. It was time to raise the next fund.

Dave Beirne did not think small. "I think we should raise a billion dollars. Seriously."

The problem with such a plan, Kagle pointed out, was not that they couldn't raise it, but that it would force undesirable changes in the kinds of deals they did, the kinds of companies they worked with.

Andy Rachleff was more receptive to Beirne's proposal. "KKR wants to get in the venture business. Softbank is raising more money. If we're not prepared to fight, we're going to get our clocks cleaned."

"You don't go on the lacrosse field without a fuckin' stick," Beirne added. "You'll get killed."

"If we raise the fund," Kagle asked, "why would you put in five million and not twenty [in a typical investment]? We might overcapitalize companies if we have a huge fund. I think we should raise money, it should be large. I'm all for that. But I don't want to follow everyone else into big-check-dom. But how do we differentiate ourselves?"

"The way you differentiate is doing the best deals," Harvey said.

"I think," said Dunlevie, "we need more guys with stones as big as Dave's. I'm not going to write a check for fifty, but I like to watch Dave do them." As for Kagle's concern, Dunlevie argued that the firm's behavior had changed already.

"We need money to play," Rachleff said. "Every one of my telecom deals is ten million. Table stakes."

"I'll be Bob for a moment," Harvey said. "Has everyone forgotten, we're in a totally hysterical market? Our companies are money losers valued at billions of dollars!"

"Everyone looks like a genius," said Kagle.

"We need to be cognizant," continued Harvey, in his own voice but extending the same theme, "this is not the way it will always be."

Kagle served as chorus. "It's been a free-capital world. It breeds behaviors—in us, in our companies."

Harvey was not urging withdrawal, however. "I say, Let's play the game that has to be played. When it corrects, we adjust accordingly."

Harvey proposed that $100 million of the new fund be supplied by the partners personally. By investing a large amount of their own money, they could signal to prospective entrepreneurs their commitment to providing excellent service and also retain 100 percent of the profits rather than splitting them with limited partners and retaining only 30 percent.

Dave Beirne, surprisingly, did not immediately embrace the proposal, not because of cautiousness but because he believed he didn't have the money—a belief that involved willed blindness.

Kevin Harvey saw that Beirne truly had no idea what his net worth now was. "You don't know what you're—" and before he could say "worth," Beirne interrupted, with a note of irritation.

"I don't know. I don't have time to think about it."

"Carry in eBay is two hundred million." Harvey did not spell it out, but that meant that disregarding the other seventy companies in the Benchmark portfolio at the time, the undistributed portion of stock in eBay alone would be more than enough to fund a $100 million kitty created by the six partners.

"Is that the Coming Environment?" Beirne asked, referring to Bob Kagle's long-standing refrain that the Coming Environment would be one of depression. "I don't spend a dollar unless I have it," Beirne said. The paper profits from eBay and all the rest were, in his view, meaningless until actually transmuted into cash.

If the partners were to choose to raise a small fund instead of a large one, Dunlevie pointed out, and if the prices for individual deals continued to go up, then "you might end up with a fund of just eight companies. You need statistical diversification in order to have the winner that carries the fund." He was inclined to pursue a billion-dollar fund because even though "we know size doesn't matter, there are some who will regard it as leadership."

Beirne had one request: "I just want to take a before and after picture before we invest a billion dollars. We'll be older, stooped, shuffling, drooling."

■

Dave Beirne told his partners the story of an acquaintance, a successful venture guy. "Has this son who isn't doing anything, just laying around at home. He introduces the kid to lots of companies, hoping he'll show an interest in working for one of them, but he doesn't. So finally he gets fed up and says, 'Here's a million dollars. Go start your own company.' The father goes abroad on a trip, and when he comes back finds his son lazing around at home. Incredulous, he asks his son, 'What happened to the million dollars?'

" 'Dad, rather than becoming an entrepreneur, I became an investor. I put the money evenly distributed into all of the public companies whose boards you sit on. Now, you're working for me.' "

The subtext of this humorous tale was left unspoken: Was this the sum of the son's understanding of a work ethic?

■

The eBoys would have to remind one another of the need to remain focused on start-ups as they settled upon a figure of $1 billion for the next fund. Bob Kagle was the one who was most fearful that Benchmark would lose sight of its founding focus on the little guys. "Writing fifty-million-dollar checks is not the answer," he said. "It's being there at the beginning."

On the eve of launching the fund-raising for the new fund—one that was more than twice as large as Benchmark's first three funds combined—each partner paused to ask himself, again, what his primary motivations were. Even Dave Beirne slowed down and spent time with his family in a way that he had found impossible since joining in 1997. Bob Kagle poured his energies into lobbying his partners to expand "from a partnership into a firm"—a firm being an institution that was not dependent upon particular individuals—with regional offices. His ambition was to make Benchmark "the McKinsey of venture capital." It was his way of coming to grips with the question of how to leave a legacy professionally, not just personally through philanthropy.

Some venture capitalists, like John Doerr, were fond of claiming that their contribution to society took the form of creating thousands of new jobs. The claim was empty bluster, however. Mike Moritz, of Sequoia Capital, peeled back the truth with mordant detachment: "One of the dirty little secrets of the Valley is that all the jobs-creation we like to talk about is probably less than the Big Three automakers have laid off in the last decade. One of the best ways to have a nice Silicon Valley company is to keep your head count as low as possible for as long as possible."

The Benchmark partners never parroted the line that venture capital gave the world the gift of new jobs; they never claimed anything grand. As long as they hewed to the we-serve-entrepreneurs theme, their self-described role in a larger scheme was limited. The individual venture capitalist in Silicon Valley did not make life-or-death decisions about promising fledgling businesses; there was simply too much capital available from too many different sources for a good idea to remain unfunded. If hospitable tax policies changed, however, or the supply of capital from institutional investors was turned off, or if any of a dozen other factors that created the underlying—and delicate—ecosystem for entrepreneurialism were altered, then the formation of new ventures would be conspicuously affected.

Venture capital investing had always been bound by a boom-and-bust cycle, and there was no reason to believe that the cycle had ceased to operate. But though a downturn was inevitable, the shrinking of recently renascent small business was not. One aspect of the most recent wave of investments that distinguished them from those in earlier high-water marks in venture capital's modern history, such as when investments clustered, at different times, in aviation, semiconductors, personal computers, and biotech, was that many of the new Internet businesses directly enabled individuals to start their own small businesses. The unanticipated growth of sellers on eBay who quit their day jobs to pursue online selling full-time was one example. Another was Vstore, a deal backed by Bill Gurley, which gave anyone who wished to set up his own e-commerce site ready access to suppliers of new goods.

A proliferation of similar companies that offered e-commerce services, and the invitations to amateur businesspeople extended from other sites, like Amazon and Yahoo, gave America the look of a land that had gone mad for commerce like never before, even when Tocqueville was jotting down notes in the 1830s. Even assuming that many of the virtual stores would not ultimately succeed—the ratio of numbers of aspiring sellers and actual buyers would have to find a natural equilibrium—there remained a good chance that a sea change was taking place, a shift in the relative power wielded by small business versus big.

For the daydreamers among us who would like to pursue an idea for a new business of their own, the entrepreneurs in Silicon Valley can always be viewed as hopeful icons. But it may be a bit discouraging to note that in Benchmark's portfolio, the entrepreneurs who were the biggest winners, such as eBay's Pierre Omidyar, Scient's Eric Greenberg, and Ariba's Keith Krach, all had prior experience. The one person who came closest to representing Everyman—Stu Weisman, at ePhysician—got his opportunity through luck as well as pluck, to use Horatio Alger's nineteenth-century formula, and his story lacked a dramatic denouement; in the fall of 1999, more than a year after its initial funding, ePhysician was still in the beta-test phase of its PalmPilot-based service for doctors and had not yet formally opened for business.

In any case, the business fates of Benchmark's portfolio companies and of its competitors could not alone define historically significant change. Venture capitalists simply did not make nearly enough investments to democratize entrepreneurship directly. Only to the degree that the venture capitalists funded businesses that, in turn, either enabled the masses to go into business for themselves (Vstore's tag line was "Commerce for Everyone") or whose financial success inspired others to try their own hand at it, would their work outlast the next turn of the business cycle.

On a daily basis the venture capitalist was not concerned with historical impact; he worked to create wealth for himself and his limited partners. However, among the Benchmark partners there was awareness that framing one's professional raison d'être in the language of financial return meant that one was hostage to the vagaries of the market—and even when the market is buoyant, there is little that is soul-quenching about mere numbers.

"The really big wins are where *all* the rewards come from," Bob Kagle once pointed out, before eBay had gone public. The rewards he was referring to were the emotional ones, not the financial ones, and they were rewards derived not from a game of assuming personal risk—the venture guys had a portfolio across which risk could be spread—but from being backers of entrepreneurs, the ones who commercialized new technology and introduced new products and services—and were the ones who really took on risk. "Nine times out of ten they're taking on some big, established system of some sort." He dropped his voice for emphasis: If the individual entrepreneur won, even for the venture guys it produced an "exhilarating feeling"—he groped for the right words—"it's confirmation that one person with courage can make a difference."

This was the minidrama Kagle and his colleagues had seen play out triumphantly again and again. The work itself did not have any neat demarcations of beginning, middle, and end. The funds seemed to be evergreen, fresh capital materializing as soon as the till was exhausted. The calendars of the partners, revolving as they did around looking at new business plans, meeting new entrepreneurs, considering new deals, gave a feeling of perennially beginning afresh. For them, it was the best place in the cosmos to get the first peek at the future.

Acknowledgments

The Benchmark partners did not really know what they had signed up for; if they had, they wouldn't have. That became clear as the project proceeded and they realized that they would be revealing all that they were professionally and personally inclined to keep private. But they were honorable individuals, they'd given their word, and they followed through on what they had promised. I am grateful to Dave Beirne, Bruce Dunlevie, Kevin Harvey, Bob Kagle, and Andy Rachleff for their cooperation, even when they wished to flee, and to Bill Gurley and Steve Spurlock, for gamely assisting in a project that had begun before their arrival.

I am indebted to many others at Benchmark. Chris Hadsell was always unstinting in giving me time and providing information. Marissa Matusich, Bernadette Wagner, and Kerri McClain met my many requests for assistance with unflagging good cheer. Renee Beaulaurier, Lisa Chew, and Suzette Phillips also showed me kind consideration.

Many generous individuals provided interviews: Tom Adams, Gary Bengier, Louis Borders, Gary Dahl, Lawton Fitt, Mark Gainey, Eric Greenberg, John Hagan, Jeff Hawkins, David Hayden, Bob Howe, Bill Lee, Peggy Lo, Burt McMurtry, Bob Moog, Pete Mountanos, Pierre Omidyar, Alan Seiler, Danny Shader, Rob Shaw, Mike Shirkey, Jeff Skoll, Jennifer Sun, Stu Weisman, Steve Westly, Meg Whitman, Curt Wozniak, and George Zachary.

In Flint, Michigan, Vivian Corlew and Michele Kagle generously shared family memories. At Kettering University, Professors John Lorenz and G. Reginald Bell provided useful historical information, and Susan VanCamp and Bill Holleran helped me mine the university archives.

At eBay, Lisa Baldwin and Anita Gaeta kept me apprised of frequently rescheduled staff meetings; Rick Rock and Victor Lonsberry kindly dug up statistics that I could not have obtained elsewhere.

Greg Stross and Lee Gomes provided lots of suggestions and questions; their encouragement went a long ways, coming as it did from natural-born skeptics.

The book was greatly improved by Gail Hershatter's eye for unexamined assumptions and her ear for disharmonious style. It was also she who prodded me to try to make the chronicle less "boy."

At Random House, Jon Karp served as a brilliant editor, a combination of cheerleader and critic, who saw, even when I didn't, that the story needed more time to ripen fully.

Margaret Wimberger, an extraordinarily sharp copy editor, saved me from many slips.

With a glint in his eye, Benjamin Dreyer gave the pages a thorough scrubbing.

My agent, Elizabeth Kaplan, was wholly dedicated to this baby, even as she prepared to give birth to her own.

San Jose State University provided stalwart institutional support, granting a leave and stipend so that I could pursue the project.

My thanks to one and all.

Notes

Introduction

xvi increasing amounts of capital: "Heat Wave: Venture Capitalists Maintained a Torrid Fund-Raising Pace in the First Half of the Year," *Venture Capital Journal*, 1 September 1999.

xvi Business-school graduates: "MBA Graduates Forego Corporate World for Internet Start-Ups," *Knight Ridder Tribune Business News*, 9 May 1999.

xvi One in twelve American adults: "Gap Exists Between Entrepreneurship in Europe, North America, Study Shows," *Wall Street Journal*, 2 July 1999. The survey was conducted by a consortium of business schools and interviewed 10,000 people in 10 countries in the spring of 1999. While 8.5 percent of Americans surveyed were trying to start a business, the numbers in Europe were much lower: Italy, 3.4 percent; Britain, 3.3 percent; Germany, 2.2 percent; France, 1.8 percent; and Finland, 1.4 percent.

xvi touted as a panacea: "Can Entrepreneurship Help to Guide Teens Toward Better Lives?" *Wall Street Journal*, 2 July 1999.

xvii also wanted to get into venture capital: "Venture Firms Are Dethroning Once-Reigning Buyout Kings," *Wall Street Journal*, 7 June 1999. The article also pointed out, however, that even at the end of 1998, buyout funds still had about $250 billion under management, compared with $84 billion for venture capital.

xvii venture guys worked in a nicer neighborhood: In June 1999 Erica Bushner, a principal at Wilshire Associates, a firm that advised foundation and endowment trustees about private-equity investments, said that her institutional clients now viewed buyout firms as commodities, lacking in glamour. "Do I want to talk about the buyout of a soda bottler and the re-engineering of the bottling line? Or do I want to talk about a hot e-commerce company being bought out by Amazon.com?" "Venture Firms Are Dethroning Once-Reigning Buyout Kings," *Wall Street Journal.*

xvii easy for the finance world: The return in 1998 for buyout funds was 10.9 percent. The annualized return in the 3 years 1996–1998 for early-stage venture investing was 37.7 percent versus 19.2 percent for buyout funds. "Private Equity Returns Rebound for Short-Term; Long-Term Returns Continue Stellar Performance," *Venture Economics News,* 18 May 1999. Looking back 10 years, the differences were smaller: 19.7 percent annually for early-stage venture funds versus 16.4 percent for buyouts. If one looks at the record over the previous 20 years, buyout funds (19.6 percent annually) actually beat the venture funds' average return (16.8 percent).

xxii market capitalization of $2.9 billion: The increase in value since Benchmark's investment was most dramatic shortly after Critical Path's IPO in late April 1999, when the company's market capitalization briefly approached $4 billion.

1: The Right Answer

6 *Vanity Fair* likened him: "The New Establishment," *Vanity Fair,* October 1997.

6 *New York Times* piece: "A High-Tech Headhunter Who Knows His Prey," *New York Times,* 2 June 1996.

6 profile in *Fortune:* Janice Maloney, "So You Want to Be a Software Superstar," *Fortune,* 10 June 1996.

2: Good People

18 "I appreciate this school": R. C. Kagle, "30 Days in the Hole," *Technician,* July 1978.

18 Happy Valley assembly plant: The plant was subsequently closed in the 1980s but remained a conspicuous eyesore until the university prevailed upon General Motors in the late 1990s to raze the buildings and plant the site in grass.

20 grant of Microsoft stock: Ten years later the stock was worth $1 million. Or, at least, could have been. But the school, too small to have a professional staff to manage equities in the endowment, had sold the stock upon receiving it. In 1997 Kagle donated $1 million—in cash, this time—to make up for the stock that had come and gone.

25 Omidyar had a shortlist: On the list, besides Benchmark, was Mayfield, an old-line firm; another venture firm, less known, which had already placed an offer on the table and was expecting a response from him soon; and a corporate suitor that wanted to buy the company whole. The eBay entrepreneurs did not mention to Benchmark that they were no longer interested in Mayfield; the partner that they had met with there, an older gentleman, did not appreciate the potential of the Web. Kleiner Perkins was not on the shortlist because every characterization of the firm that Omidyar had heard related to the shark family, and KP had already invested in another online auction company, Onsale.

3: Go Big or Go Home

31 sold the company to Kmart: For an interesting oral history of the early years of Borders Books, see "The Bookstore in America: Borders," *Review of Contemporary Fiction,* Summer 1997.

35 "It's not the money": Borders could have self-funded Webvan at its inception, and so too Mike Farmwald, the founder of Rambus, could have self-funded subsequent ventures, Epigram and Rhombus, both of which he invited Benchmark to back because they were "experts at helping you build a company." See Andrew P. Madden, "The New VCs," *Red Herring,* November 1999.

4: Accidents Happen

53 he hadn't spent anything: "www.ebay.philanthropy," *San Jose Mercury News,* 23 April 1999.

5: Don't Get Screwed

62 "can in no case stigmatize": Alexis de Tocqueville, *Democracy in America,* J. P. Mayer, ed. (Garden City, N.Y.: Anchor Books, 1969), p. 622.

62 more aware than most: For a profile of Steve Jurvetson, see Po Bronson, "Surfing on the Slippery Skin of a Bubble," *New York Times Magazine,*

20 June 1999. Jurvetson also makes an appearance in Bronson's account of Hotmail's success in *The Nudist on the Late Shift and Other True Tales of Silicon Valley* (New York: Random House, 1999), pp. 78–97. For a look at Jurvetson's two partners, Tim Draper and John Fisher, through the eyes of one entrepreneur, see Gary Rivlin's "This Guy Needs Two Million Now; These Guys Have It; Let the Games Begin," *San Francisco Focus,* August 1997.

62 Twain was financially ruined: Joseph Epstein, *Ambition: The Secret Passion* (Chicago: Ivan R. Dee, 1989), pp. 71–72.

6: Room at the Top

75 first to go public: Benchmark did not want to follow Kleiner Perkins in one way that a 1998 *Fortune* profile of KP pointed out: Between 1990 and 1997, the stock of KP-backed companies tended to drop after the IPO. "KP took public 79 infotech and life sciences companies that have not been acquired since. If you'd bought each of those stocks immediately after the first day of trading, you would have lost money on 55 of them. That's right, a loser rate of 70 percent." Melanie Warner, "Inside the Silicon Valley Money Machine," *Fortune,* 26 October 1998.

76 *The Economist* estimated: "Going, Going . . . : On-line Auctions," *The Economist,* 31 May 1997.

76 his memoir, *Startup:* Jerry Kaplan, *Startup: A Silicon Valley Adventure* (Boston: Houghton Mifflin, 1995). For an article that highlights Kaplan's tendency to overdramatize and claim credit for advances achieved by predecessors, see Lee Gomes, "Story of Go Is Juicy, But Is It History?" *San Jose Mercury News,* 26 June 1995.

76 creating a bidding experience: "Making the Sale," *Wall Street Journal,* 17 June 1996.

76 Doerr publicly derided Kaplan: "Nowhere to Go but Up," *PC Week,* 23 October 1995.

76 "Just because you make *Waterworld*": Quoted by Michael Lewis in "Millionerds," *Slate,* 21 January 1998.

76 offerings were eclectic: "Nowhere to Go but Up."

77 prices declined daily: In an SEC filing Onsale described the problem with dry objectivity: "Due to the inherently unpredictable nature of auctions, it is impossible to determine with any certainty whether an item will sell for more than the price paid by the Company. Further, because minimum bid prices for the merchandise listed on the Company's Web site generally are lower than the company's acquisition

costs for such merchandise, there can be no assurance that the Company will achieve positive gross margins on any given sale." See Forms S-1 for Onsale, Inc., filed on 20 December 1996.

77 "they kill it": "Are You Bidding? What You Need to Know to Work the Online Auctions," *Boston Globe,* 11 February 1999.

77 "We're shocked": "Making the Sale."

7: Privileged

85 no one today can recall: A student of the industry's history traces distinct talk of "venture capital" to 1939, when a professional identity began to take form, distinct from the adventurous personal investing of wealthy individuals. See Martha Louise Reiner, "The Transformation of Venture Capital: A History of Venture Capital Organizations in the United States," Ph.D. dissertation, University of California, Berkeley, 1989.

86 permitted it to charge 30 percent: Tom Perkins explains Kleiner Perkins's shift in 1980 from a carry of 20 percent to 30 percent as the suggestion of KP's primary limited partner, who urged the adoption of the higher carry to persuade the KP partners not to deviate from the investment course they had been following up until then. See David A. Kaplan, *The Silicon Boys and Their Valley of Dreams* (New York: William Morrow, 1999), pp. 200–201.

89 Wolff's 1998 book: Michael Wolff, *Burn Rate: How I Survived the Gold Rush Years on the Internet* (New York: Simon & Schuster, 1998).

89 two thirds of the entire firm's carry: "Building a Future: Venture G.P.'s Groom Tomorrow's Partners Through Today's Training," *Venture Capital Journal,* 1 July 1998.

89 "must have been a senior partner": "Building a Future."

91 "put into a cell with Charlie Manson": David Sheff, "Don Valentine Interview," *Upside,* May 1990.

8: Name Your Price

110 eluded everyone else: Bruce Schneier, head of Counterpane Systems and an author of several books on cryptography, rejected TriStrata's claim. Schneier explained: "A true one-time pad uses a random key that is distributed through a separate secure channel. [It] gains its unbreakable security from the fact that the key is as long as the message. . . .

And both the sender and the receiver must have this secret key, which must be exchanged in some fashion which the attacker cannot penetrate. . . . Because the key has to be as long as the message, there is no way to use an established system to exchange more keys, since in order to securely send a 1 MB key a user needs 1 MB of additional pre-agreed key. (And if users can exchange these keys [via a network], why can't they just exchange the messages?) This means that all keys have to be exchanged via some other mechanism (such as a courier). This kind of system was used for the U.S.-Soviet teletype 'hot line' and it is occasionally used for paper ciphers and spies, but that's it. There is no way in which a true one-time pad can be implemented over a computer network." From Schneier's "Review of TriStrata Public Information," 5 October 1998.

9: World Class

130 Wahl's predecessor, Klaus Besier: "Wahl Leaves SAP for Tech Startup," *Information Week*, 7 September 1998.
130 "opportunity of a lifetime": "Wahl Leaves SAP."

10: All e-, All the Time

132 new issue of *Forbes*: *Forbes ASAP*, 6 April 1998.

12: The Art of the Deal

170 a "capitalist in a sea of communists": "Photography House Getty Images to Buy Art.com," *Wall Street Journal*, 5 May 1999.

13: Getting Out

179 range for this offering: The share prices are contemporaneous, without adjusting to take into account a three-for-one split on March 2, 1999.
180 Amazon was up 17 points: The share price is contemporaneous, without adjusting to take into account a three-for-one stock split effective January 5, 1999.
180 Yahoo, 14: The share price is contemporaneous, without adjusting to take into account a two-for-one stock split effective February 8, 1999.
180 would disappear altogether: "A Cloud Behind eBay's Bright Day," msnbc.com, 24 September 1998.

14: Techniqued

184 totaled $150 million: The "total" referred to in the text is an artificial construct. In limited-partnership accounting, each of Benchmark's funds has a separate balance sheet. The totals here were the current sums from Benchmark I, II, and the just-started III.

186 "the book I was reading": Bruce Schneier, *Applied Cryptography: Protocols, Algorithms, and Source Code in C* (New York: John Wiley & Sons, 1996).

186 "website is all about TriStrata": "Review of TriStrata Public Information," 5 October 1998 (www.counterpane.com/tristrata.html), which was based on the scanty information that was publicly available about the TriStrata system. Schneier concluded that he could not perform a complete evaluation until TriStrata had released the necessary technical information, but his preliminary findings were scalding:

> There is a huge amount of hype and very little substance to the documentation. Many of the statements made are incomplete, vague, or suggest facts that cannot be true. The cryptographic claims are wild and unsubstantiated. Parts are clearly written by someone who does not understand modern cryptography, and who is not well versed in the cryptographic literature. Certain areas of the documentation give the impression that they were written with the intent to deceive the reader, but ignorance is probably a better explanation. Based on past experience with systems that made similar unsupported security claims, we are very skeptical about the security of the TriStrata system.

190 finally released its software: The company chose to call this "System 2.0," claiming that the first "release" of the software had been in June 1998, at the time of the company's nominal launch, but in fact the software was not released commercially at the time.

191 "a little too excited": "TriStrata Tries Again with Security Management," *PC Week,* 22 March 1999.

16: One Monkey Don't Make No Show

209 17 million shares: "Hype Machine Went into High Gear for eBay's Launch," *San Jose Mercury News,* 28 October 1998.

210 "We do not expect": "Hype Machine."

211 "done a terrific job": "Wall Street's Love Affair with eBay Could Be a Fling, Not a Long-Term Romance," *Barron's,* 3 November 1998.

211 "400 home runs in a row": Christopher Byron, "The Psychedelic Trip of a Net Stock," msnbc.com, 11 November 1998.

213 split the gain equally: In Dave Beirne's case, since he had arrived late in the first fund's life, his share was to be split equally with the partner who had departed before his arrival.

216 math was rather simple: On 12 April 1999, Omidyar sold $187 million of eBay stock as part of the company's secondary stock offering, leaving him with more than 36 million shares; at the same time Whitman took $50 million off the table and still held 6.8 million shares.

216 "still bouncing down the street": "EBay's IPO Return Is Just Peanuts to Some," *San Jose Mercury News*, 28 January 1999.

217 local paper suggested: "www.ebay.philanthropy," *San Jose Mercury News*, 23 April 1999. One could make another argument why philanthropies should receive grants of stock earlier, rather than later: Everyone else in the Valley received stock options in lieu of cash—not just lawyers and corporate recruiters, but also building contractors, landlords, website developers—even restaurateurs. See a humorous story about the phenomenon, "Bartering for Equity Can Offer Sweet Rewards in Silicon Valley," *Wall Street Journal*, 2 September 1999.

17: Off the Dole

221 "almost every way perfectly": "Yahoo May Be Eyeing eBay, Too," *ZD Net*, 23 March 1999.

224 would eventually be called: Accept.com was adopted later and is used anachronistically here to avoid confusion; the original name of the company was Emptor.

19: "R" Toys Us?

248 preparing to add toys: Moog's appointment was announced on 12 May 1999; Amazon, as expected, added toys to its website on 13 July 1999.

250 *The Innovator's Dilemma*: Clayton M. Christensen, *The Innovator's Dilemma: When New Technologies Cause Great Firms to Fail* (Boston: Harvard Business School Press, 1997).

258 partnership between Toys and Benchmark: "Toys 'R' Us Ends Partnership Effort for Web Venture," *Wall Street Journal*, 17 August 1999.

259 "prenuptial agreement": "On the Internet, Toys 'R' Us Plays Catch-up," *Wall Street Journal*, 19 August 1999.

259 Nakasone was forced out: "Toys 'R' Us CEO, Nakasone, Resigns," *Wall Street Journal*, 27 August 1999.

259 "just as dynamic": "Nordstrom a Shoe-In to Expand Its Online Sales," *Seattle Post-Intelligencer,* 25 August 1999.

20: Crash

262 Amazon acquired Accept: "Amazon's Accept.com Deal Cost About $101.7 Million," *Seattle Times,* 11 June 1999.

266 "guppy eating the whale": "Auction House Gets Bid by eBay," *San Jose Mercury News,* 27 April 1999.

266 "not good enough anymore!": "Meg Muscles eBay Uptown," *Fortune,* 5 July 1999.

269 "until the baby gets better": "Defining the Online Chief at eBay," *New York Times,* 10 May 1999.

272 "beyond anyone's control": "Seller, Investor Defections Plague eBay's Comeback," *San Jose Mercury News,* 15 July 1999.

21: Hoover Dam

276 the resulting article: "Co-Founder of Borders to Launch Online Megagrocer," *Wall Street Journal,* 22 April 1999.

277 had spent $24 billion: "July 20, 1969: The Day Mankind Took Its Biggest Leap of All," Associated Press, 20 July 1999. The cost of the *Apollo* program also included the lives of three astronauts who died in a fire during launch rehearsal.

277 $5 billion investment: "For Iridium, A Quick Trip to Earth," *New York Times,* 14 August 1999. Iridium filed for bankruptcy protection in August 1999.

280 off more than 10 percent: "NASDAQ Enters Correction Territory as Internet Stocks Keep Tumbling," *Wall Street Journal,* 5 August 1999.

280 Chancellor's history of financial manias: Edward Chancellor, *Devil Take the Hindmost: A History of Financial Speculation* (New York: Farrar Straus Giroux, 1999).

282 "unprofitable for a long time": "Hot Strategy: 'Be Unprofitable for a Long Time,'" *Inc.,* 1 September 1997.

282 "I don't see any reason": "Co-Founder of Borders."

286 Shaheen had made comments: "George Shaheen Ruled a Digital Army at Andersen Consulting. Why Give It Up?" *Forbes,* 18 October 1999.

286 SEC deemed inappropriate: "The 'Quiet' Question: A Debate Reopens over Disclosures During a Stock Offering," *Wall Street Journal,* 8 October 1999.

286 disseminated publicly by Adam Lashinsky: "A Special Delivery Direct from Webvan's Roadshow," *TheStreet.com,* 7 October 1999.

286 an amended prospectus: Adam Lashinsky, "What's Inside Webvan's Amended IPO Filing," *TheStreet.com,* 12 October 1999.

286 publicity had worked in Webvan's favor: Tom Davey, "Webvan Profits from SEC Problem," *Redherring.com,* 14 October 1999.

22: Built to Win

290 *Fortune* magazine article: "America's Richest 40 Under 40," *Fortune,* 27 September 1999.

291 fourth place: Omidyar's $3.69 billion was behind Michael Dell ($21.49 billion), Amazon's Jeff Bezos ($5.74 billion), and Gateway's Ted Waitt ($5.44 billion); and immediately ahead of Yahoo's David Filo ($3.12 billion) and Jerry Yang ($3.05 billion).

291 current value of $3.9 billion: This was an extraordinary figure, even after making allowances for the fine print: The $3.9 billion represented, for the most part, illiquid investments. Equity in private companies could not be readily traded for cash, and shares of newly public companies that Benchmark held were subject to lockup agreements set by the underwriters and could not yet be freely traded. The exception was Benchmark's investments that had already led to stock distributions. These were worth cumulatively to date $775 million at the time of distribution and were the only gains that were certain. The rest were subject to the whims of the market, down or up, until the stock was distributed to the general partners and the limited partners. The same held true for the other firms on Sand Hill Road.

293 "This is a discouraging business": Among McMurtry's earliest investments, one of the companies that succeeded in keeping its original identity intact was KLA Instruments. But in 1997 even it succumbed, after 20 years, to a merger with Tencor Instruments; the new entity goes by the name of KLA-Tencor.

295 remained below the offering price: For a peek at the post-IPO disappointment experienced by 1-800-Flowers.com employees, see "1-800-Flowers.com's IPO Lesson: Coping with Wilt," *Wall Street Journal,* 19 August 1999.

298 "One of the dirty little secrets": Kaplan, *The Silicon Boys and Their Valley of Dreams,* p. 321.

Index

About the Author

RANDALL E. STROSS teaches business at San Jose State University and is a contributing editor to *U.S. News & World Report*. He is the author of four previous books, including *The Microsoft Way* and *Steve Jobs and the NeXT Big Thing*. He lives in Menlo Park, California, and can be reached via his website, www.randallstross.com.

DATE			